D0758218

TRAVELS

TO THE

NANOWORLD

MINIATURE MACHINERY IN NATURE AND TECHNOLOGY

TRAVELS

TO THE

NANOWORLD

MINIATURE MACHINERY IN
NATURE AND TECHNOLOGY

MICHAEL GROSS

PLENUM TRADE • NEW YORK AND LONDON

Library of Congress Cataloging-in-Publication Data

Gross, Michael, 1963–
    [Expeditionen in den Nanokosmos. English]
    Travels to the nanoworld : miniature machinery in nature and
technology / Michael Gross.
        p.   cm.
    Includes bibliographical references.
    ISBN 0-306-46008-4
    1. Microelectromechanical systems.   2. Nanotechnology.   I. Title.
TJ163.G7613   1999
620'.5--dc21   99-13756
                                                                  CIP

This book is an expanded and updated translation by the author of his book published in
German under the title *Expoditionen in den Nanokosmos*,
© 1995 Birkhäuser Publishing Ltd., Basel, Switzerland.

ISBN 0-306-46008-4

© 1999 Plenum Trade
A Division of Plenum Publishing Corporation
233 Spring Street, New York, N.Y. 10013

10 9 8 7 6 5 4 3 2 1

A C.I.P. record for this book is available from the Library of Congress

Printed in the United States of America

Contents

Preface: Of Nature and Technology

> The lilies of the field toil not, neither do they calculate, but they
> are probably excellent structures, and indeed Nature is generally
> a better engineer than man.
>
> James E. Gordon, *Structures, or Why Things Don't Fall Down*

Shipwrights of the pre-engineering era liked to make their masts of entire
tree trunks, which they changed as little as possible. Then came the engineers, who told the shipwrights to cut up the tree and glue it together in a
more efficient shape, like a hollow tube, or an I-shaped beam. Only a few
decades ago, scientists found that the old, "superstitious" shipwrights
were right and the modern, "rational" engineers wrong. A tree, after all, is
shaken by the wind as much as the mast of a ship. When it is bent over, the
wood is compressed on the leeward side and extended on the windward
side to the same extent, but the wood as a material can cope with the
tension much better than with the compression. As the tree cannot tell in
advance from which direction the winds will blow, it cannot reinforce the
lee side. But it solves the problem in a very clever way. It makes sure that
the trunk is prestressed in such a way that the outer parts are under

tension and the inner parts under compression—as if an outer ring of wood had been forced on an inner core just a little bit too big to fit in without being compressed. Thus, the maximum compression on the lee side will be partially compensated by the preexisting tension, and the tree can withstand the wind considerably better than it could without this help. And this, of course, is the reason why unaltered tree trunks make the best masts and spars.

This is just one of the many amazing things that I have learned recently from Gordon's book, which, although written by an engineer (naval architect manqué in his own words) and mainly concerned with structures designed by human engineers, never fails to point out the analogies with the similar structures that evolution has come up with over the past 3 billion years. The mesh of a few bones and a lot more tendons and muscles that keeps us in shape is, according to Gordon, not so very different from the rigging of a sailing ship, which also contains many more ropes than masts and spars, and does so for very good engineering reasons. Similarly, the sail of a Chinese junk works like the wings of a bat, and if thrushes could study engineering they would find out why the difficulty of pulling a worm out of the lawn does not depend on the length of the former. (As a warning I should perhaps mention that the book is not suited for fainthearted air travelers.)

Gordon's "popular engineering" book *Structures*, which is still in print today, was first published in 1978, at a time when there was already a certain awareness of the fact that technology does not always know better than nature. Unfortunately, I only came across this book 20 years later, after reading an obituary about the author, who died in June 1998 at the age of nearly 85. It so happened that I read it while I was putting the finishing touches to the book you're reading right now, which is also concerned with structures designed by evolution on the one side and by humans on the other. What has changed over the past few decades, however, is that now there is a rapidly growing interest in structures that are rather a lot smaller than a sailing ship, or the human skeleton—a lot smaller even than a bat's wing.

The structures I am going to tell you about are so small that one cannot see them even with an ordinary microscope. Millions of such structures can be found in each living cell. Their crude shapes can be "photographed" using electron beams instead of light, but their details can only be visualized indirectly if at all. The lengths concerned are normally measured in nanometers (billionths of a meter), which is why various words with the prefix *nano* are often used to describe them. We will, for instance, deal with nanotubes, nanoscale particles, and the anticipated development of nanotechnology. The use of this prefix actually allows us to assess the progress that science has made toward the world of the invisibly small, the nanoworld. While the late 1980s saw an average of 200 to 300 publications per year with *nano* in the title, the number has increased steeply since 1991 and is bound to approach 4000 for 1998 (see Fig. 1 of Chapter 10). The nanoworld is both intriguing for the curiosity-driven, and promising for the application-oriented, as we shall realize when we explore it on an armchair travel.

The introduction presented in Chapter 1 will set the scene and sketch how the structural elements of the nanoworld, the molecules, relate to other units, such as atoms, cells, or organisms. Then, Chapters 2–4 will introduce the natural nanoscale structures, the biomolecules, which are found within every living cell, and which can carry out the most amazing tasks. Of course these biomolecules are also dealt with in textbooks of biochemistry and molecular biology, but here we shall always keep in mind that we are investigating these systems not only for the sake of their intrinsic beauty and importance for the understanding of biology, but also so that we can compare them with artificial nanoscale systems that have recently been created, and to find inspiration for even more powerful nanosystems that we are only beginning to dream of.

When it comes to taking stock of what nanoscale systems can be created by human design efforts (Chapters 5–7), it will become clear that nature's superiority is much more obvious on the nanoscale than in large-scale engineering. Perhaps this has partly to do with the fact that evolution has been acting on cells for more than 3 billion years, and that building cells is what it is good at. At the beginning of life on Earth, the step from nothing at all to the first cell took much less time than the step from cells to multicellular organisms. Human engineers, in contrast, are at their best with things corresponding to the length scale they can grasp with their hands and eyes, and are only beginning to learn how to work their way down to the cellular scale. In short, we will encounter many examples of natural systems whose achievements cannot be replicated even by the most advanced human technology available today.

This, however, may change within a few decades or so, if the predictions of a few visionary thinkers come true. As will be explained in Chapters 8–10, scientists believe that a new technology operating on the nanometer scale, and therefore called *nanotechnology*, will become reality soon and that this will have extremely profound impacts on economy and society. At best, it could mean a long life without worries for 10 billion people, but at worst it could lead to the end of biological life on our planet. Promises and risks have to be discussed very carefully as early as possible, even though we cannot yet be sure that the "nanotechnology revolution" will take place any time soon.

This is—in a nutshell—the story I am going to expound on in this book, and it is essentially the same story told to readers of the German version, *Expeditionen in den Nanokosmos*, which came out in October 1995. In the details, however, quite a few things needed updating or expanding, as many of the research fields I am touching here are moving quite rapidly. During this process of translating, rewriting, adding to, and as I hope generally improving the book, I have benefited from the help of a number of people who were kind enough to provide details or broaden my horizon. Significant improvements have resulted from the helpful suggestions made by the first two readers of the draft manuscript, namely, Ken Derham at Plenum's London office, and my friend and colleague Kevin Plaxco who is now at the University of California, Santa Barbara.

Thanks to the pleasant and constructive interactions with everybody involved, and also the fascinating nature of the subject matter, I've had an enormous amount of fun writing this book, and I hope this will at least partially surface through its pages. From the "nano-"related papers that are piled up to a height of roughly a billion nanometers in my little office at home, I have learned many things that I never even dreamed about. If there is one disadvantage in this, it is what I call the balloon theory of knowledge, although I am sure that some clever philosopher of science had a better name for it. As I accumulate an ever larger volume of knowledge (and write it down in books so I don't have to carry it around in my head), the surface between the known and the unknown expands as well, and I become aware of more and more things that I know nothing about. Thus, I am certain that there are a few really nice and important research papers about nanoscale systems out there that I have shamefully overlooked, forgotten to mention, or not understood properly. My sincere apologies to any scientific colleagues who find their work outside my knowledge balloon. And please don't hesitate to bring such faults to my attention. No human being is perfect, and therefore, no popular science book can be perfect either. At the time when I was struggling to accept this fact of life, I found great comfort in reading a sentence written by Gordon 20 years ago in the foreword of his book (which in my opinion is as good as it gets): "Some of the omissions and oversimplifications are intentional but no doubt some of them are due to my own brute ignorance and lack of understanding of the subject." At least during the last few weeks of finishing this book, I would have happily signed this declaration.

While the scientific community may think I have left out one crucial detail or the other, the lay reader could easily come to the opinion that there's a detail or two too many on these pages. If you're among the latter, you could always skip a section that gets too demanding. It is worth bearing in mind that the more detailed parts of the book (Chapters 2–7) contain the pieces of two jigsaw puzzles that will one day fit together to reveal an understanding of how cells work, together with a technology that could perform as well as a living cell. As yet, we don't have all of the pieces for the former puzzle and only very few of the latter one. It is particularly obvious for the technology side of the nanoworld that we do not yet know how these pieces will fit together one day. I have tried to link the pieces as best I could and present them in an arrangement that appeared logical to me, but if you would like to consider them in a different order or selection from the one I have chosen, that is quite as well. In a sense, Parts II and III of the book should allow everybody to take their own customized tour around the nanoworld. Whatever you do, I hope you enjoy the trip.

I

Introduction

1

Welcome to the Nanoworld

Imagine a motor measuring a few hundredths of a thousandth of a milli-meter, running on and on and on. Or a data storage device squeezing the equivalent of five "high-density" floppy disks into a thousandth of a millimeter. Or a catalyst converting the inert nitrogen gas from the air into nitrogen fertilizer at room temperature and atmospheric pressure. Such extraordinary achievements are sometimes dreamt up when scientists discuss new technologies operating in the nanometer area of the length scale, which are therefore collectively referred to as *nanotechnology*. While this has become a buzzword of the 1990s, scientists have been using the prefix *nano* for decades to refer to a billionth (10^{-9}) of a metric unit. Thus, one nanometer (1 nm) is a billionth of a meter, or a millionth of a millimeter (Fig. 1).

We are talking about complicated and highly efficient machines hav-ing a size of only a few millionths of a millimeter. Unbelievable? Not at all, for evolution solved these problems more than a billion years ago. The motor mentioned above is already in existence—it is a system mainly consisting of the proteins actin and myosin, and serves to power our

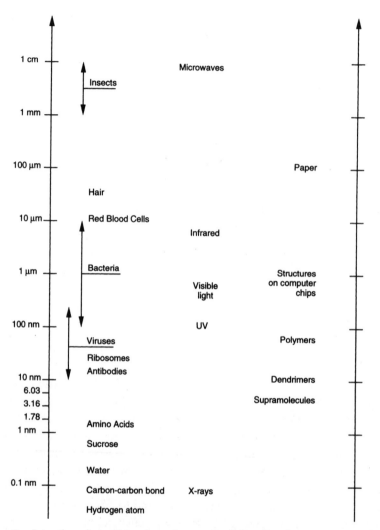

Figure 1: Length scale reaching from the atomic (0.1 nm) to the macroscopic. Note that the length increment is represented on a logarithmic scale, each tick on the axis indicating a 10-fold bigger scale than the previous one. The Ångstrom (Å) length unit corresponds to 0.1 nm. Any items that may not sound familiar right now will be explained in detail later on in the text and also in the Glossary. Antibodies will reappear in Chapter 2, ribosomes in this chapter and in Chapter 3, dendrimers and supramolecules in Chapter 5. Thus, it may be useful to refer back to this figure when these structures have become familiar.

muscles. The data store, or chromosome (i.e., a very long stretch of DNA wound up in a complicated way), determines your genetic identity as well as that of every other living organism on this planet. And the catalyst, the enzyme nitrogenase, is a specialty of the nodule bacteria, which live in symbiosis with certain plants and provide them with freshly made nitrogen fertilizer produced from air and water.

These are just three examples out of an enormous number of tricky technical problems that living cells can apparently handle with little effort. The secret behind this success story, the underlying principle that has been proven the best (if not the only) way to efficiency on a small scale by 3 billion years of evolution, is the modular design principle. Nature's nanotechnology relies on long, chainlike molecules, fabricated from a small set of building blocks. The whole management of genetic data is based on an alphabet of just four letters. Most functions of a living cell are performed by proteins consisting of only 20 different amino acids. However, this simplicity is rather deceptive, as the combination of these building blocks to a long chain can happen in an astronomical number of different ways. If we wanted to "invent" a rather small protein with 100 amino acid residues, we would have a choice of 20^{100} (i.e., 10^{130}, or a number with 131 digits) possibilities. Thus, modular design allows the cell to create a wide variety of structures from a very small number of basic units. In terms of complexity (i.e., content of functional or information elements) per space, nothing ever produced by human engineering efforts comes anywhere near the performance of these biological systems.

Let us have a first look at these "natural nanomachines," to see whether they could serve as models for scientists and engineers trying to develop new technologies. We will start with the smallest parts, the molecules, and then work our way up the length scale into the world of the cell.

Molecules: The Building Blocks of Life

Atoms are generally regarded as the fundamental building blocks of matter. Although physicists can split or fuse them under extreme conditions, they will stay intact in all biologically relevant environments and in all technological applications short of a nuclear power station. (They may win or lose a few electrons in chemical reactions, but that doesn't change their mass very significantly.) The physical properties of atoms are crucial for the way in which they assemble to form molecules. Molecules, their formation, reactions, transformations are the domain of chemistry. But if the early stars of our universe had not fused an awful lot of hydrogen atoms to provide a whole range of different (heavier) atoms, there wouldn't be much chemistry to talk about.

Molecules can consist of as little as two, or of as many as thousands of atoms. The latter may be called *macromolecules* (i.e., "big" molecules) although they are still far too tiny to be visible through a light microscope. (Technically, this can be explained by the fact that their dimensions are smaller than the wavelength of visible light, which ranges from 400 to 800 nm.) Macromolecules are normally put together through repeated reactions of small molecules, a process called *polymerization*. When chemists first produced polymers, they made long chains of just one type of building blocks and ill-defined length, called *homopolymers*. Many well-known plastic materials fall into this category, such as polyethylene and poly-(vinyl chloride). In contrast, biological macromolecules are made of a meaningful sequence of different building blocks selected from a limited set. Therefore, they are referred to as *heteropolymers*. Heteropolymers can store information and carry out functions, the combination of which makes them the perfect material for life. Without molecules, there wouldn't be any life.

But just how small are atoms and molecules? Atoms can't really be measured, because they are wrapped in clouds of electrons, which don't have sharp boundaries. But if you take half of the distance between two atoms of the same kind in a molecule as a measure of their radius, they are all less than 1 nm. By this definition, the diameter of a hydrogen atom is 0.06 nm, while the sulfur atom, which is 32 times heavier, measures 0.2 nm across. Small molecules may be up to several nanometers long. Macromolecules can extend up to micrometers, or be wound up to compact shapes with diameters in the range of 10 to 100 nm (see Fig. 1 for some examples).

And it is on this length scale that the macromolecules of the living cell store information, process it, and convert it into function. Deoxyribonucleic acid (DNA), possibly the most prominent molecule of our time, is in charge of the information storage, while proteins fulfill the mechanical or chemical functions. Ribonucleic acid (RNA) can do both: It serves as an information carrier between DNA and the machinery making proteins, and it has functional roles both in protein synthesis and in editing of genetic information. (It is therefore regarded as a promising candidate for the role of the ancestral molecule, which made evolution possible before the complex DNA–RNA–protein machinery was fashioned.)

For the purpose of this book, it will serve you to regard the nucleic acids, DNA and RNA, as just strings of letters, but there are one or two things I need to tell you about proteins. On one level, proteins are strings of letters too, and they normally have 20 different kinds of letters called *amino acids* as previously mentioned. The order in which they are arranged along the string is called the *sequence* or *primary structure* of a protein. As the latter term suggests, there are some deeper levels of complexity (Fig. 2). Protruding from the linear "backbone" of the polypeptide are those parts of the amino acid building blocks that protein chemists call the *side chains*. These come in various shapes and sizes ranging from a simple hydrogen atom (glycine) to a double ring structure (tryptophan). Because of differences in their chemical nature, these side chains can make the chain curl up in a variety of ways. Certain stretches of the chain will form elements of "secondary structure," such as flat spreads called *beta sheets*, or screwlike coils called *alpha helices*. In most proteins, there will be several such elements, held together in what biochemists call the *tertiary structure* by interactions between the side chains. I will explain the nature of these interactions in the next section. The process by which a linear protein chain forms its secondary and tertiary structure is called *protein folding* and it will be explained in some detail in Chapter 3.

Proteins and other biological macromolecules normally act individually carrying out one highly specific task in the nanometer-sized network of the cell's business. Some examples of well-defined molecular function units will be discussed in Chapter 2. In contrast, if *we* handle molecules, we normally have huge numbers of them. An amount of protein that is visible to the naked eye and can be weighed out on a laboratory balance, can contain millions of billions of molecules. For instance, a milligram of the enzyme uricase, which is commonly used to measure the concentration of uric acid in the blood, contains 6 million billion molecules—and when a physician is using the enzyme for a diagnostic assay, they are all doing the same thing. It is as if we were only able to see a tree when it comes in the company of the whole South American rain forest. To construct machines on the nanometer scale, we will have to build macromolecules that are nearly as efficient as their biological counterparts, and we will have to learn to give each individual molecule a task, and to check that it performs well. First advances in that direction will be described in Part III of this book.

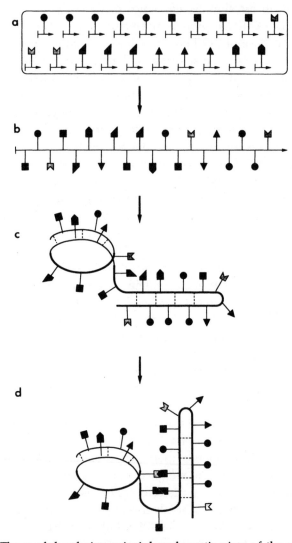

Figure 2:   The modular design principle: schematic view of the structural elements and hierarchic levels of structure formation in proteins. (a) Amino acid building blocks with geometrical forms indicating different chemical properties in the side chains. (b) Linear polypeptide resulting from peptide bond formation between the amino acids. (c) Formation of secondary structure elements such as alpha helix (left) and beta-pleated sheet (right). (d) Formation of tertiary contacts between elements of secondary structure. *NB*: This is a grossly oversimplified representation with the main objective of helping to explain the modular design and structural hierarchy. For a more accurate account of the folding process, see Chapter 3.

However, sticking atoms together to make macromolecules does not necessarily produce nanomachines. Because the latter owe their strength—somewhat paradoxically—to weak interactions.

Interactions: The Weakest Are the Best

Legend has it that organic chemistry was born when the German chemist Friedrich Wöhler (1800–1882) demonstrated that the molecules of life are normal chemical species in the sense that they can be synthesized from inanimate substances—in the first instance, it was urea, which he obtained from ammonium cyanate in 1828. Since then, organic chemists have been making and breaking bonds between carbon atoms and half a dozen other species such as hydrogen, oxygen, nitrogen, sulfur, and phosphorus, so as to create new or interesting molecules, or just to re-create natural products. However, with their classical methodology of making, breaking, and rearranging firm chemical bonds between atoms (known as *covalent bonds*), they will never be able to create anything remotely similar to a cell. Although biological macromolecules are built from covalently linked atoms, this type of binding is much too rigid and inflexible for their three-dimensional functional architecture and for interactions with other molecules in the cell. Breaking a stable covalent bond requires either a catalyst, a large excess of one of the reacting species, or—in the laboratory—high temperatures and nonaqueous solvents.

In the cell, three-dimensional folds (such as the secondary and tertiary structures of proteins mentioned above) and assemblies of several molecules are typically held together by the so-called weak interactions (Fig. 3). These include:

- Hydrogen bonds, in which a hydrogen atom, which is normally bound to just one atom of oxygen or nitrogen, starts an affair with a second atom. (This effect is also the reason why water has an extremely high boiling point considering its modest molecular weight. If hydrogen bonding did not exist, water would be a gas at ambient temperatures, and life would not be possible on Earth.)
- Electrostatic attraction between parts of molecules having opposite electrical charges (also known as *salt bridges*).
- The so-called van der Waals' forces between the negatively-charged cloud of electrons of one atom and the positively-charged nucleus of the other.

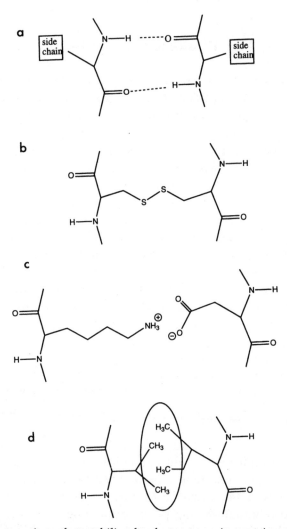

Figure 3:   Interactions that stabilize local structures in proteins: (a) hydrogen
bonds (secondary structure); (b) disulfide bridges (tertiary or even intermolecular);
(c) salt bridges (dto.); (d) hydrophobic interaction (dto.). The oval shape symbolizes
the hydrophobic area from which water is excluded.

- The hydrophobic interaction, which is the tendency of oily, water-avoiding molecular surfaces to stick together and shut out any water molecules (Chapter 3).
- As an exception to the rule, there is also one kind of covalent chemical bond that helps in stabilizing three-dimensional structures in the cell. It is the so-called disulfide bond, which is easily formed and broken under physiological conditions.

Hydrogen bonds, for instance, provide the force that keeps the two strands of the DNA double helix together. In the three-dimensional structures of proteins, they help with the formation of structural elements such as the alpha helix and the beta-pleated sheet. Salt bridges often help an enzyme recognize its substrate. Van der Waals' interactions are so short-ranged that they only become effective when two molecules or parts of molecules have complementary shapes and click into a jigsawlike association. The hydrophobic interaction keeps the lipid double layer together, forming the membrane surrounding every cell and some special compartments within cells. It also plays an important role in the structure formation (folding) of proteins (Chapter 3).

All of these bonds can easily be dissolved and rebuilt by subtle changes in conditions. In many cases, their quality of being as easy to open as a Velcro tightening is a major requirement for the function of the systems they help to build and stabilize. The DNA double helix, for instance, has to be opened locally so that it can be "read" by the enzymes that either copy it to make more DNA or transcribe it to make RNA. And when the oxygen-storage protein of the muscle, myosin, carries an oxygen molecule, the latter is deeply buried within the structure of the protein. To be able to take it up or set it free, the protein has to rearrange its structure in such a way that a tunnel is opened between the oxygen-binding site and the rest of the world. Weak interactions are needed not only for these relatively rapid local rearrangements, but also enable the association of macromolecules to form highly complicated systems without any help from molecules that are not part of the final structure. This phenomenon is known as *self-organization*.

Self-Organization: Together We Will Make It

The factory in which the gut-colonizing bacterium *Escherichia coli* produces its proteins is a compact particle some 25 nm in diameter (and

somewhat reminiscent of a sculpture by Henry Moore) known as the
(bacterial) *ribosome*. It consists of two subunits, containing a grand total
of 52 protein molecules and three long strands of RNA. Although more
than a dozen research groups have been trying for more than two decades
to determine the exact structure and function of this machinery, elucida-
tion has not been achieved.

Researchers have divided the particle into its molecular components,
separated all 55 types of macromolecules, and studied them individually.
More surprisingly, they found that if they recombined the aqueous solutions of those components coming from the smaller subunit, they obtained
fully functional small subunits (Fig. 4). The recipe for the larger subunit is
only a little bit more complicated, involving two subsets of components,
one of which should only be added after the other one has had time to
assemble, and a shift in the buffer conditions. Having assembled the two
subunits, one can proceed by mixing these and will end up with complete
ribosomes that will synthesize proteins as if nothing ever happened. This
extremely complex structure has formed just like that, by four mixing steps.
Obviously, no blueprint, scaffolding, or input of additional information
about the target structure is needed for the assembly of this molecular factory.

This example may be spectacular, but it is by no means unique. It
points to an important principle in the nanotechnology of life. All machine
parts are built in a way so that they can associate to functional machinery
on their own. They don't need an instructions, template, or engineer. They
carry their destination encoded in their structures. In a similar way, scientists can reassemble complete viruses, such as tobacco mosaic virus (TMV),
or complex cellular structures such as microtubuli, the tubelike threads of
the cell's skeleton. However, you should not try this with your computer
or VCR. It would be a rather expensive way of demonstrating how twentieth century engineering falls short of the standards set by nature.

A remarkable example of how researchers have learnt their lesson
from nature and used self-organization to create an artificial ion channel
will be discussed in Chapter 5. However, this is a rather singular case.
Although the reconstitution of natural systems that tend to self-assemble
in a similar way as the ribosome was performed in the reaction tube
decades ago (TMV 1972, large ribosomal subunit 1974, small subunit 1968),
this phenomenon has only rarely been used to construct artificial molecular systems. The new branch of chemistry that mainly deals with weak
interactions and self-organization—supramolecular chemistry—is still in
its infancy (see Chapter 5).

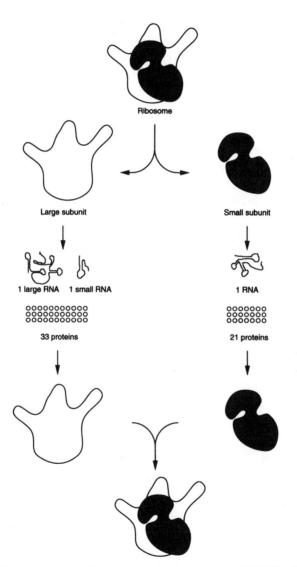

Figure 4:   Disintegration of ribosomes into their protein and RNA building blocks can be carried out reversibly in the test tube. Provided with the right conditions, the molecules will reassemble into fully functional ribosomes.

Having watched the cellular nanomachines as they put themselves together, you may wonder what these tiny marvels do when they are finished.

Catalysts: Making Chemical Reactions Fast and Accurate

Proteins can, for instance, serve as structural elements in the cell's architecture or as carriers for small molecules or ions (the best-known examples for these being tubulin and hemoglobin, respectively), but most of them have the task of speeding up (catalyzing) chemical reactions. In extreme cases, they can make reactions that would otherwise require millions of years to run to completion within seconds. Proteins with a catalytic function are called *enzymes*. The dogma that *only* proteins can play this role was overturned in the 1980s, when researchers discovered catalysts constructed exclusively of RNA and called them *ribozymes*.

Why does a cell need enzymes? The obvious answer is that it doesn't have the time to wait for slow reactions to occur. But there is another equally important reason: It needs enzymes to direct the production processes in its chemical factory. Catalysts are—by definition—not allowed to govern the direction of a reaction. They only accelerate the arrival of the equilibrium distribution between states, which is defined by conditions such as temperature, pressure, and so on, by lowering the energy barrier between the initial and the final state (Fig. 5). However, this apparently modest influence can move quite a lot. For instance, if one chemical could theoretically get involved in alternative reaction paths, an enzyme could catalyze only one of them. In this way, a highly specific catalyst—and enzymes tend to be the most specific catalysts we know—could completely change the range of products obtained from a given reaction mix. Furthermore, enzymes can couple one reaction to another. Thus, reactions that would require a lot of energy (e.g., the synthesis of macromolecules) can be driven forward by energy-providing reactions, such as the cleavage of certain small molecules.

Many enzymes outperform the corresponding technical catalysts by orders of magnitude. For instance, there is no technical catalyst producing ammonia from the elements (hydrogen and nitrogen) at ambient temperature and pressure, as the nitrogenase of nodule bacteria does (see Chapter 2). Some enzymes are used in households, for stain removal, as additives

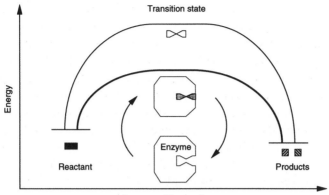

Figure 5:   Energy profiles of a chemical reaction with (lower curve) and without (upper curve) catalysis, e.g., by an enzyme. By binding to the reactant in a way that favors the transition state, the catalyst reduces the height of the energy hill that separates the products from the starting point of the reaction, the so-called activation barrier. It thereby increases the number of the molecules that at a given temperature carry enough energy to surmount the barrier. Note that, like any true catalyst, the enzyme is not changed in the overall reaction and can be recycled, as indicated by the arrows.

in washing powders, or for curdling milk to make curd cheese. Enzymes that can degrade proteins (proteases) are used in cosmetics, and hair perms can be laid with the help of the enzyme urease.

Some enzymes have even created their own specific applications in the laboratory, in procedures that scientists could not even have dreamt of before a specific enzyme was discovered. Among the best-known high-flyers are the restriction endonucleases developed by bacteria to fight viruses. Now they are indispensable for molecular biologists, who use them to fragment nucleic acids into well-defined pieces. Even more spectacular, the availability of extremely heat-stable DNA polymerase from thermophilic bacteria paved the way for the polymerase chain reaction (PCR) of *Jurassic Park* fame, which enables molecular biologists to make millions of copies starting from just one piece of DNA. While a small sample containing only a "countable" number of DNA molecules was utterly useless in pre-PCR times, the so-called amplification procedure enables researchers to do anything with it—at least anything short of cloning dinosaurs.

And some enzymes are already used in industrial production, mainly in simple reactions, such as the degradation of starch to make sugar. More than 20 million tons of sugar are produced this way every year, requiring 15,000 tons of the enzyme amyloglucosidase. In Brazil, the fermentation of carbohydrates to produce technical ethanol has been boosted as part of a national program to reduce the country's dependence on petroleum imports. Furthermore, enzymatic processes are becoming more and more important in the production of pharmaceuticals as well as in food processing.

Although nature has millions of different enzymes and we are far from using this potential to a significant degree, many technical applications would benefit if we could make similarly specific catalysts to measure, especially to speed up reactions that do not occur in biology. One might also hope that these synthetic enzymes could have a longer shelf life than their natural counterparts. Various routes to this goal will be discussed in Chapter 5.

Directing the chemical reactions of metabolism by selective catalysis is a really clever feat, but to avoid getting things messed up, the cell also has to allocate spaces for each process.

Compartmentation: Keeping Your Cells Tidy

The first step toward the confinement of this network of chemical reactions that we call life was taken when cells started being cells. They surrounded their precious little selves with a double layer membrane (which can in many cases be further shielded and reinforced by a cell wall, and further layers) so that their own chemical processes would not so easily be disturbed by the outside world.

But we also find walls and barriers within cells. We (people, cats, yuccas, yeasts, and very many other species) belong to the group of life forms enjoying a cell nucleus, collectively called the *eukaryotes*. While this nucleus contains most of our DNA, there are other compartments in the eukaryotic cell, which all have a specific set of functional tasks and often a fairly involved name, such as *endoplasmic reticulum* or *mitochondrion* (Fig. 6; see Chapter 4 for a comparison with bacteria). All that matters for our current purpose is that the cell appears to have secluded areas for specific functions, resembling the way in which houses are divided into living room, dining room, kitchen, bedrooms, and so forth.

Obviously, this organization requires even more different sorts of

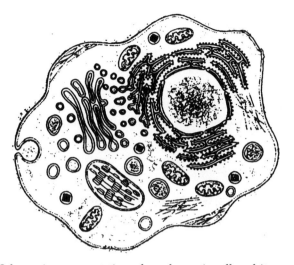

Figure 6:   Schematic representation of a eukaryotic cell and its compartments.

nanomachines. Walls between compartments must be built, or rather build themselves, as we would suspect after the earlier discussion of self-organization. So we won't need cranes or scaffolds. But once the walls are there, we will need means of transport between the rooms. A door or cat-flap won't do, as we want to control the traffic between the rooms. A simple regulated valve might do if we just want molecules to get from one room with plenty of their kind to an empty one. However, quite often the cell needs to transport molecules against this trend of equal distribution. In this case it could use the principle of coupling the transport with an energy-consuming process, as discussed above.

Within the rooms of the house as well as in the single-roomed bacterial cell, some scientists have expected to find a chaotic random mixing of all molecules. However, it begins to emerge that even the soluble enzymes have some kind of spatial organization as well. Nanomachines are sometimes arranged in an assembly line, where the product of one step can be directly passed on to become the raw material of the next. For instance, molecular chaperones known to supervise the folding of freshly synthesized proteins have been found in close contact with the ribosomes that make the proteins (Chapter 3).

Only a few years ago (1994), scientists succeeded in arranging biological macromolecules or similarly complex systems with nanometer precision, at least in two dimensions. Using the method presented in Chapter 6, nanobiotechnologists will be able to construct a biotechnological assembly line, along which the substrates can be handed on from one enzyme to the next without any loss of time or substance.

Although, with the discussion of whole cells, we are leaving the nanoscale and heading toward the visible world, we shall now have a quick look at the macroworld of life before returning to the molecular scale.

Evolution: Molecules to Organisms

From the big bang through to the rise of green plants and vertebrates, matter has increasingly become organized in bigger and more complex structures. Subatomic particles became atoms, atoms fused to form bigger atoms, which reacted to form small molecules (which could form big things like planets, but not complex things like living cells), small molecules became macromolecules, which gave rise to cells, which evolved to form multicellular organisms, which grouped together to form herds, flocks, or learned societies, and so on.

This admittedly rather crude account of the history of our universe covers 15 billion years on the time scale and 14 orders of magnitude on the length scale. The theory of evolution by the interplay of mutation and selection provides convincing connections for a major part of this way, at least from the first macromolecule that catalyzed its own duplication—possibly a variant of today's RNA—through to the current population of the Earth with millions of species.

Some researchers even believe that the evolutionary principles started shaping our history even further back in time and down in scale. Atomic-scale defects in the otherwise regular lattices of clay minerals may have been the first kind of hereditary information. This hypothesis proposed by A. G. Cairns-Smith implies that a pre-evolution has taken place in the realm of atoms and inorganic solid states, which then may have provided a scaffold for the first organic information molecules. Even today we observe stunning capabilities of proteins and cells, directing the precipitation of inorganic minerals in crystalline as well as in amorphic phases, leading to such diverse structures as bones, teeth, eggshells, mollusk shells, or pathogenic urate crystals (Chapter 2).

Strictly speaking, the question of how cells form complex organisms is beyond the nanoscopic focus of this book. However, it should be noted that communication between cells, which is essential for every multicellular organism, relies on complex molecular systems, many of which may be useful models for information scientists and computer developers. The "one to all" function, for instance, is often performed by hormones and the corresponding receptors. Self-organization is, again, involved when receptor complexes integrate into membranes. Molecular recognition with the help of weak interactions is needed for the specific binding between hormone and receptor, which then triggers a reaction cascade.

For the site-directed delivery of information, our body has its own telephone network, namely, the nervous system. In addition to the phenomena discussed above, electric voltages and currents play a major role here. At the best-described site of the nervous system, the retina of the eye, light is one further information carrier to be considered. Signal conversion between light, electricity, and chemical energy on the length scale of cell receptors certainly is one of the targets to be set for future technological developments. Not to mention that computer technology has thus far failed to match that (generally underused) masterpiece of evolution, the human brain. Thus, while every "primitive" bacterial cell holds rich lessons for future engineers to learn, higher organisms contain additional levels of complexity, which could provide additional inspirations for advanced technologies.

Technology: Back to Molecules

In a sense, scientists are now walking the way back on which humankind evolved. Fifteen billion years took us from femtometers to meters, from subatomic particles to human beings, who are now trying to go back to the small worlds, using the relatively recent invention of technology, or the art to make tools, which allow you to make even better tools, and so on.

Technology began, of course, as "macrotechnology." The first tools made and applied by early people were on the scale of their natural tools, their hands and arms. They may have used sticks if their arms were too short to reach a fruit. Or stone blades if their fingernails were too blunt to dissect a prey.

Later on, early cultures used pulleys, levers, wheels, and the like to erect amazing buildings on the gigantomanic scale of the pyramids or

Stonehenge. And unknowingly, they used microorganisms to produce beer and bread. But they did not try to observe or manipulate the invisibly small parts of the world. The atoms proposed by the Greek philosopher Democritus (ca. 460 BC) remained a philosophical postulate for more than two millennia.

The microworld only opened up when the light microscope, which was invented in the Netherlands in 1590, became a fashion during the seventeenth century. The Dutch shopkeeper Antonie van Leeuwenhoek (1632–1723) was the first to develop a microscope good enough to discover microbes (1675). Remarkably, he made his discoveries, which constitute the foundation of the entire discipline of microbiology, as a total outsider to the science establishment of his time. He did not even know any Latin, which was the official language for scientific publications. Despite this handicap, he eventually became a fellow of the Royal Society.

Even in the nineteenth century, watchmakers were the only people to fabricate small structures. They were operating down to the 0.1 mm scale, using a magnifying glass. Chemistry, which evolved to become an exact science during the early nineteenth century, and a leading industry afterwards, had a strong tendency to go for big things, rather than for small ones. Although nineteenth century chemists could not work out what molecules were in a physical sense, they found comfort in the observation that these chemical entities behaved in a predictable way, if you had billions of billions of them in your reaction tube. To be on the safe side, they defined their standard quantity of matter, the mole, in a way that it contains ca. 6×10^{23} molecules.

Only when electronic components became important in the second half of the twentieth century and miniaturization became crucial for the development of more useful and faster equipment did fabrication on the micrometer scale become a mass industry.

Windows into the nanoworld have been opened since the middle of our century by techniques such as electron microscopy, X-ray crystallography, neutron scattering, and nuclear magnetic resonance. Chemists have learned during the past 200 years to handle molecules, describe their structures, and create novel molecular structures. However, they have always dealt with macroscopic amounts of the substances, containing billions of billions of molecules. And there have always been limits to the size and complexity of the molecular systems that could be analyzed. Furthermore, the science of the huge molecules—macromolecular chemistry—has always been a stepchild of chemistry. It could not aspire to become a classical subject, as inorganic, organic, and physical chemistry are, or an independent discipline like biochemistry.

Making tools for fabrication on the nanometer scale is something we are only just beginning to learn to do. Only now do the subject areas of biochemistry, chemistry, physics, and biology, which deal with natural nanoscale systems or try to produce artificial ones, approach one another. Only now have chemists started using the power of weak interactions and the principle of self-organization to make synthetic molecules similarly efficient as biological systems. Only now have methods in materials sciences been miniaturized to a degree that nanometer-scale structures can be etched out of semiconductor material and electronic elements as well as mechanical machine parts can be produced on this scale.

When technology enters a new dimension, this can potentially change the world. The development of microscopes led to the discovery of microbes, which revolutionized our ideas about fermentation, hygiene, and disease. The invention of microchips led to the breathtaking developments in computer applications that we have witnessed over the past few decades, and that will indeed continue to change the way people live and work for some time. Similarly, the technologies that will result from the conquest of the nanoworld may revolutionize not only the world of science but also daily life as well. Whether or not nanotechnology is likely to become the next industrial revolution will be discussed in Part IV. Current prophecies will be critically assessed. Predicted applications of nanomachines range from medicine to space travel, from data processing to the protection and healing of the environment. We shall once again realize that the nanoworld, although invisible, shapes our visible world.

II

The Role Model
The Living Cell as a Nanotechnological Factory

2

Proteins: The Cell's Nanomachines

Cells can do everything. Well, not each of them individually, of course. But for every task that a mischievous examiner could possibly think of setting for a microscopically small something, there probably is a cell that can perform it. You want a living compass? No problem, as magnetotactic bacteria know which way is north. A remedy against oil spills? There are bacteria for this as well. A transport vehicle for oxygen? Our red blood cells are doing that for a living. A molecular motor? Our muscle cells contain hundreds of them. Two mirror-symmetrical kinds of molecules form separate but apparently identical crystals—can one tell them apart? Cells can. No matter whether you want to mine for silver, dispose of organic solvents, or produce highly toxic substances, whether you want to deposit a mineral substance in its amorphous or in its crystalline form, whether you want to convert chemical energy to motion, heat, or light, or vice versa, nature has a small-scale solution for each of these technical challenges. Thus far, technology is unable to duplicate most of these achievements.

Within the cell, most of the smart solutions that could serve as role models for future technologies, fall into the realm of proteins—especially those from the areas of mechanical action and chemical reactions. Proteins are the action molecules of all living things. Hence, if scientists want to know how a cell carries out a given task, the key to a deeper understanding lies in finding out the detailed structures of the protein molecules involved. The structures are all different, because they have evolved to fulfill different tasks in different ways. More than 7000 structures of proteins have now been determined, and the number is growing at an ever-increasing rate, but many new structures are still revelations. Although the first protein structure (myoglobin) was solved in 1957 and the first enzyme (lysozyme) in 1965, many proteins believed to hold key positions in the workings of the cell have proven extremely difficult targets and are only now understood after decades of massive research efforts. Some of the difficult cases solved during the 1990s will be discussed in this chapter and in Chapter 3. Having solved the structure, scientists can proceed with a more sophisticated analysis and manipulation of the molecules than would have otherwise been possible.

Even a relatively simple cell, like our all-time companion, the gut bacterium *Escherichia coli*, produces several thousand kinds of proteins all the time. Small ones and relatively large ones, water-soluble and lipid-soluble ones (which find their place within the water-avoiding interior of the cell membrane), acidic and alkaline ones, ball-shaped and rodlike proteins, and many more. Each kind of protein—as specified by the relevant gene—is an individual, and it is difficult to make generalizations beyond the basic chemical principles specifying how proteins are made up as chains of amino acid building blocks. While Chapter 3 will outline the "curriculum vitae" of a protein by describing research topics lining its path from the cradle to the grave, the present chapter aims to provide a picture of what proteins can do, how they do it, and how we find out how they do it. This will be illustrated by selected examples—somewhat the way that biochemists tend to choose certain "model proteins" as their pets to investigate general issues while being careful not to overgeneralize from these. From these examples, we shall get an impression of what certain proteins are able to do. As we are traveling a vast, mostly unexplored land, these are just small excursions, but they will provide us with some insight into the functioning of the natural nanoworld and with some ideas about how engineers could set about constructing the first technological structures and factories in the nanoworld, overcoming the technical difficulties we still have today.

Molecular Motors: Muscle Research Moves On

Some people tend to be exceedingly proud of their powerful muscles, inflated by years of hard training to the most intriguing shapes and sizes. Biologically speaking, however, this pride seems to clash with the snobbish attitude with which we as members of the species *Homo sapiens* tend to look down on other creatures. Not only the skeletal muscles of the vertebrates—with whom most of us would acknowledge some kind of kinship—but also the closing muscles of mussels and other invertebrates essentially function in the same way as our power packs. Whether Arnold Schwarzenegger shows off his biceps or whether a scallop snaps its shell shut to swim a couple of centimeters, it is all the same to a biophysicist.

If you want a 100,000-fold magnified rough model of what happens, just stick the heads of two toothbrushes together so that the bristles are intermingled while being parallel. In a similar way, two different kinds of bristles, the so-called thick filaments and the thin filaments, are arranged in the muscle cell. If we want a precise model, we need three sets of bristles, though: two brushes of thin filaments opposing but not touching each other, and the thick filaments bridging the gap between them and intermingling with both. Now, a muscle shortens (by approximately a third of its length in the relaxed state), because in each individual cell the bristles of one kind move a little bit alongside those of the other kind—as if you moved the brushes a little bit closer together. The protein myosin, composed of a long tail and a roundish head, makes up the thick filaments and is regarded as the motor driving this sliding movement, using the most widespread energy currency of the cell, adenosine triphosphate (ATP), as a fuel. (Note that this is a linear motor as opposed to the rotatory motors that we are more familiar with. Both types occur in cells.) Each molecule of myosin is firmly anchored with its long tail in the thick filaments, and its head can grab the thin filaments, which mainly consist of the protein actin.

The "sliding filament model" of muscle function was developed by Andrew Huxley and R. Niedergerke, and independently by Hugh Huxley and Jean Hanson in the 1950s and 1960s. However, the driving force, i.e., the mechanism by which the chemical energy released from the degradation of ATP can be converted into the motion energy of the sliding filaments, remained elusive for decades. Muscle research seemed to proceed in slow motion. This changed radically in the years 1993–1994, when structural biologists provided most of the detailed information about the structures of motor proteins that muscle researchers could wish for, and biophysicists developed clever ways of watching individual motor molecules in action.

Muscle research moved over to the fast lane in July 1993, when Ivan Rayment and his co-workers at the University of Wisconsin published the crystal structure of the myosin head. To crystallize the protein, which they had obtained from chicken muscles, the researchers had to remove the tail in its entire length of some 160 nm and carry out minor chemical modifications on the head, which contains all of the important functional elements and can interact with the actin filaments even in the absence of the tail. From the atomically detailed structure of the myosin head, together with that of actin (solved in 1990), Rayment's group developed a molecular model of the interaction between the two compounds, which brought the sliding filament model to the level of molecular detail (Fig. 1). From the spatial arrangement of the moving parts of the actin–myosin motor, the researchers could set limits to the step length for each functional cycle (corresponding to the degradation of one molecule of ATP per myosin head): It was predicted to lie in the range from 6 to 20 nm.

Another breakthrough was achieved at first with a different motor molecule, the protein kinesin, which has nothing to do with muscles in particular, but is extremely important for transport and motion within all kinds of cells in higher organisms. Normally, kinesin travels along the tubelike fibrils of the cell's skeleton, the microtubuli, and drags along relatively big things like chromosomes or organelles, for instance. Karel Svoboda and his group, however, got kinesin to work on a microscope slide with glued on microtubuli and to drag along a little ball made of silica gel in such a fashion that it moves through the two parts of a laser beam split into two partially overlapping rays—a so-called optical trap. (It is important that the half-beams have different polarizations, i.e., their light waves are oriented differently.) By comparing the way in which the two parts of the beam are affected by the moving particle, the researchers could reconstruct the movement with a resolution of 1 nm. They came to the conclusion that kinesin moves in individual steps that are 8 nm in length.

Sadly, this finding could not be interpreted in molecular terms when it was published in October 1993, as the structure of kinesin was not yet known (about a third of it would be published in April 1996). Therefore, it was another big leap, when James A. Spudich's group at Stanford could improve on the interferometry method and apply it to single myosin molecules. Their study included the application of a minute counterforce, which could be adjusted so that it brought the movement to a halt. Thus,

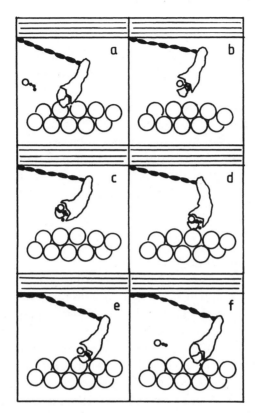

Figure 1: Schematic representation of the reaction cycle of myosin during muscle contraction. The horizontally striped element at the top of each box represents the thick filament, in which the myosin tail (black twisted rope) is anchored. (a) The myosin head is bound to one of the actin subunits (circles) of the thin filament, and it carries no nucleotide. (b) ATP binds to the myosin head and makes it let go of the actin. (c) Cleavage of the outermost phosphate group from ATP results in ADP-myosin, which (d) stretches out and grabs a more distant actin subunit to which it binds only weakly at the beginning. (e) Removal of the cleaved phosphate group allows the myosin to bind more firmly and to contract. This is the power stroke that actually generates the muscle movement. (f) Removal of the ADP leads back to the initial state.

they could not only measure the step width, which turned out to be 11 nm in that case, but also the force generated by an individual muscle molecule. It was determined to be 3 to 4 piconewtons, i.e., three to four times a millionth of a millionth of the force that you would need to hold an object weighing 102 grams—let's say an apple, as a tribute to Newton. This also means that lifting that apple would require at least 0.3 trillion molecules to work at any one time.

Shortly afterwards, another X-ray structure of a muscle protein was published. This time, a small part of the motor protein that enables scallops to move their shells (and thereby swim) was analyzed. It was the domain that regulates the ATP degrading function of the myosin head—the gas pedal of the muscle motor, so to speak. Whether this pedal is being kicked down or released depends on the concentration of calcium ions in the cell. Interestingly, this regulatory domain does not exist in vertebrate myosin. Therefore, the structure solved by Carolyn Cohen at Brandeis together with several other groups provided additional insight into the mechanisms of power regulation in muscles that could not be obtained from the earlier studies on chicken myosin. Furthermore, the scallop myosin did not need chemical modification to crystallize, and in some regions it is better resolved than the chicken myosin.

In the following years (1995–1997), further studies in basically the same directions, i.e., structural work using X-ray crystallography and electron microscopy, and single-molecule biophysics using optical tweezers kept the research field of linear molecular motors going in fast forward mode as witnessed by the regular appearance of these nanomachines, especially myosin and kinesin, on the pages of *Nature* and *Science*. In April 1996, for instance, it was reported that the crystal structure of the kinesin motor domain showed more similarity with the corresponding part of the myosin head than most researchers would have anticipated. The major difference between the functional behavior of the two different motors— apart from the fact that each of them requires a specific type of rail to move on, made of actin for myosin, and of tubulin for kinesin—seems to stem from the different "duty ratios," that is, the fraction of time that the molecules spend in tight association with the rail they move on.

Another piece of evidence that could only be obtained after decades of frustrated attempts was the molecular structure of the tubulins, the building blocks of microtubules that are not only among the most important structural elements of higher cells, but also the support system for several kinds of motors including kinesin. In January 1998, Eva Nogales and her co-workers at the Lawrence Berkeley National Laboratory reported the final success of solving the structures not by classical X-ray crystallography, but by sophisticated electron scattering analysis on two-dimensional sheets of the proteins. Although this method does not quite reach truly atomic resolution, it does allow fitting the known sequence of amino acid building blocks into a reliable three-dimensional model of the overall protein conformation. We will look at the structure of tubulin in more detail in Chapter 4.

There is one other fascinating protein in muscle that I will only mention in passing as it is not directly involved in motor activity. If a muscle gets overstretched beyond the reach of the sliding filaments, the structural units are still held together by the protein titin, which is by far the biggest single-chain protein known so far. In its relaxed state it spans more than 1 μm, and it can extend to a multiple of that length. If worst comes to worst, some of the more than 300 "domains" (folding units the size of a small protein) making up this giant molecule could unfold reversibly to allow some extra length. Titin does not possess any active role—it is thought to act simply as a molecular rubber band that brings the gliding filaments together if they accidentally slide off the end of the scale. In May 1997, several groups presented single-molecule studies on titin unraveling the strange mechanisms of its elasticity.

Thus, after a long and often frustrating effort, structural biologists now have access to detailed data on the most important parts of the major motor systems required for muscle contraction and for motion and transport within cells and during cell division. In a sense, this is only the first step on the way to a full understanding of the workings of these molecular marvels. However, with the most important pieces of the jigsaw in place, achieving this goal has moved into the realm of the feasible.

The Enzyme that Feeds the World

Plants are facing a paradoxical supply problem. One of the chemical elements they require most urgently for their growth is nitrogen. And the air around them is mostly made up of exactly this element. However, as the nitrogen in the air occurs in its molecular form, which is extremely reluctant to take part in chemical reactions, plants cannot make use of this immense supply. The conversion of molecular nitrogen into nitrogen compounds usable for plants, animals, and humans happens largely in two different ways.

Each year, roughly 100 million tons of the element are technically forced to react with molecular hydrogen to form ammonia, the basic compound for the production of all nitrogen-containing synthesis chemicals and especially for the production of fertilizers. This reaction is carried

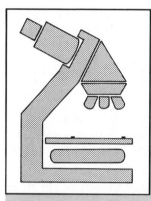

Ways and Means

Structure Determination
by X-Ray Crystallography

Until well into the twentieth century, proteins were a kind of biological goo, and controversies were raging on issues such as whether they had a defined chemical structure or not. Nowadays, not only the chemical structures are generally known, but also the conformation it is most likely to adopt in three dimensions can be looked up in the protein database for more than 7000 different kinds of proteins. Most of this is the achievement of biophysicists who have analyzed the way that X-rays get bent from their path when they meet a protein crystal, as I will explain below. An increasing fraction of new structures is provided by NMR spectroscopy (see Ways & Means on p. 80–81).

First of all, X-ray crystallographers need a crystal, which is far from being a trivial requirement. Considering the "soft" and irregular shape of proteins, it is intriguing that many of them do form well-defined crystals, much more than that many others just don't. For instance, literally anybody can crystallize lysozyme in a kitchen simply by combining egg white with a concentrated brine of table salt. Other proteins of immense biological importance, such as tubulin, have had biophysicists struggling for decades in vain attempts to obtain satisfactory crystals.

Once they have the crystal in hand, they place it in a well-defined orientation to a screen covered with an X-ray film and to the X-ray beam with which it will be irradiated. On the film, a multitude of black dots will show up, the so-called diffraction reflexes, which are an encoded description of the spatial distribution of electron density in the repeating unit of the crystalline array. One can translate the dots back to a picture of the electron density distribution using a mathematical operation known as Fourier synthesis. This procedure is necessary, because there is no way of focusing X-rays as one would focus light in the eyepiece of a microscope to reproduce an enlarged picture of the object studied. Thus, the X-ray "picture" one gets is necessarily "unfocused" and one needs mathematics to produce an image of the electron density that has caused the particular X-ray diffraction. This, however, requires a second data set, obtained with a similar structure containing a few heavier atoms in well-defined places. Getting protein crystals with the "heavy atom replacement" has in some cases been the trickiest bit of the structure determination. Max Perutz, who developed this method in Cambridge in 1953, wrote later that he had optimistically expected that many protein structures would be determined soon after he solved this fundamental problem. In fact, only three structures were solved by 1965: myoglobin, lysozyme, and hemoglobin. Only in the 1970s did the number of available crystal structures begin to rise exponentially as it has done to this day.

Once the crystallographers have produced the three-dimensional map of the electron density from the diffraction pattern, this is already a "structure" in a crude sense, as it outlines the overall shape of the molecule. However, one still has to work out which blob corresponds to which atom or which amino acid residue in the chemical structure of the polypeptide. That is, one has to know the amino acid sequence of the protein first—feasible but not trivial in the 1960s—and then try to fit a chain with this sequence into the electron density map. This means a couple of days for a silicon graphics workstation in the late 1990s, but years of hard work for the pioneers of protein crystallography back in the stone age of computing.

In principle, the atomic structures proudly displayed in the papers are just hypotheses. They are models of conformations the protein chain could adopt and which would fit the experimentally observed electron density. One should always bear in mind that errors in these models can and do occur. One problem is that not all protein crystals give diffraction patterns allowing optimal resolution. Thus, a very highly resolved study would nowadays have a resolution of say 0.165 nm, while crystals of lesser quality may only diffract to 0.35 nm.

out on a huge scale and with rather poor efficiency. The synthesis originally developed by the German chemist Fritz Haber (1868–1934) and
adapted to the industrial scale by Carl Bosch (1874–1940) requires high
pressures (200 atmospheres), high temperatures (500°C) and expensive
catalysts, to convert as little as 18% of the nitrogen involved to ammonia.

Another estimated 100 million tons of nitrogen per year are converted
to nitrogen compounds by unicellular microorganisms such as cyanobac-
teria, and the nodule-forming bacteria of the genus *Rhizobium*. They use
the nitrogen from the air to build nitrogen-containing biomolecules such
as proteins, nucleic acids, and others. Through the leguminous plants
(such as beans, peas) with which nodule-forming bacteria live in symbiosis, nitrogen compounds get into the food chain and thus reach all
living beings (apart from those that can get it directly from the air).
Nature's process appears to be much more elegant than the Haber–Bosch
synthesis. The reaction—called *nitrogen fixation* in this context—is carried
out at ordinary temperatures and atmospheric pressure, and the catalyst is
the highly specialized enzyme nitrogenase.

Although the initial motivation for developing a technical synthesis of
ammonia and establishing the first 30,000 ton per year factory at Oppau,
Germany, had certainly more to do with gunpowder than with fertilizer,
the agricultural use of the Haber–Bosch process became big business on a
global scale, after technical improvements in the 1960s made the production more economical. By 1988, half of the production of nitrogen fertilizer
was used in developing countries. Today approximately every third nitrogen atom in our food (and hence in our bodies) comes from a factory rather
than from a nitrogen-fixing microbe. In other words, two billion people
alive today owe their existence to Haber and Bosch. (Note that among all
of the chemical cycles that keep our biosphere going, it is not those
involving the much discussed greenhouse gas carbon dioxide, but rather
those involving nitrogen that have been most spectacularly changed
through our industrial activities.)

Economically speaking, the process was a major success story on a
global scale, even though the environmental impact of fertilizer overuse
has also grown with the increase in production. But still it must have been
frustrating for chemists working in this field to realize that they couldn't
come up with a technical catalyst that achieves what seems to be straightforward in nature, namely, breaking up nitrogen molecules at ambient
conditions. At least, their chances of learning some of nature's tricks
improved in 1992, when the group of Douglas C. Rees at Caltech presented

the crystal structures of both of the protein subunits of the nitrogenase enzyme after years of extremely difficult work. As the nitrogenase enzymes are very sensitive to oxygen, they had to be kept under inert gas (argon) during every step of the process, from protein purification through to the X-ray analysis.

Up to this point, one only had a crude picture of how the catalysis work was distributed between the two proteins. First there is the iron protein, which owes its name to an iron–sulfur complex contained in its active site. It is thought to pump electrons over to the molybdenum–iron protein. This second compound of the nitrogenase enzyme is the place where the actual conversion of the nitrogen molecule takes place, and it boasts a cofactor that also includes the relatively rare heavy metal molybdenum, apart from iron–sulfur compounds. Each stroke of the iron protein's electron pump drives the molybdenum iron protein one step ahead on a circuit including the intake of nitrogen, release of ammonia, and back to the binding of the next nitrogen molecule. Scientists believe there are eight steps to this reaction cycle, because eight electrons are required to turn one molecule of nitrogen (N_2) together with eight hydrogen ions (H^+) over to form two molecules of ammonia ($2\ NH_3$) and one molecule of hydrogen (H_2). (Strictly speaking, nitrogenase also is a hydrogenase, an enzyme reducing protons—the form of hydrogen common in water and acids—to molecular hydrogen, the gas that can be used as a fuel.) While the electron transport processes can be explained in analogy to the corresponding processes in photosynthesis, the details of the nitrogen chemistry in this cycle are largely mysterious. Only a single reaction intermediate is known, namely, the halfway reduced compound hydrazine, which contains two nitrogens and four hydrogens.

The molybdenum–iron protein, however, is not only driven around in circles by the electrons pumped into it, it can also store them, acting like a sponge for electrons. This becomes obvious when researchers carry out the catalytic reaction in the test tube. The first batch of the product is already released before all of the eight electrons required for the reaction have been pumped. This suggests that the metal complexes in the active site of the protein have a certain storage capacity for electrons. This kind of chemical curiosity, along with the enormous economical importance of nitrogen fixation, has of course aroused the interest of biologically minded inorganic chemists even long before the structures of the proteins were known. For years they have been playing around with compounds of iron, molybdenum, and sulfur, which are called *clusters* because the chemical bonding between the atoms is more like that in a metal than in nonmetallic molecules. These clusters were somehow inspired by the nitrogenase problem and often yielded interesting findings, but failed to come up with the ultimate answer.

Even with the structures of the proteins known and some reasonable hypotheses about the exact structure of the metal centers (Fig. 2) proposed, bioinorganic chemists keep scratching their heads. G. J. Leigh of the University of Sussex in Brighton noted in 1997 about new findings concerning the chemical reactivity of the dinitrogen molecule: "Rather than clarifying the reaction modes of nitrogenase, these reports add to the list of possibilities." One of the new possibilities was presented by Catalina Laplaza and Christopher C. Cummins of MIT, who reported in 1995 a reaction of molecular nitrogen taking place at a molybdenum center at moderate temperatures. Leigh commented that this finding, although surprising and interesting for chemists, was not the key to the nitrogenase reaction. Similarly, other unusual reactions that the nitrogen molecule has undergone in these years, including a "fixation" reaction at 55°C using the heavy metals tungsten and ruthenium reported in early 1998 by researchers from Tokyo, have enriched the chemistry of nitrogen and may even result in

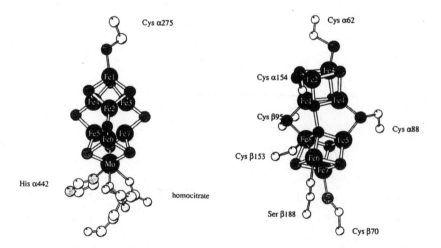

Figure 2: Model representations of the metal clusters in the active sites of the enzyme nitrogenase. (Left) The iron–molybdenum cofactor, which is thought to be directly involved in the reduction of nitrogen. (Right) The so-called P-cluster of the iron protein, which delivers the electrons needed for the reduction of nitrogen.

some improvement of technical procedures in the future, but they failed to spark a major eureka effect as far as the mechanism of the enzymatic pathway is concerned.

It has become clear from this case that the availability of a protein structure with atomic resolution does not necessarily answer all of the questions immediately. After all, chemical reactions have to do with change over time, and crystal structures tend to be static images of an unnaturally immobilized state of the molecule(s) involved. As we shall see in the next section, the step from the static picture to the real life movie still is a major challenge.

Protein Movies: Snapshots of an Enzyme Reaction

Structural images based on the exact location of the many thousands of atoms in a protein or nucleic acid have shaped the appearance of the modern, the molecular, variety of good old biology (see Profile on Irving Geis). Classically, these pictures arise from the results of the X-ray diffraction analysis of the crystallized material (see Ways & Means on pp. 32 and 33). The younger competitor, structural NMR spectroscopy, will be discussed below and in Chapter 3. Crystallography can fix the atoms in space with a resolution close to the diameter of a hydrogen atom (0.1 nm), and it provides crucial information for the understanding of complex molecular systems such as the molecular motors and the nitrogenase enzyme discussed above.

On the other hand, fixing the atoms in space can give a false impression insofar as proteins in the real world are far from being static frameworks of fixed atoms. The problem arises from the fact that X-ray diffraction measurements take hours or days, so they fail to see dynamical motions taking place in seconds or minutes. Even relatively slow chemical reactions may escape the analysis, and rapid structural fluctuations can only be seen as an averaged position with a standard deviation.

To be able to follow the structural changes involved in an enzyme-catalyzed reaction, one would have to shorten the measurement time drastically, slow down the reaction rate, and start the reaction in all of the molecules contained in the crystal at the same time. Crystallographers have spent a lot of effort on each of these goals. They have, for instance, invented "caged" substrate molecules, which could be liberated by a very short laser flash and thus start off the reaction at a well-defined time, they

Profile
Irving Geis—
The Art of Protein Architecture

The nanoworld is by its very definition invisible. As the kind of electromagnetic radiation that we use for vision and therefore call *visible light* has wavelengths of 400 nm and more, no one will ever see the structures of proteins or nucleic acids. All we can do is to collect physical data and reconstruct the structures that are most likely to have caused the particular X-ray diffraction or NMR cross peak pattern that we observe (see Ways & Means on pp. 80 and 81 for details).

And yet, we now have very strong visual images of "what proteins look like." This is of course partly the merit of structural biologists, who measured the structural coordinates in the first place. But their results are essentially long columns filled with numbers. The way we now visualize them has been shaped by a man who was trained not as a scientist but—of all things—as an architect.

Irving Geis was born in New York City in October 1908. He studied architecture, design, and painting, but graduated in the midst of the Depression, without much of a job prospect. Eventually, free-lance illustrating became his main profession, and from 1948 to 1983 he worked regularly for *Scientific American*. His "scientific career" began essentially with the zeroth hour of structural biology. In 1961, after John Kendrew and his co-workers at Cambridge University had elucidated the first-ever crystal structure of a protein—that of sperm whale myoglobin—Geis was asked to illustrate the article that Kendrew wrote for *Scientific American*. (The title "The three-dimensional structure of a protein molecule" illustrates nicely how sensational it was at the time to have a peep at *a* protein structure—no matter which one.) Some years later, he also drew the pictures for the article by David Phillips on the first enzyme structure ever solved, that of hen egg white lysozyme.

In the summer of 1964, a man knocked on his door to buy some linoleum prints that he had seen at an exhibition in the New York Hilton. During conversation, it turned out that he, too, had a link with Kendrew and myoglobin—he had been a postdoc at Cambridge. Thus, a work of art and a protein were the catalysts that initially brought together the two names that most biochemists would instantly recognize as a pair: Dickerson–Geis. Most famous for the 1969 book *The Structure and Action of Proteins*, the duo of the biochemist Richard E. Dickerson and the artist/architect/scientific illustrator Irving Geis collaborated for 33 years, until Geis's death in 1997, on all fronts. In an obituary published in *Protein Science*, Dickerson summarizes this experience saying: "It was never clear whether Irv illustrated my books or I wrote Irv's captions. In the end it didn't matter; together we could do more than either could have done alone."

While his first representations of molecular structures contained the exact position of each of the thousands of atoms like a ball-and-stick model would show them, he later developed abstract ways of symbolizing higher-order structures, such as the arrows for beta strands, the coiled ribbons for helices, and the twisted string ladder for the DNA double helix. Nowadays, computer programs such as the ubiquitous "Molscript" automatically implement these symbols when scientists feed them with the structure coordinates and the sequence limits of the structural elements.

While this kind of graphical depiction of structures has become so commonplace that it is easy to forget it had to be invented by somebody in the beginning, many of Geis's drawings still make a strong impact as works of art. For instance, among the examples reprinted in the December 1997 issue of *Current Biology*, there is one of the protein cytochrome *c*, in which the central iron atom is the sole source of light. Like a strange solar system with lots of interlinked planets, the protein is arranged around this shining metal ion.

Apart from the works with Dickerson, Geis also illustrated several major biochemistry textbooks (including Matthews/van Holde, and Voet/Voet), and provided cartoons for miscellaneous other works such as *How to Lie with Statistics*. Above all, he will be remembered as the man who taught us to "see" proteins, or as Dickerson put it, "the Leonardo da Vinci of protein structure."

have used low temperatures to slow down enzymatic reactions, and they have followed the reaction in relatively short time intervals using high-energy radiation only available at synchrotron facilities. (A synchrotron is a particle accelerator in which electrons are sent around in circles with very high energies. The emission of X-rays is a side effect of this experiment.) These efforts have led to a limited body of time-resolved crystal structures, obtained at a rather prohibitive cost.

In 1993, however, Bauke W. Dijkstra and his co-workers at the University of Groningen, the Netherlands, demonstrated that a bit of chemical wizardry can at least in some cases provide time-resolved information even for people who don't happen to have a synchrotron in their backyard. They manipulated the enzymatic reaction to run within the crystal and then to stop at a certain stage to allow the structural analysis. Haloalkane dehalogenase, the enzyme that was of interest to the Dutch researchers, removes the chlorine from halogenated hydrocarbons and is therefore considered as a potential catalyst in a biotechnological degradation of these chemicals, which are a threat to our planet's ozone layer (Fig. 3). The bacterial species from which the enzyme is obtained, *Xanthobacter autotrophicus*, can grow in media containing chlorinated hydrocarbons such

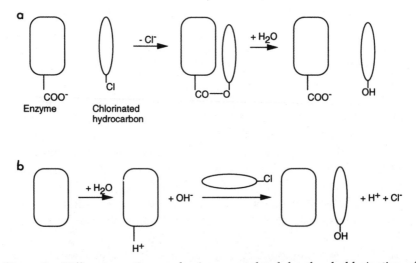

Figure 3: Different reaction mechanisms postulated for the dechlorination of chlorohydrocarbons by the enzyme haloalkane dehalogenase. The intermediates observed in the crystallographic "snapshots" show unambiguously that mechanism (a) is the correct one. Only this mechanism involves the transient formation of a covalent bond between the enzyme and the hydrocarbon.

as 1,2-dichloroethane as the only source of carbon and of energy. Considering that the bacteria also get their own nitrogen from the air, they should be fairly self-sufficient and easy to use in biotechnological cleanup processes.

If a crystal of this enzyme is soaked with a solution of a suitable substrate (i.e., the kind of molecule the enzyme can act on) such as dichloroethane at acidic pH (5.0) and 4°C, the substrate gets bound to the active site of the protein, but not turned over. The X-ray diffraction of this crystal then provides a snapshot of the first step of an enzyme reaction, the binding and recognition of the substrate. If, however, one conducts the same procedure at 20°C, the reaction proceeds one step further and stops at an intermediate state in which the hydrocarbon is covalently bound to the enzyme, while the chlorine has already been cleaved off and remains near the active site as a chloride ion. The third snapshot is then obtained from a crystal that has been soaked with substrate solution at room temperature and only weakly acidic pH. In this case, the hydrocarbon has separated from the enzyme and left the active site, while the chloride ion is still present. Together with the crystal structure of the uncharged enzyme, this provides us with four stills, which describe the mechanism of the enzyme-catalyzed reaction in considerable detail. Moreover, it enabled researchers to make a clear decision between the two possible mechanisms that had previously been discussed, as only one of them includes a covalently bound intermediate as the one observed in the second snapshot.

Although this little "enzyme movie" has but four frames, it provides a much better time resolution than any TV or cinema screen (let alone our dreadfully slow eyes). That's because the enzyme reaction would normally run to completion in just a couple of milliseconds. Thus, our film runs at 1000 frames per second, and as the enzyme goes through the same reaction cycle again and again, we could use multiple copies of the four frames to make a feature-length enzyme action movie. Considering the poor time resolution of our eyes and brains, however, we should better watch it at a 1000-fold reduced speed.

Compared with the possibilities of classical crystallography, this mini-movie represents a significant and cleverly obtained progress. While traditional investigations of enzyme mechanism would have relied on binding a "dead-end" substrate mimic to the enzyme, the new method not only provides more information, it also stays on the reaction path rather than in some possibly remote cul-de-sac. And in comparison with the "big science" approach of using laser photolysis and synchrotrons, this method is cheap and easy.

In December 1996, the showing of another protein movie on the pages of *Science* could have been announced with the headline "The Empire Strikes Back." Instead, it read: "Nanosecond Crystallographic Snapshots of Protein Structural Changes." Working at the European Synchrotron Radiation Facility at Grenoble, France, Keith Moffat and his co-workers investigated how the conformation of the binding site in myoglobin changes when the firmly bound carbon monoxide molecule is suddenly set free by a laser flash. They recorded data sets describing the structural differences after six different time delays ranging from 4 nsec to 1.9 msec.

At about the same time, another alternative method able to obtain data that are well resolved both in structural detail and in short time intervals has emerged in the shape of crystallography's younger competitor, NMR spectroscopy (see Ways & Means on pp. 80 and 81). While time-dependent studies by NMR face in principle the same problem as those using crystallography—namely, that the acquisition of the data needed for a detailed structure takes a lot of time—compromises have been found that promise reasonable resolution in both space and time. In 1995, Jochen Balbach, working as a postdoc in Christopher M. Dobson's group at Oxford, developed a mixing device that allows rapid changes in the sample while it is already positioned within the magnet of the NMR spectrometer. Thus, a reaction can be started by injection of the substrate, and acquisition of spectra can begin within a second after the mixing. The compromise that researchers have to make consists in not using the option of recording nicely resolved two-dimensional spectra, which would give more information about structural aspects, but only the more overlapped and hence less easy to interpret one-dimensional spectra, one of which can be recorded roughly every other second, and thus permit following of reasonably fast reactions, although with a restricted yield of structural information.

Subsequently, the same researchers developed a more sophisticated analysis, which involved recording two-dimensional spectra while the reaction was proceeding and observing how the change during the acquisition of one data set distorts the line shapes obtained. Both approaches were originally applied to the protein folding reaction (which we will meet again in Chapter 3), but should in principle also be applicable to other targets such as enzyme catalysis. Pushing back the frontiers of time and structural resolution at the same time remains one of the most important challenges in structural biology.

G Proteins: The Cell's Switchboard

Obtaining information about its environment is crucial for the survival of any cell—be it a bacterium trying to swim toward a source of nutrients, or a cell in the human body that has to react to external signals such as light or hormones. This means that the cell must have elaborate mechanisms of transporting signal information across its membrane, and converting it into chemical signals that the systems within the cell will understand. While the mechanism of signal transduction is a fundamental problem of cell biology, the conversion of signals from one medium to another is also immensely important for all kinds of technical applications including sensors, computer memories, communication technology, and others. So let's have a look at the cell's switchboard—maybe future engineers can borrow a switch or two from here.

Cells receive all of these stimuli and signals with the help of a variety of antennae, each of which specifically responds to one type of impulse. These antennae are proteins embedded in the cell membrane, the so-called receptors. They forward the signals to switchboards located at the internal surface of the membrane, which are surprisingly uniform: the G proteins. Figure 4 shows a typical signal transduction pathway for the case of a cell that receives a signal from the hormone epinephrine (adrenaline).

The first messenger (hormone) carries the information that the body urgently needs glucose to produce energy. When the hormone arrives on the outer surface of the cell membrane, it activates the specific receptor, which would typically be a rather big protein located within the membrane and sticking out on both sides of it. At the inside surface of the membrane, the receptor then induces the G protein G_s to switch on the so-called effector, which in this case is an enzyme that converts ATP to the most common "second messenger," cyclic AMP (cAMP). The presence of this molecule triggers a cascade of enzyme reactions that eventually leads to a change in cell behavior, in this case, secretion of glucose into the bloodstream.

In the 1970s, Alfred Gilman and Martin Rodbell with their co-workers discovered the central role of G proteins in the signal transduction of all cells, which earned them the Nobel Prize for physiology/medicine in 1994. Since these pioneering studies, researchers have discovered more and more processes in which G proteins or other related GTP-degrading enzymes are involved. G proteins in a narrower sense exist for vision, taste,

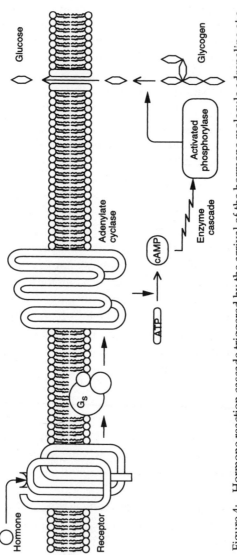

Figure 4: Hormone reaction cascade triggered by the arrival of the hormone molecule adrenaline at a transmembrane receptor on the surface of a liver cell. The receptor activates the membrane-anchored stimulatory G protein (G_s), which carries the message to the effector, adenylate cyclase. This enzyme converts ATP to the most widespread second messenger molecule, cyclic adenosine monophosphate (cAMP). cAMP diffuses through the cell and triggers an enzyme cascade that ultimately leads to the degradation of the storage carbohydrate glycogen and the release of glucose from the cell.

hormone reception, and other processes related to the signal transduction pathways. The wider family of GTPases also includes the elongation factors of protein biosynthesis (see next chapter) and the building blocks of microtubuli, alpha- and beta-tubulin (see Chapter 4).

The reaction cycles of the G proteins were described using qualitative methods of cell biology, and they turned out to fit into a general scheme that can even be applied to most members of the wider GTPase family clan. Basically, the G protein or GTPase is switched back and forth between its active form (in which GTP is bound to the active site) and its inactive GDP-bound form. The empty form exists only fleetingly, as it has a very high tendency to bind the first GTP molecule it can find. The cleavage of GTP to GDP, which leads the protein from its active to its inactive form, is controlled by a second protein, the GTPase activating protein (I will call it *activator* in the following, but biochemists prefer to think in acronyms and thus call it *GAP*). Similarly, the release of GDP from the inactive form may be controlled by a guanine nucleotide release protein (GNRP). In the case of the signal transduction G proteins, the alpha subunit is the GTPase, the beta–gamma complex is the release protein, and the enzyme that produces the second messenger cAMP is the activator.

Although the biochemical evidence had clearly established this general mechanism, the molecular details of this important functional element in the workings of the cell remained in the dark, as the proteins proved notoriously difficult to crystallize and were too big for NMR analysis (although certain fragments of the structure have in fact been solved by NMR). Only in 1995 were the structures of two typical G protein complexes (containing one alpha, one beta, and one gamma subunit, i.e., the GTPase in association with its release protein) solved. The groups of G protein veteran Alfred Gilman and crystallographer Stephen R. Sprang obtained a crystallizable G protein complex by expressing the rat proteins in bacteria, which meant that some modifications, which the rat cells would have introduced after the synthesis, were missing, but otherwise the proteins were intact. They published their structure in December 1995 in *Cell*, just 6 weeks before a similar study by the groups of Heidi Hamm (University of Illinois at Chicago) and Paul Sigler (Yale University) came out in *Nature*. These researchers had used a slightly different strategy, which involved a mixture of removing some offending parts of the proteins and expressing certain parts in bacteria. In the end, however, both teams arrived at essentially the same result.

Both structures show that the signal transduction apparatus of the cell is more than just a chain of dominoes, in which one event triggers the next. Instead, an intriguingly complex mesh of structural interdependencies and interactions was revealed, which David E. Clapham described as a "G-protein nanomachine" in his commentary accompanying the paper by Hamm and Sigler in *Nature*. Not the least surprising was the finding that one of the subunits has the shape of a seven-bladed propeller—a structure that is an irresistible invitation to speculate about how it might interact with other "machine parts."

Two weeks after the Hamm–Sigler paper, *Nature* published another crystal structure of a GTPase with its associated release protein. This time it was the protein biosynthesis elongation factor EF-Tu together with EF-Ts, solved by Reuben Leberman's group at the EMBL outstation in Grenoble, France. Together, the three structures should give molecular biologists more than enough data to work out the exact details of how GTPases interact with release proteins, but the race was still on for a complex containing an activator.

In 1997, this race saw a tight finish, with three structures published within a few months:

1.   Gilman and Sprang cracked it for the signal-transducing G proteins.
2.   Alfred Wittinghofer's group (at the Max Planck Institute for Molecular Physiology in Dortmund) solved the structure of Ras—the protein that is notorious for being mutated in (and thus presumably guilty of) a quarter of all human tumors—in a complex with its activator RasGAP.
3.   Stephen J. Smerdon's group at the National Institute for Medical Research in London obtained the analogous structure for the RhoA protein, which controls building work in the cell's skeleton.

Although the three activators are regarded as unrelated, they share a structural element, the "arginine finger," which thus must be the product of convergent evolution. This finger actually moves the trigger for rapid turnover from GTP to GDP. Without it, the GTPases would only process one molecule of GTP every half hour, on average. With the matching activator protein and the finger in the right place, they can cleave some dozens of them every minute. Again, crystallographers are facing the problem of time resolution discussed above, which in this case they resolved by replacing GTP with a combination of GDP and an aluminum compound that together are thought to mimic the conformation of the transition state of GTP cleavage reasonably well.

Some answers to longstanding problems could be directly derived from the crystal structures. For instance, that of the Ras protein with its activator clearly showed the reason why any mutation in position 12 would make the protein carcinogenic. In the healthy protein, this position is filled with a glycine, whose "side chain" is simply a hydrogen atom. Any other amino acid would be bulkier and would hinder the binding of the activating arginine finger; hence, the G protein would remain permanently turned off.

Other aspects will take more time to analyze in detail. As always with crystal structures of biological macromolecules, they don't answer all of the questions, but they provide a major breakthrough in that they enable molecular biologists to address problems specifically on the basis of struc-tural knowledge. Having three-dimensional maps of all of the little bits and pieces of the "G protein nanomachine," and even better, of three examples for each of the two important complexes, will teach them which bits are especially interesting to mutate and look at the outcome. Although less spectacular than the structural work, this detailed analysis will even-tually lead to a full understanding of how the nanomachine works.

Crystals Made to Measure: Proteins Directing Crystal Growth

Let us time-travel to Paris in 1848. There we find a 25-year-old recently graduated chemist who is seriously puzzled. Why, he keeps wondering, why could the racemic acid rotate the plane of polarized light, while (by all chemical criteria) identical tartaric acid would leave it unchanged? He made oversaturated solutions of the optically inactive compound and left them to crystallize overnight on the window sill of his laboratory. When scrutinizing the crystals with a microscope the next day, he found that there were two types of crystals, had the same geometry but were mirror images of each other, like a right and a left glove. Painstakingly using a pair of tweezers while watching through the microscope, he sorted the two types apart, redissolved them separately, and checked what the solutions did to polarized light. Those crystals that had the same "handedness" as crystals obtained from tartrate solutions gave a clockwise rotation the same way that tartrate did. And the other solution turned the plane of polarized light by the same angle—but in the opposite direction. Thus, at a time when atoms and molecules were still elusive postulates, our chemist had established a direct connection between the chirality (handedness) of molecules (as witnessed by the optical activity) and the chirality of the crystals they form. And of course this was only the beginning of the career of Louis Pasteur (1822–1895).

A little less than one and a half centuries later, researchers in Lia Addadi's group at the Weizmann Institute in Rehovot, Israel, seemed to be following Pasteur's footsteps in that they were busy sorting crystals formed by mirror-image molecules (enantiomers) under a microscope. This time, the chiral substance is a salt of tartaric acid, namely, calcium tartrate. It appears to be impossible to tell the crystals of the enantiomers apart, as they are symmetrical in appearance, not chiral. If, however, the researchers brought certain types of living cells, such as cultivated kidney cells of the clawed toad *Xenopus laevis*, in contact with the mixed crystals, these seem to be very well able to discern the apparently identical crystals. In the first phase of the experiment they settle exclusively on a certain surface of crystals formed by the RR enantiomer. With a Pasteur-style sorting procedure, measuring the optical activity of solutions derived from the crystals that the cells chose to grow on in comparison with the others, Addadi and co-workers could prove that cell growth on the crystal surface is a reliable criterion for enantiomeric separation of otherwise indistinguishable crystals.

However, the cells that chose the RR crystals in the early hours of the experiment came to experience the downside of their choice after a day or so. The binding of their cell surface molecules to the crystal surface was so tight and rigid that the cells died like insects on flypaper. On the crystals of the other enantiomer, in contrast, smaller and less tightly bound cell cultures began to thrive on the second day and survived for several more days.

This demonstration of how molecules of the cell surface can distinguish the chirality of the constituent molecules within macroscopically identical crystals is just one example of the manyfold and often amazingly specific interactions between biological macromolecules and small molecule crystals. In 1994, Addadi and her co-workers showed that antibodies they had raised against different salts of uric acid and against the neutral analogue allopurinol can specifically promote the formation of the type of crystal they had been raised against (Fig. 5). Although the specificity of the antibodies was selected for the recognition of fully grown crystals, they

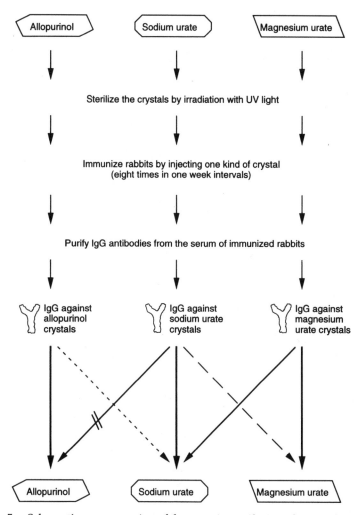

Figure 5: Schematic representation of the experiment designed to test the specificity of the antibodies raised against crystals of uric acid and analogous substances.
Immunization of rabbits with the crystals of allopurinol, sodium urate, or magnesium urate leads to antisera from which antibodies (IgG class) can be purified that
specifically catalyze the growth of the crystal form they were raised against (arrows). Cross-checks showed either much weaker or no effect on crystal growth of
the nonmatching substances, in one case even inhibition of growth.

seemed to stabilize the very first assemblies of say 20 to 30 molecules during the nucleation of crystal growth. In a similar way as for antibodies that researchers have raised against transition state-analogues of simple chemical reactions and that were found to act as catalysts by lowering the energy of the transition state like enzymes do, Addadi's antibodies seem to be specific catalysts for the more complex assembly reaction that leads to crystal formation. In one case (allopurinol) the antibodies also led to shape changes of the grown crystals (Fig. 6).

More recent work from her group has resulted in monoclonal antibody preparations, which consist of just one specific protein sequence each, so that structural investigations become possible. Structure predictions for one particular antibody against cholesterol crystals revealed an intriguingly sharp kink in the recognition site, which exactly matches the edges found on the surface of the cholesterol crystal.

Thus far, one might be forgiven for thinking that such antibodies are just fascinating biochemical toys. But in fact, they may turn out to be models for a physiological process of immense medical relevance. The symptoms experienced in a fit of the joint disease gout are thought to arise from crystals of a uric acid salt accumulating in a joint, which are then recognized by the antibodies of the immune system as intruders (even though the same compound in soluble form does not trigger an immune response), which in turn leads to an inflammatory response in the joint. The specificity results from Addadi's group suggest that a similar recognition in the affected joint is the most likely cause for the inflammation. They also invite the speculation that the immune system may be making things worse by supplying large numbers of antibodies against the offensive crystals, which unintentionally catalyze the formation of more crystals. This might explain why the threshold for fits of gout is lowered as the disease progresses—a case of immunity gone wrong. Moreover, the immune response cannot make the offending crystals disappear, as its cleanup systems are optimized to be efficient against cells, viruses, and biomolecules, rather than against small molecule crystals.

However, interactions between proteins and crystal surfaces can also be immensely useful for organisms that depend on controlling crystal growth, as is the case in biomineralization and in protection from freezing. Living beings that are not as warm-blooded as we are can avoid frost damage by two apparently opposite strategies. Some of them stop their body fluids from freezing by mixing an antifreeze into them. Biological antifreeze formulations can be small molecules, e.g., glycerol in the case of

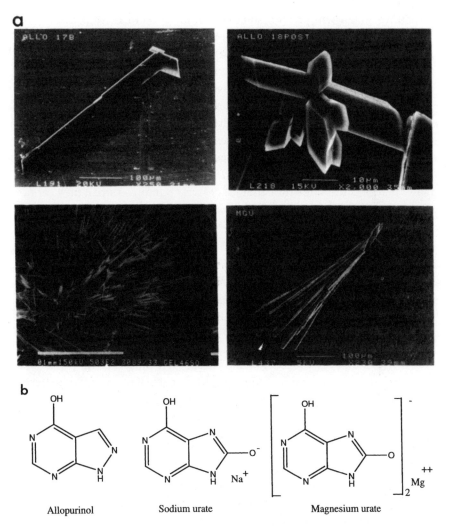

Allopurinol   Sodium urate   Magnesium urate

Figure 6: (a) Electron micrographs of crystals of (clockwise from top left): allopurinol (grown in absence and in presence of specific antibodies), magnesium urate, and sodium urate. In the latter two cases, the presence of specific antibodies does not change the shape of the crystals. (b) Chemical formulas of the three compounds.

the remarkably frost-hardy insect larvae. However, they are often found to consist of proteins that specifically recognize the repetitive molecular structures in growing ice crystals and bind to them to stop them from growing. Various kinds of these antifreeze proteins are found in many fish species that live in arctic or antarctic waters.

The opposite strategy is exclusively based on proteins that bind ice nuclei (the "seeds" of crystallization) and encourage them to grow. This is the way several species of frogs and tortoises in Canada cope with subzero temperatures—they freeze voluntarily. Canadian researchers found that the animals can be thawed after 2 weeks in the freezer with up to 65% of their body water turned into ice, and get on with their life as if nothing ever happened. Their ice nucleation proteins induce ice nuclei to form in so many places at the same time that ice crystals remain so small they cannot cause physical damage. Macroscopically this results in the whole animal freezing stiff within a fraction of a second.

Ice nucleation proteins are also found in bacteria, or outside bacteria to be more specific. The genera *Pseudomonas*, *Xanthomonas*, and *Erwinia* secrete such proteins so as to control ice formation in their direct environment and avoid damage to their cells. *Pseudomonas syringae* is being used on a technical scale for the production of artificial snow—a procedure that has been criticized because of its possible impact on the environment, as the bacteria may infect plants.

Current models concerning the mechanism of ice-binding proteins predict that the polypeptides, which typically consist of repetitive patterns of short blocks of amino acid sequence, form a beta-sheet structure with a periodicity corresponding to that of one of the surfaces of an ice crystal.

Finally, there is a further group of extremely important natural processes relying on the interactions between biological macromolecules and the crystalline or amorphous phases of solid substances. It includes the processes that form our bones and teeth, and those that provide invertebrates such as mollusks and snails with a rigid outer shell, covering the formation of more than 60 different minerals and a wide range of phenomena, which are collectively called *biomineralization*.

The biomolecules controlling these processes can decide whether deposition of the mineral from the solution leads to an amorphous or to a (micro)crystalline phase, they can trigger crystallization, shift a bias between different crystal forms (morphologies), guide or limit the crystal growth directions in space, and stop the process altogether. In most cases (but not in our bones) the controlling agents belong to a class of proteins that are so exotic that they are often referred to as *unusually acidic macro-molecules*. (The first example was a protein retrieved from teeth during the 1960s, which was found to contain 40 mole % of aspartic acid.) Generally, these molecules have aspartic acid in every third or every other position, and they also contain exceedingly high percentages of phosphorylated amino acids, mainly phosphoserine. All of these unusual properties lead to the problem that these proteins are extremely difficult to analyze and characterize with conventional methods. Often even determining the molecular weight causes problems. Presumably they can form extended beta-sheet structures similar to those of ice nucleation proteins. Although the control of mineralization by these molecules can be mimicked in the test tube, their mechanisms are still controversial. It would be conceivable that the acidic proteins act at membranes and/or in free solution by influencing the formation and orientation of nuclei and/or the growth of the crystals.

In many cases—just think of the spirals of snails' shells always wound up in the same direction—the control of crystal growth by chiral biomolecules leads to macroscopic objects that have a chirality just as Pasteur's crystals. Intriguingly, this may even happen if the molecular building blocks (calcium phosphate in the case of the snail) are achiral.

3

From Genes to Proteins

By now you will have realized that proteins are quite useful things to have. The question becomes: How do we make ours? The cell manufactures its proteins, the way it does most of its jobs: with the help of other proteins (although nucleic acids also play an important role in this case, as we will find out below). The next question is: Technologically speaking, can we produce nanomachinery of similar efficiency with nonbiological systems? To better appreciate the technological approaches described in the second half of this book, we shall now investigate how the cell builds its nanomachines.

The production line for these "biological nanomachines" has been up and running for more than 3 billion years and is quite well understood (in general terms if not in atomic detail). It starts with the blueprint (DNA), involves various helpful biomolecules (RNAs and proteins) along the way, and eventually produces a linear molecular chain that folds up to a biologically active protein molecule. Similarly, when the protein is no longer needed or has passed its use-by date, a disassembly line takes it to pieces, which can then be recycled.

This pathway is also an ideal route to travel through many hot research fields, from genome research, through folding helpers, and to the degradation machinery. First, we shall follow the life cycle of a single protein—the hormone insulin—from the cradle to the grave in one section. Then we will retrace our steps and visit some of the current research fields along the way in much more detail. On all stages we shall again find proteins acting as makers, helpers, or destroyers.

Five Minutes for a Vital Mission: The Short Life of an Insulin Molecule

Of all biological molecules, proteins show the greatest variety in structures and functions, as we have already seen in some examples presented in Chapter 2. Nevertheless, they share some basic principles in the way they are synthesized, folded, and eventually degraded. We shall now explore these common aspects in the curriculum vitae of a protein in a very time-economical way using a protein that on average only survives for 5 minutes in our body. It is the well-known hormone insulin, the lack of which is a cause of diabetes. Insulin concentrations in the blood must be so tightly controlled that the molecule is degraded immediately after it has conveyed its message. While this short life span is typical for hormones, other proteins can live substantially longer, and some, like those in the eye lens, can last a lifetime.

The short life of an insulin molecule begins like that of any other protein, namely, with protein biosynthesis, a serial chemical reaction, in which the amino acid building blocks are linked up to form a long chain. Human cells can, in principle, produce up to 100,000 different proteins, but each cell type only produces a selection of this total genetic program, and thus, some types of proteins are only made by one special group of cells or at a certain time in the organism's development. To find the one special group of cells that make insulin, we will have to delve deep into the body.

Just behind your stomach, stretched out from left to right, is the pancreas, a hand-sized organ most of which is busy pumping more than a liter per day of digestive secrets into the duodenum (the upper part of the small intestine), where they help break down the food that is being digested. A minority of the cells in the pancreas, grouped in roundish, islandlike assemblies called *Langerhans islets* after their discoverer P. Langerhans (1847–1888), are distinctly different. These cells do not produce digestive enzymes for the gut, like the rest of the organ, but hormones that go into the bloodstream. There are two types of cells in these islets. The A cells make glucagon, and the B cells are the ones we need to look at now, because they are the ones that make insulin.

In passing I should mention that the pancreas's secretion of digestive enzymes, which would destroy the insulin if they got near it, made the discovery of its hormone production extremely difficult. Thus, it was only in 1921 that Frederick Banting (1891–1941), a Canadian surgeon, and Charles Best (1899–1978), then a graduate student in pathology, could prepare pancreas extracts that were active against diabetes. Much has been written about this truly dramatic chapter of medical history, so I don't need to dwell on it any further.

Within the B cells (and having accommodated our inner eyes to the nanometer scale), we find the machine that makes the proteins, the ribosome, which is itself composed of dozens of different protein molecules and several strands of RNA. The ribosome can slide along the messenger RNA (mRNA), the intermediary between DNA and protein, read from it the information specifying which amino acid residues should be incorporated in which order, and assemble the protein chain according to this instruction. Because this process involves converting genetic information from the 4-letter code of nucleic acids into the 20-letter code of proteins, it is also referred to as *translation*, and the ensemble of the ribosome with all of the associated factors involved in protein biosynthesis is called the *translational apparatus*. The intensive investigation of protein biosynthesis and ribosome structure by a relatively small number of specialized research groups over the past three decades has yielded a schematic picture of the structure and function of most of the molecules involved, but many details have remained elusive, as will be shown in more detail in the third section of this chapter.

The ribosomes of the B cells produce—among all of the other proteins that these cells will need—a precursor molecule of insulin as a single chain with 103 amino acid residues. As they incorporate about 5 amino acids per second, the synthesis will only last 21 seconds from the first to the last amino acid. As there can be many ribosomes lined up on a messenger RNA, each strand of insulin mRNA can actually deliver a full copy of the protein every few seconds. The first 19 building blocks of the sequence are a kind of zip code specifying into which part of the cell the freshly made protein should be sent. As soon as this so-called signal sequence has emerged from the ribosome, the cell's transport machinery gets activated

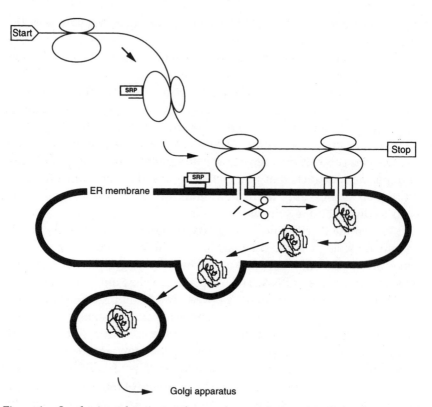

Figure 1:   Synthesis and export pathway of a protein (e.g., insulin) to be secreted by a eukaryotic cell. The first few amino acids emerging from the ribosome are recognized by the signal recognition particle (SRP), which directs the ribosome toward the membrane of the ER, where it is docked to a ribosome receptor. Within the ER, the signal sequence is cleaved, the protein folds, and gets packaged into vesicles to be transported toward the Golgi apparatus.

(Fig. 1). A sorting helper (the signal recognition particle) catches hold of the signal sequence, interrupts translation for a short time, and directs the emerging protein with the ribosome toward the membrane of the cell's export harbor, the endoplasmic reticulum (ER). The ribosome gets attached to this membrane, and the protein threaded through a pore into the ER. Once inside the ER, the signal sequence is no longer needed and gets snipped off.

The remaining chain of 84 amino acids then spontaneously begins to fold to its complex and unique three-dimensional structure, which the protein has to adopt if it is to fulfill its biological function. How and why this happens will be explained in later sections of this chapter. For the time being, it is only important to note that the folding occurs without any information input from outside, as all of the information needed to define the final folded structure is already encoded in the sequence of the amino acid building blocks. Our insulin molecule then gets packaged into a small sphere that buds out of the ER membrane and transports it to the cell's sorting office, the Golgi apparatus. Here, our protein, which is still a tied-up version of insulin and not yet ready to use, is cleaved again. A stretch of 30 amino acids is cut out of the middle region of the sequence, leaving two parts known as the A and the B chain, which are only connected by disulfide bonds (covalent chemical bonds that are formed by the sulfur atoms in the amino acid cysteine) and their entangled arrangement in the folded structure.

The result of this operation is the active hormone insulin with 54 amino acid residues. This molecule is the active ingredient of the pancreas extracts first prepared by Banting and Best and used for the treatment of diabetics for decades. Active insulin was also the first ever protein for which the amino acid sequence was determined. For this achievement the British biochemist Frederick Sanger received the Nobel Prize in chemistry in 1958. Furthermore, it was among the first proteins to be studied by X-ray crystallography, although not among the first successfully solved structures (see Profile on Dorothy Crowfoot Hodgkin).

The active insulin is again packaged into small membrane globules, which are this time called *storage granules*. The concentration of insulin within these little balloons can become so high that the protein forms small crystals. If our B cell notices that the level of glucose in the blood is too high—as it might well be after a meal, for instance—it has to act to make sure the excess glucose gets either burned up by metabolism or incorporated in polymeric form (glycogen, which serves as a fuel store for times of need). Therefore, the cell makes the granules merge with the outer membrane so that the insulin is set free into the bloodstream. With the blood it reaches its target, an insulin-binding protein (receptor) in the membranes of liver cells, which specifically recognizes and binds insulin molecules and then acts on other molecules inside the cell to pass the message on. For the liver cell, having insulin bound to its insulin receptors means that it receives the order to take up glucose from the blood and do something with it.

Once the insulin has fulfilled its mission, liver cells will inactivate it by

Profile

Dorothy Crowfoot Hodgkin

X-ray crystallography of proteins owes its existence to a pair of breakthrough discoveries, which lie some 20 years apart. The later, which enabled the first structure to be solved, was the isomorphic replacement developed by Max Perutz, which I explained in the crystallography Ways & Means in Chapter 2. The earlier, not immediately fruitful but no less important discovery, that protein crystals do in fact generate regular X-ray diffraction patterns, is associated with the name of Dorothy Hodgkin, nee Crowfoot.

Born to archaeologist parents in Cairo, she spent most of her scientific life at Somerville College in Oxford, except for her Ph.D. work with J. D. Bernal in Cambridge that resulted in the half-page report published in *Nature* on May 26, 1934, which heartwarmingly begins with the sentence: "Four weeks ago, Dr. G. Millikan brought us some crystals of pepsin prepared by Dr. Philpot in the laboratory of Prof. The Svedberg, Uppsala." Those were the days. More to the point, the paper then describes how ill-treatment of crystals may have prevented others from seeing regular diffraction patterns, and how the far-traveled pepsin crystals in question were giving X-ray pictures that immediately allowed estimating the particle size and the arrangement of protein molecules in the crystal lattice. Analysis of the detailed molecular structure encrypted in these patterns, however, had to await both the work of Perutz in the 1950s, and the analysis of polypeptide sequences introduced by Frederick Sanger in the 1950s. In 1934, it was by no means clear that the particles known as *globular proteins* were really single molecules, namely, linear polypeptides folded up in space. Thus, the emergence of well-defined diffraction patterns pointing to long-range repetitive patterns gave them at least a certain degree of respectability as well-defined physical entities.

In the following year, she turned to the analysis of crystals of the peptide hormone insulin, which features prominently in the first section of this chapter. She obtained well-resolved diffraction patterns and had the crystals analyzed for insulin activity. Thus, she could demonstrate that a biologically active protein had a well-ordered structure, but the exact details of this structure remained elusive for more than three decades. With her almost proverbial patience and persistence, she remained interested in insulin, solved the structure in 1969, and finally published an improved crystallographic structure at high resolution in 1988.

Back in the 1930s, as she realized that the technical problems with the insulin crystals would not go away soon, she patiently worked her way up from small biomolecules to middle-sized ones. Smaller but no less important natural products provided more tractable targets, including cholesterol, penicillin, and vitamin B_{12}, and each of them was a substantial challenge in its time, which she managed to overcome with skill and persistence. One has to bear in mind that in those days the matching of a chemical structure with a three-dimensional electron density map was not carried out by a computer as it is today. Dorothy Hodgkin was famous for her skills at "seeing" the right chemistry behind blobs of electron density.

Between crystals, she also managed to bring up three children, and play an active role in the Pugwash movement (a loose association of scientists from East and West founded in 1957, who warned of the risks of technology misuse and mass destruction weapons). She was awarded the 1964 Nobel Prize in chemistry—not shared, and the only British woman so far to get a Nobel Prize in one of the natural sciences.

Dorothy Hodgkin died at her home near Oxford in July 1994. Thus far, her name is essentially only known by crystallographers and protein biochemists. A biography of her remarkable life that came out in the fall of 1998 may be on the track to change this.

cleaving the disulfide bonds that join the two chains. The separate chains can never form active insulin again, as part of the folding information was in the middle part, which was clipped out back in the ER of the B cells, is now missing. They will be degraded by specialized enzymes (which we will meet at the end of this chapter) down to the level of individual amino acids, which may be recycled for the synthesis of new proteins.

In summary, insulin conveys the message that there is enough glucose in the blood to the cells of the liver (as well as to all other kinds of cells that possess a receptor for it). If the pancreas cannot produce enough insulin, diabetes ensues. In the diabetic metabolism, nutrients cannot be used efficiently, as the message of their availability is not passed on. Instead of being either metabolized or stored, glucose accumulates in the blood and is excreted with the urine. Before the 1920s, diabetes was incurable and eventually fatal for more than half of the people affected. However, the preparation of insulin extracts by Banting and Best in 1921 quickly led to its therapeutic application. Since 1923, pig insulin could be produced in large quantities and used to help most diabetes sufferers. For those who are sensitive to the small difference between the pig and the human hormone (only one amino acid is different), biotechnological conversion into the human sequence was introduced in 1983, followed by the mass production of human insulin by genetically altered bacteria in the late 1980s.

Thus far, I have only given a quick tour of the protein life cycle. If this is all you want to know about proteins, you can safely jump to Chapter 4 from here. If, however, you're somewhat more ambitious and want to find out more details and recent research developments, read on. We are now going to return to the beginning and to look at the blueprints for making proteins, the genes.

The Language of the Genes: Linguistic Methods Help to Make Sense of DNA

How can one build a human being? A student of natural philosophy by the name of Victor F. tried it the rough-and-ready way. Bones from the abattoir and from the dissecting room were the building blocks from which he tried to fabricate a man. Published reports say that his experiment narrowly failed, resulting in a monster that eventually killed its creator and laid the foundation for an image problem with which science is still struggling today.

As Mary Shelley's famous novel *Frankenstein* came out in 1816, her protagonist, Victor Frankenstein (whose name often gets mixed up with the monster he created), could by no means have known that the blueprint for making human beings is available in billions of duplicates in each representative of our species. And that each tiny cell contains the complete information necessary for the whole development from the fertilized egg to the adult human being.

Each of our cells has a small compartment, the cell nucleus, that contains a double set of our chromosomes, the total hereditary information, with some 80,000 to 120,000 genes determining the sequences and structures of all of our proteins and thereby, indirectly, characteristic properties from eye color to abilities and body functions.

In 1988, the human genome project (HUGO) was launched as a worldwide research collaboration aiming to decipher this blueprint in its entirety. Rather than searching for genes for a certain hereditary disease—a needle-in-the-haystack kind of operation that has often frustrated researchers for decades—molecular biologists are now taking the haystack down and sorting all of the straws and needles systematically. The project appeared quite megalomanic in the beginning, and was criticized both for ethical and for practicability reasons. Using the sequencing technology that existed in 1990, it would have taken more than 100,000 researcher years to complete.

Since then, however, genome researchers have steadily improved their methods, including the development of automated facilities, and the application of novel strategies such as shotgun sequencing, which in 1995–1996 allowed the Maryland-based Institute for Genomic Research (TIGR) led by Craig Venter to score the first three sequences of complete microbial genomes within months (see accompanying Ways & Means, pp. 64 and 65). The first organism of the much more complex eukaryotic type, bakers' yeast, followed soon after, and by the end of 1997 there were more than a dozen full genome sequences recorded in the databases (see Table 1), the HUGO enterprise thus appearing much less Babylonian than in the beginning. The plan is to proceed stepwise to more complex organisms, with yeast and the tiny worm *Caenorhabditis elegans* at the beginning, the rice plant *Arabidopsis* and fruit fly in the middle, and mice and men at the end.

While the initial plans aimed at finishing the human genome by 2005, some researchers have suggested this may be achieved even earlier. As the first milestones on the way to the human genome sequence, a complete schematic "map" of the human genome was published in 1996, and the full

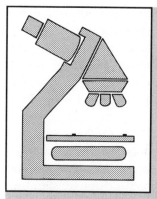

Ways and Means

**DNA Sequencing
and Genome Analysis**

Imagine you have millions of paper strips with the same message written on them in one long line. You take out a bunch of them, cut each one at the first place where you happen to see the letter "A" in the text, discard the end, and put the beginning of the text into a box labeled "A." You do the same for "B," for "C," and for the rest of the alphabet. Perhaps for gaps, hyphens, full stops as well. Then you will need a huge table that will also serve as a table in the mathematical sense. At the top end you will place the boxes A–Z, and in the column underneath them the paper strips sorted by length in the way that the shortest strip will be in the first row (and still in the column underneath its corresponding letter), the second shortest in the second row (and presumably in a different column), and so on. At the end of the procedure, you can read the text that was written on the original paper strip without reading a single letter from the fragments. How can you do that? You look at row 1, find the square with the paper strips, read the letter on the box at the top of the column, proceed to row 2, find the box out of which the strip in row 2 came, and so on. Just by checking which squares of the table have a paper strip on them, you can read the message.

Well, this box isn't really talking about paper messages, so you will have guessed by now that the above protocol describes how the sequence of DNA is read. Except that it is easier for DNA, as it only contains four letters and no punctuation, so one only needs four columns in the table. Cutting the strand after a specific letter can be achieved either chemically or by specific enzymes. Sorting by length is accomplished by gel electrophoresis, a common laboratory technique in which the macromolecule is dragged by the traction of an electric field through a porous gel where smaller molecules move faster than larger ones. To make sure that only the length of fragments including the beginning of the message is measured, the detection is based on a radioactive compound attached to the beginning of the DNA strand to be sequenced. Any fragments from the other end or from the middle if a strand has been cut several times, will also be separated on the gel, but they will not show up on the film, which the molecular biologist will bring in close contact with the gel and which will blacken in those squares of the table where the radioactive marker is present.

This method has a couple of shortcomings. For one, it can only read less than 1000 DNA bases in one go, thus a larger gene would have to be split enzymatically into manageable fragments to be sequenced. Furthermore, although radioactive markers are the most sensitive detection method available and thus allow one to work with extremely small samples, some 10 billion molecules of a given DNA sequence would still be required to be able to read it this way. This limitation has been overcome by the development of the polymerase chain reaction (PCR; of *Jurassic Park* fame), which allows molecular biologists to produce any amount of DNA with a desired sequence starting from only a couple of molecules. Thus, if a sample is too small for DNA sequencing, one can still blow it up by PCR.

Further problems arise as molecular biology proceeds from genes to entire genomes. While the first viral genome sequenced by Frederick Sanger in 1977 only contained 5375 letters, simple bacteria have 500,000 to several million base pairs, and bakers' yeast has 13 million. Automated sequencing procedures were developed, which involve the use of fluorescently labeled DNA building blocks chemically modified in such a way that they terminate the chain without the need for enzymatic cutting. This development led to a rapidly increasing output of sequence information, which could only be handled and processed thanks to the equally fast progress in computer technology.

Table 1. The First Full Genome Sequences Published as of July 31, 1998 (in Chronological Order of Publication)

Organism (domain)	Significance	Genome size (million basepairs)	Institution
1995			
Haemophilus influenzae (b)	Causes ear infections and meningitis	1.83	TIGR
Mycoplasma genitalium (b)	Parasite; smallest bacterial genome	0.58	TIGR
1996			
Methanococcus jannaschii (a)	First archaeon	1.66	TIGR
Synechocystis (b)		3.57	Kazusa DNA research institute
Mycoplasma pneumoniae (b)		0.81	University of Heidelberg
1997			
Saccharomyces cerevisiae (e)	First eukaryote; important model organism	13	International consortium
Helicobacter pylori (b)	Causes ulcers	1.66	TIGR
Escherichia coli (b)	Important model organism	4.60	University of Wisconsin
Methanobacterium thermoautotrophicum (a)		1.75	Genome Therapeutics & Ohio State University
Bacillus subtilis (b)	Model for gram-positive bacteria	4.20	International consortium
Archaeoglobus fulgidus (a)	First sulfur-metabolizing organism	2.18	TIGR
Borrellia burgdorferi (b)		1.44	TIGR
Aquifex aeolicus (b)		1.50	Diversa
Pyrococcus horikoshii (a)		1.80	NITE
Mycobacterium tuberculosis (b)		4.40	Sanger Centre
Treponema pallidum		1.14	TIGR & University of Texas

Source: TIGR website. More than 50 microbial genomes are listed as "in progress."

genome sequence of bakers' yeast *Saccharomyces cerevisiae* was released in the same year, representing the first genome of a eukaryotic organism and by far the largest of the genomes sequenced so far.

As these pages are written, it looks as if HUGO might even face strong competition from the private sector. In May 1998, Craig Venter whipped up a storm by announcing plans for a private sequencing of the essentially complete human genome within 3 years. Using 230 state-of-the-art automatic sequencing machines provided by the market leader Perkin-Elmer, the new company is scheduled to sequence fragments representing 99% of the genome within a year (starting in April 1999) and then spend 2 years fitting these pieces together. Critics have argued that the privately sequenced genome will be far from perfect, as it will contain a few thousand small holes (which would be too expensive to close). Furthermore, debates are raging about how accessible the genome sequence will or should be to other researchers. Thus, as there are still doubts as to whether the private venture will really provide the genome sequence faster than the multinational genome project, the latter will continue as scheduled for the time being.

Of course, reading the 3 billion letters lined up in the chromosomal DNA, although a daunting task, is far from being a final solution once it is achieved. In fact, not all of our DNA makes sense in that it encodes proteins or RNA molecules. While there are certain hallmarks by which researchers can usually identify the beginning of a gene, this method does not guarantee that all of the information encoded in a given sequence will be found. For the task of sorting the genes from the junk DNA, an unusual interdisciplinary approach could become useful, which was reported by Graziano Pesole and his co-workers at the University of Bari in Italy in 1994. Statistical methods derived from linguistics should help to find those bits of DNA sequence that actually represent a message. Furthermore, these methods could help in deciphering these messages and relating them to other sequences that may describe similar functions.

Parallels between the language of the genes and natural languages are manyfold. Essentially, both are made up of linear strings of symbols, which express a meaning following a complex set of rules. Thus, it is no coincidence that geneticists and biochemists use many metaphors derived from language. Words like genetic *code, translation, reading* frame, *message,* and others are quite commonplace and will reoccur along the life cycle of proteins later on in this chapter. Strings following certain formal rules are common in both poetry and genetics. While in the former patterns like rhyme, alliteration, and metron are important, the latter have a penchant for palindromes—strings that read the same forward and backward (Fig. 2).

The language of the genes only contains four letters: A for adenine, C for cytosine, G for guanine, and T for thymine. (Each of them is an organic ring-shaped molecule that protrudes from the chemically uniform backbone of the DNA macromolecule. The famous "double helix" structure is held together by the specific interactions between A and T, and between G and C.) The genetic "words" are called *codons* and consist of three letters each, with the word boundaries defined by the reading frame, which is set at the beginning of the gene.

There are $4^3 = 64$ different codons, although only 20 would be needed to specify the different amino acids. Thus, there is a redundancy in that several codons may specify the same amino acid, but each species has strong preferences and dislikes in the use of equivalent codons. Similarly, the observation of longer stretches of DNA also shows that only a small fraction of the huge number of possible sequence combinations is commonly used. Typical start signals for the transcription of a gene to messenger RNA contain seven letters, so they are just a few possibilities out of $4^7 = 16,384$. From the finding that only a fraction of the possible combinations of a given length actually occur in natural genes, the gene linguists conclude that there must be something like a DNA grammar, but lacking the possibilities of structuring the string of information by punctuation and by gaps. In this, and in its redundancy, gene language more closely resembles spoken than written human language.

Beyond this level of intuitive similarities between genetic and natural language, the methods of linguistic statistics that are to be transferred to genome analysis are highly abstract and could only be described with the help of a pile of mathematical equations. Gene linguists analyze, for instance, ways a given sequence of DNA letters can be cut into shorter "words." However, as they don't know a priori whether the sequence in question does or doesn't carry a message, they have to consider all possible subdivisions and analyze them statistically. They may be looking at the "linguistic homogeneity" of a given genetic text, which they subdivide into "Markow chains" (a concept derived from the mathematical investigation of probabilities), or they may be describing the complexity of a sequence by replacing recurring motifs with simple symbols.

Using such methods, they can derive complicated algorithms for the description of genetic sequences and prediction of their biological rele-

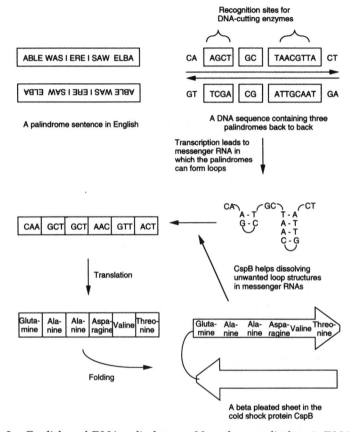

Figure 2: English and DNA palindromes. Note that a palindromic DNA strand is not symmetric in itself but rather with respect to the double strand. If you turn one of the boxed regions by 180 degrees, you will end up with the same pair of sequences. On the level of the (single stranded) RNA, the base complementarity makes palindrome sequences form loops. While this is desirable for stable RNAs (transfer and ribosomal RNAs), it tends to be a nuisance in translation of the messenger RNA as it would block the way of the ribosomes. For this reason, cells have "RNA chaperones" to keep the RNA in a linear shape. The cold-shock protein CspB, from whose gene this example is taken, is thought to act on mRNA in this way.

vance. These algorithms bear some similarity with those used by evolutionary biologists to detect kinship between species. Small wonder, as both human languages and the genetic code are products of evolution. In the next section we will continue to use linguistic analogies when we proceed from the analysis of DNA as such to the rules for its translation into the protein language, which are laid down, of course, in the genetic code.

Death of a Dogma: The Genetic Code Is *Not* Universal

Francis Crick, who shot to fame with the double helix structure of DNA that he and James Watson worked out in 1953 using X-ray data acquired by Rosalind Franklin and Maurice Wilkins, was never short of brilliant ideas. On one occasion, he thought the genetic code, which sets the rules for translating the sequences of DNA into proteins, should be operating without any punctuation marks. That is, the words (codons) consisting of three letters (bases) each would have to be made up in a special way such that there was no risk that a shift of the word limits would lead to a misreading of the message. In other words, if AAU and GAA were allowed codons, AAA, AUG, and UGA had to be forbidden. Crick began to work out how many of the 64 ($4 \times 4 \times 4$) three-letter codons would be allowed in such a system, and to his own surprise he arrived at the result 20, which matches exactly the number of amino acids to be coded for.

Sadly, this hypothesis of the "commaless code," published in 1957, just 4 years after the double helix structure that made Watson and Crick immortal, was too good to be true. In the first half of the 1960s, it emerged that the real genetic code is much less elegant than the version that Crick imagined. In fact, several amino acids are assigned to several (up to six) codons, some only to one (Table 2). And if the reading frame (which is established on recognition of the first codon, as it turned out) is shifted by one letter forward or backward, the information still translates into an amino acid sequence, but into one that will unfortunately have no similarity whatsoever with the correct sequence—not even the same length.

With all of these shortcomings, the code that was unraveled in the 1960s appeared to have one major advantage (especially for biology students): Results obtained with the gut bacterium *Escherichia coli* seemed to hold equally well for viruses, plants, and animals including humans.

Table 2. Genetic Code[a]

First nucleotide base	Second nucleotide base				Third nucleotide base
	Uracil	Cytosine	Adenine	Guanine	
Uracil (thymine)	Phenyl-alanine	Serine	Tyrosine	Cysteine	Uracil
	alanine	Serine	Tyrosine	Cysteine	Cytosine
	Leucine	Serine	Stop	Stop	Adenine
	Leucine	Serine	Stop	Tryptophan	Guanine
Cytosine	Leucine	Proline	Histidine	Arginine	Uracil
	Leucine	Proline	Histidine	Arginine	Cytosine
	Leucine	Proline	Glutamine	Arginine	Adenine
	Leucine	Proline	Glutamine	Arginine	Guanine
Adenine	Isoleucine	Threonine	Asparagine	Serine	Uracil
	Isoleucine	Threonine	Asparagine	Serine	Cytosine
	Isoleucine	Threonine	Lysine	Arginine	Adenine
	Methionine	Threonine	Lysine	Arginine	Guanine
Guanine	Valine	Alanine	Aspartic acid	Glycine	Uracil
	Valine	Alanine		Glycine	Cytosine
	Valine	Alanine	Glutamic acid	Glycine	Adenine
	Valine	Alanine		Glycine	Guanine

[a]Repetitions within the same square indicate that the third base of a codon has little or no influence on the amino acid encoded. Some of the deviations from the "universal" code are also indicated.

Having confirmed this uniformity with a couple of random checks, biochemists declared the universal genetic code to be one of the dogmas of molecular biology. Crick explained this somewhat surprising universality with his theory of the frozen chance event. After the common ancestor of all living beings had developed a functional code, the theory went, any change in the rules would have been catastrophic, as it would have changed many proteins at the same time and thus inactivated several of them. As with the commaless code, this theory sounded quite plausible, but reality got the better of it eventually.

The dogma of the universal genetic code was already shaken a bit during the 1980s, when exceptions had to be defined for the newly discovered 21st amino acid selenocysteine, and for the different definitions of stop codons found in mitochondrial protein biosynthesis. As mentioned in Chapter 1, mitochondria are cell compartments specializing in energy metabolism. It is thought that they are the descendants of bacteria that originally lived in symbiosis with the ancestor of the complex eukaryotic cell. One of the several pieces of evidence pointing in this direction is the fact that mitochondria still run their own protein biosynthesis, although this is hardly worth the effort, as they import most of the proteins they use. Interestingly, only the mitochondria of green plants use the "universal" genetic code for their protein synthesis. In the mitochondria of all other eukaryotic species, changes in codon assignment are so frequent that researchers have taken to using these variations to trace evolutionary lineages. Yet, this wasn't enough to convince hard-boiled dogmaticists. After all, mitochondria have lost their autarky billions of years ago. As they only produce a few dozen proteins themselves, a change in codon assignment would be much less catastrophic for them than for a free-living organism.

Further exceptions to the rule were discovered in 1985 in *Paramecium*, *Mycoplasma*, and *Tetrahymena*, but they only affected codons that would normally have been stop signals and were read as amino acid specific codons in these particular organisms. Three years later, August Böck's group at the University of Munich found that the stop signal UGA can in certain cases call for the incorporation of the rare amino acid selenocysteine in *Escherichia coli*. As this was essentially an untypical and quite expensive way of introducing a specific modification into certain proteins, it came to be regarded rather as the exception that proves the rule than as the end of the universality dogma.

A more worrisome observation was made by researchers who tried to combine some parts of the protein synthesis apparatus from the yeast *Saccharomyces cerevisiae* with others from the related organism *Candida albicans* (a fungus that most people carry around with them and that only becomes annoying if its overgrowth manifests in thrushes in the mouth or in more private parts) to build up a system that would make proteins in the test tube (*in vitro*), i.e., in the absence of living cells. The protein produced by the *in vitro* system differed from the natural protein, and at first it was far from obvious why they did. In 1989, a research group at the Tokyo Research Laboratory found evidence indicating that another *Candida* species, *Candida cylindracea*, reads the codon CUG as serine instead of leucine as any biochemistry textbook would suggest. Using genetic engineering and state-of-the-art analysis methods, Manuel Santos and Mick Tuite at the University of Kent in Canterbury could in 1995 directly prove that this codon has a different meaning for *Candida cylindracea* than for most organisms.

This result has finally established that the universality dogma was plain wrong. It's not only that there are differences between the codes used by different organisms, but also that evolutionary change of codon "meaning" happens all the time to this day, as can be deduced from the differences between closely related species in the genus *Candida*. While researchers now agree that the code does change with evolution, they are still arguing about how this can happen. While some believe that a codon can only adopt a new amino acid after it has been out of use for some time (which can happen with those codons that are not unique for their original amino acid), others think the shift goes via an intermediate stage in which the codon could be used for both the old and the new amino acid. A more detailed understanding of the evolution of both tRNA and the enzymes that recognize their specificity and charge them with the appropriate amino acid will be needed, before a final answer to this question can be given.

Whichever way the reassignment happens, it has shown up that the redundancy of the genetic code is really an advantage over the more sharply defined commaless code. It allows any DNA base to undergo mutation, as all possible codons are permitted, and it allows selection pressures for criteria on the DNA level (such as the heat stability of the double helix, which is governed by the content of G and C) as well as the obvious selection for the optimal final protein product. Of course, the variability of the genetic code is not quite so good news for biotechnologists, as we shall find out in Chapter 7.

Round and Round the Ribosome

Considering the immense importance of proteins for almost every function of a living cell, it is intriguing how incomplete our knowledge about their biosynthesis is. The central piece of the translational apparatus, the ribosome, has still not been described at atomic resolution, which also implies that the mechanism of protein biosynthesis is only known schematically, not in detail.

If we consider the making of a protein from its very beginning, the first step is to bring the machinery into the starting position. Biochemists call this the initiation of protein biosynthesis (Fig. 3, left-hand side of the upper circle). Around the RNA with the specific initiation site, a crowd of molecular machines and factors assembles, including the two subunits of

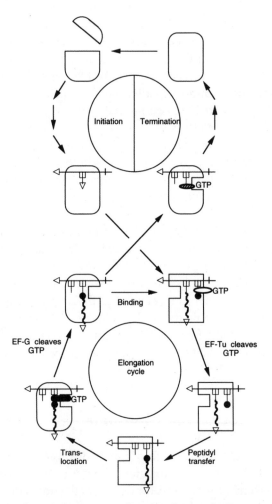

Figure 3: Schematic representation of protein biosynthesis according to the allosteric three-site model developed by the group of Knud Nierhaus at the Max Planck Institute for Molecular Genetics in Berlin. Starting at the top, the ribosome goes through the upper left half-circle (initiation), then through the lower circle as many times as there are peptide bonds to be formed (elongation), and finally through the upper right half-circle (termination).

the ribosome, the first amino acid to begin the protein chain, bound to its specific carrier, the initiation tRNA, and several specialized protein helpers, the initiation factors. All of these molecules and molecular complexes assist in binding the charged tRNA to the message and locating it on the ribosome in such a position that the next amino acid coming in with its own specific tRNA will be able to form the first peptide bond with the carbonic acid group of the first amino acid. This bond formation will be carried out by the peptidyl transferase, the only enzymatic activity attributed to the ribosome, during a complex circular reaction known as *elongation* and schematically described in Fig. 3. Although functional models have been established that specify the role of each part of the machinery and the interactions between them, the molecular details of the reactions involved have remained largely elusive so far. Some aspects became clearer in the mid-1990s, when several structural studies of important molecular assemblies from the translational apparatus were published.

In 1995, for instance, researchers were stunned by the pictures of the complex that delivers the amino acids to the ribosome, consisting of the protein EF-Tu, the nucleotide GTP, and the tRNA with the amino acid bound. The overall shape of this assembly was remarkably similar to that of another elongation cycle helper, EF-G, with just GDP bound. The structural elements contributed by the tRNA in the ternary complex are precisely mimicked by a protein domain in EF-G. This "molecular mimicry" could carry some important clue to the evolution and molecular mechanism of protein synthesis, although it remains a rather well hidden clue so far.

The biggest problem (in more than one sense), however, remains the ribosome itself. As crystallographers are having serious trouble with this highly complicated and sensitive particle, the best structural data available to date are derived from electron microscopy, and their resolution (2.5 nm) is still far from reaching the atomic scale (0.25 nm). As yet, structural data don't even allow tracing the chains of the RNA strands or the proteins (except perhaps for those proteins whose structures have been determined separately). Still, current structures are good enough to localize important functional sites and to confirm the existence of a tunnel through which the newly synthesized chain emerges from the large subunit of the ribosome.

The function of the ribosome was initially thought to reside in the proteins, but is nowadays mostly attributed to the large RNA molecules that account for roughly two-thirds of its mass. Partly, this development followed the logic of the drunkard who famously searched for his key below the streetlight rather than in the place where he thought he lost it. Biochemical methods and thinking were more geared toward protein enzymes in the 1960s, and more toward nucleic acids in the 1980s, when catalytic RNAs were all the rage. Following these developments, the hypothesis that the ribosome has evolved from a catalytic RNA (which because of its enormous size took on some proteins to keep its structure organized) has become more and more popular in the 1990s. While a lot of circumstantial evidence for this case accumulated during these years, it was only in 1998 that the final proof could be presented. Kimitsuna Watanabe's group at the University of Tokyo showed that naked molecules of the major RNA strand from *E. coli* ribosomes (23 S RNA) can in fact promote the formation of peptide bonds. Dissecting this large RNA molecule into its folding units (domains), they could further show that all of the activity resides in just one of the six domains.

With every round that the system travels along the elongation cycle (Fig. 3), another amino acid residue is attached to the growing polypeptide chain, and the translational apparatus glides along the mRNA for the length of one codon. If it comes across a stop codon, the synthesis is terminated and the completed polypeptide chain is released from the ribosome. In this process, too, we find protein helpers, which are called *release factors*.

Now, the protein still has to fold up to attain its biologically active three-dimensional structure. For some small and simple proteins, folding may occur during synthesis sequentially as the chain emerges from the ribosome tunnel—or to some extent even within the tunnel. Other proteins need assistance from a special class of helper proteins, the molecular chaperones, which we will discuss below. First, though, we shall investigate the folding problem as such, which is complicated enough already.

Skiing the Energy Landscape: The New View of Protein Folding

"Everybody believes an experimental result—except the person who performed the experiment. And nobody believes a theoretical result—except the person who developed the theory." Such and similar aphorisms can often be overheard at conferences dealing with the folding of proteins. Discussions between skeptical experimentalists and enthusiastic theoreticians have a long tradition in this field. After all, the two foundations of protein folding as a research discipline were a simple experiment and a surprising theoretical statement, which, of course, contradicted each other.

The experimentalist was Christian B. Anfinsen (1916–1995), who, in the early 1960s, studied the structure and function of the enzyme ribonuclease A. (This work, which was fundamental for the investigation of enzymes in general, earned him the Nobel Prize in chemistry in 1972.) First he knocked out the enzyme by dissolving it in a solution containing urea, which would disrupt the weak interactions that stabilize the folded state, and a reducing agent, which would open the four disulfide bridges. Then he managed to restore the enzymatic activity by dialyzing the urea away while permitting oxygen from the air to help with reestablishing the disulfides. Thus, he became the first person to "refold" a protein, as the process is called in today's jargon. More importantly, his experiment proved that all of the information required for the correct folding of the protein is contained in its sequence. No other information-carrying molecules were present in his simple experiment.

Since then, thousands of scientists have carried out similar experiments refolding proteins in the test tube, without paying heed to the warnings of a theoretician who essentially stated this experiment should not work within the span of a human lifetime. Cyrus Levinthal (1922–1990), who in a sense is for folding theory what Anfinsen is for experimental studies, made calculations to find out how many different conformations a polypeptide chain can have in space, and how much time it will need for its correct folding, if it were to perform a random search through all of these. For middle-sized proteins he arrived at folding times that easily exceeded the age of the universe. This consideration, which seemed to suggest that Anfinsen should never have seen his ribonuclease refold, is widely known as the *Levinthal paradox*.

With this, the folding problem was born. Strictly speaking, researchers are facing three distinct problems:

1. To explain how natural proteins can refold so rapidly (Levinthal paradox)
2. To predict the folded structure from the amino acid sequence (the prediction problem)
3. To design protein sequences that will adopt a desired folded structure (the design problem)

Of the latter two, the design problem has turned out to be in some ways more tractable than the prediction problem, as I will explain in Chapter 5.

Prediction, in contrast, has been hindered by the lack of understanding of the folding language as such, including the ways in which it evades the Levinthal paradox. Successful predictions of some structural elements can now be made on the basis of statistical analysis of how likely a given sequence is to adopt a certain type of structure. However, a true understanding of the ways in which the sequence specifies both the folded structures and the means to reach the structure in a short time is still far off.

The first attempt at a solution for the Levinthal paradox was made by Levinthal himself and followed up by many others. It consisted in postulating well-defined routes through conformational space on which the protein could proceed swiftly toward its native state rather than wandering about randomly. In the 1970s and 1980s, folding researchers concentrated on identifying such "folding pathways" by identifying intermediate states, which should serve as milestones along the way. However, the whole idea of well-defined folding paths has a fundamental flaw. While the end of the pathway—the native state—is well known and described, the beginning—the unfolded state—is not really a state in the sense that all molecules behave the same way. It is rather a mixture of billions and billions of different conformations. Suppose only some of them can serve as a starting point for a folding path. The problem of finding this starting point would be just another variant of the Levinthal paradox.

This fundamental dilemma is one of the reasons why the one-dimensional description of folding pathways has been replaced by something much more complex, which Robert "Buzz" Baldwin has called the "new view" of folding. Researchers now talk about ensembles rather than states, they describe multidimensional energy landscapes—in which the protein can be imagined as a ball rolling downhill toward the deepest trough—rather than folding pathways. To describe the conformation of the polypeptide backbone alone (never mind the side chains), one needs two angles for each peptide bond, that is, $2n - 2$ parameters for a chain of n amino acid building blocks. For schematic representations like the ones shown in Fig. 4 this number has to be reduced to 2 (as we tend to have problems visualizing 200 dimensions), with the total free energy of the protein on the z axis.

This new representation, which was first used by Peter Wolynes at the University of Illinois in Urbana to describe experimental results, has its foundations in both experimental and theoretical results obtained in the early 1990s. Experimental work carried out in the laboratory of Chris

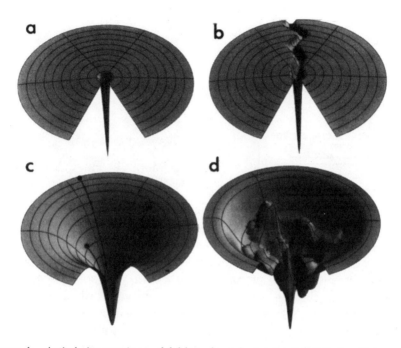

Figure 4: Artist's impressions of folding funnels: (a) the Levinthal golf course representing a uniform unfolded state and just one steep hole for the native state; (b) introducing a "folding pathway" to address the Levinthal paradox; (c) a true folding funnel for an extremely well-behaved protein that could refold rapidly from virtually any point in conformational space; (d) more realistically, a "rough" energy landscape indicating that the conformation of the initial state does matter, so different molecules may follow different paths and indeed need different lengths of time to complete folding.

Dobson at the University of Oxford, for instance, has shown that even for a relatively small and simple protein like hen egg white lysozyme, there is not just one path leading to the unique native state. Studies using advanced methods of NMR spectroscopy (see accompanying Ways & Means, pp. 80 and 81) and of mass spectrometry have shown that different molecules within the same sample can travel along parallel pathways and pass through different intermediates on their way. Furthermore, improvements in the time-resolved analysis of early folding events have yielded the insight that the first rapid steps in folding do not lead to a well-defined intermediate, but to an ensemble of compact, but poorly ordered conformations.

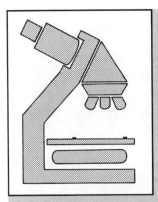

Ways and Means

Nuclear Magnetic Resonance (NMR) Spectroscopy

Nuclear magnetic resonance is a very weak effect that can be observed in the nuclei of certain kinds of atoms on placing them in the field of a very strong magnet. Within the magnetic field, these particles can adopt two different states of slightly different energy. A quantum-mechanical property called the *nuclear spin* (because it resembles in some ways a rotational movement which could be defined by its rotational momentum) makes the nucleus behave like a very small magnet. As magnets like to line up with each other, the nuclear spin can essentially be oriented either with the direction of the magnetic field, or against it. Nuclei can flip between these two states when they interact with suitable electromagnetic waves. As the energy difference is extremely small, the waves required lie in the range of radio waves, which have a much lower energy than, for instance, visible light.

What happens in an NMR spectrometer is that the atoms of the sample you want to analyze will be exposed to a strong magnetic field, and then be irradiated with short flashes of radio waves. Those atoms that are in the lower energy state can absorb energy from the radio waves to get in the higher state. After some time they will fall back to the lower state and dispose of the extra energy by sending out some radio waves themselves. Now each kind of atom will respond to and produce radio waves of one specific frequency (corresponding to its energy difference) only, and this wavelength will also be slightly altered for identical atoms put in a different chemical environment. Furthermore, atoms can "talk to each other": They can alter each other's response through chemical bonds or even through open space.

All of these phenomena are extremely subtle—the frequency differences, for instance, are typically measured in parts per million (ppm). Nevertheless, if they are assayed with a sufficiently powerful magnet, they allow the NMR spectroscopist to deduce information about the relative arrangement of atoms in space. From this, they can deduce the structures of small- to middle-sized proteins (up to 25 kDa) in aqueous solutions as opposed to the conformation in the crystal, which is what crystallographers determine. Although in most cases solution and crystal structures are in excellent agreement, it is very useful to have these two methods at hand. Especially for proteins that are small yet difficult to crystallize, NMR spectroscopy has become indispensable. In addition, its capacity to resolve each hydrogen atom of a given protein individually can also serve the analysis of other biophysical methods such as hydrogen exchange kinetics.

Technically, the performance of protein NMR is limited by the magnetic field that can be achieved. Since the introduction of supraconducting magnets in the mid-1960s, the maximum field strength available has quadrupled, increasing the frequency to which hydrogen nuclei respond from 200 MHz to 800 MHz. While most of the protein NMR work is currently done with 500- and 600-MHz instruments, the limits of the feasible are constantly being pushed forward, so there is no doubt that a gigahertz spectrometer will be available some time soon. However, because of the astronomical cost of such magnets, there will probably be relatively few of them, likely organized in national facilities, while the bulk of the research will continue to run on the equipment that is already in operation.

At the same time, the theoreticians Ken Dill and Hue-Sun Chan at the University of California in San Francisco managed to simulate certain characteristic aspects of foldings in simple computer models that basically describe a string of beads fixed to certain positions in a three-dimensional lattice. These model chains only contain 2 types of beads (instead of 20 different amino acids) and generally have to be much less complex than real proteins, as the currently available computing facilities would only allow simulating some picoseconds in the life of a real protein and are thus quite far from able to simulate real folding. Nevertheless, these so-called lattice models can have native states, collapsed intermediates, and several other features found in the folding of real proteins.

The new view allows one to explain the development of the folding field and the shortcomings of the early models. The original Levinthal view of a random search through conformational space for just one correct arrangement corresponds to the folding funnel shown in Fig. 4a: a vast plain of states with equal energy, which the chain has to search through to find the one hole it wants to fall into. Therefore, this model is also called the *Levinthal golf course*. Levinthal's remedy of a defined folding path can be represented as a riverbed running through the plain and leading to the hole (b). Panel c, in contrast, shows a simple case of a folding funnel according to the new view: a protein that can fold with little effort from almost any position in conformational space by following the slope downhill toward the native state. In most cases, however, there are bound to be complications, such as bumps in the way, troughs that could trap the chain in a wrong conformation, and so on (d). These are the features that lead to all of the parallel pathways and stable intermediates that folding researchers have been busy describing.

These complexities are also blamed for the fact that many proteins refold poorly in the test tube, in that only a fraction of the sample reaches the native states. Cells have a remedy against this, which we will consider in the next section, namely, folding helper proteins also known as *molecular chaperones*.

Safeguarding Adolescent Proteins: Molecular Chaperones Prevent Dangerous Liaisons

In the 1970s, when people began refolding proteins in the test tube, the finding that proteins can refold without help from outside was tacitly extrapolated to the cell. After all, if protein chains contained all of the information for the folded state, what else should they need? Only in the late 1980s did researchers realize that folding may need help in the cell despite Anfinsen's demonstration of autonomous folding in the test tube. And they provided an old word that had almost become obsolete with an entirely new meaning.

"A person (generally of a respectable age) who accompanies a girl or a young woman for the sake of propriety" has, according to the French dictionary *Le Petit Robert*, been designated since 1690 with a word that originally stood for a certain kind of hood: *chaperon*. Other languages including English have adopted the word for the ladies who in the old times kept an eye on the daughters of the better-off families to make sure they were not involved in inappropriate interactions.

Similarly, a group of proteins named *molecular chaperones* after those ladies is thought to prevent indecent interactions between protein molecules. Although it is still true that proteins can in principle fold without help, as their sequence contains all of the information they require, their folding in the cell faces several obstacles. As I explained above, the ribosome makes the protein as a linear chain of amino acids, which have a well-defined sequence but have not yet acquired the correct spatial structure. This means that binding sites that are meant to be placed at the inside of the final native structure and hold it together through weak interactions, are still exposed. At the same time, there is an incredibly dense crowd of other biomolecules around the not yet folded chain, including other newly made proteins exposing similar sites. Thus, it can easily happen that such binding sites destined for interactions within the same molecule come across sticky sites of other molecules and get involved in a mésalliance. This will lead to a lump of incorrectly folded and associated polypeptide chains, which will be completely useless for the cell and thus a regrettable waste of its resources.

To prevent this from happening, one protein from the molecular chaperone family already greets the protein chain when it just emerges from the ribosomal tunnel. In *Escherichia coli* this protein is DnaK, after the systematic name of the gene that codes for it. As Ulrich Hartl's group demonstrated in 1992, the protein is then passed on from one kind of chaperone to the next, proceeding on a sequential pathway of assisted folding that ends up in the barrel-shaped protein complex termed *GroEL* in *E. coli*, or *chaperonin-60* in a more general nomenclature. It consists of two rings, each made of seven identical subunits. For this barrel, there is also a lid, which is a single ring of seven smaller protein subunits, called *GroES* or *chaperonin-10* [L/S and 60/10 refer to the fact that the barrel subunits are quite large proteins (molecular mass of 54 kDa), while the lid proteins are smallish (10 kDa)]. While cell extracts normally contain complexes of a barrel with a single lid (i.e., 14 units of GroEL, 7 of GroES), symmetrical "footballs" with two lids form under some conditions. Their biological relevance has been hotly debated.

Along the pathway of assisted protein folding, the early chaperones are regarded as mostly protective in their function. The folding as such is believed to occur while the proteins interact with the GroEL complex. Just how this happens has been a matter of much research and debate. Like the ribosome and many other important biochemical reactions, the GroEL reaction seems to proceed in circles, and it uses the substantial amount of 14 molecules of the energy carrier ATP in each round. For more details of the GroEL reaction cycle, see Fig. 5.

During the first years, the investigation of the mechanisms of GroEL was seriously hindered by the lack of structural data. Considering the sevenfold symmetry of the complex, which cannot be packed into any space-filling arrangement, some researchers doubted that it would ever yield crystals suitable for high-resolution structure determination. Electron microscopy of this system was driven to reveal a remarkable amount of detail by Helen Saibil and her co-workers at Birkbeck College, London, but it was always clear it would not achieve amino acid resolution. For NMR, on the other hand, the system was much too big.

In this apparently hopeless situation, crystallographers had a streak of luck—two streaks, to be precise. The first was in 1993–1994, when Arthur L. Horwich's group at Yale managed to identify a variant of GroEL (a mutant in which two amino acid residues were exchanged) that happened to be nicely crystallizable, but still functionally active, and thus presumably very similar to the normal version. In collaboration with the crystallographer Paul Sigler, who is also based at Yale, they worked out almost the complete structure of the barrel. Only a few amino acid residues of each end of the chain were too disordered to show up in the electron density map. These "loose ends" are thought to hang around in the middle of the hollow interior of the barrel. Obtaining good crystals from GroEL was a major breakthrough in that it also enabled researchers to investigate functionally important assemblies, such as GroEL–GroES, chaperones with and without ATP, and others, to be analyzed by X-ray crystallography. Further structures of GroEL complexes were published within the

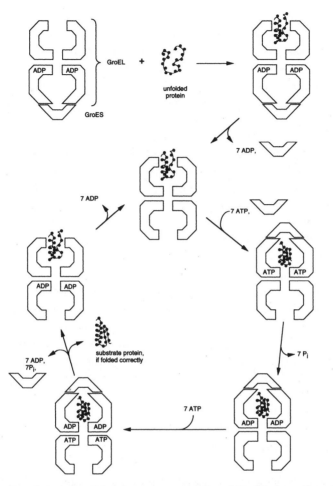

Figure 5:   Reaction cycle of the chaperone complex of GroEL (barrel) and GroES (lid). The substrate protein to be refolded runs through this cycle of binding, release, and rebinding as long as it still exhibits unfolded structures recognized by GroEL. It can only be released from the complex when it is correctly folded.

following 2 years, yielding a detailed description of GroEL "in all of its states," at least as far as its interaction with ATP and GroES was concerned.

A major issue remained, however, which still appeared to be intractable by X-ray crystallography—the conformation of the substrate bound to GroEL. This was expected to be far too disordered for analysis, even if such a complex could be crystallized. Therefore, indirect biophysical methods were developed to study bound substrates. I was personally involved in an approach to this problem using isotope exchange monitored by mass spectrometry in my first years at Oxford, working as a postdoctoral fellow with Sheena Radford.

Then, however, Fortuna made her second big contribution to chaperone research. This time, Alan Fersht's group at Cambridge University was hit by a truly remarkable piece of luck. For their studies, they had selected from the original GroEL crystal structure a small part of the GroEL subunit as a potential site for substrate binding, and produced the molecular fragment by genetic engineering techniques. Having succeeded in growing crystals of this fragment and solving the crystal structure, the researchers at Cambridge realized they had obtained much more than they had bargained for. Each molecule in the crystal had grabbed hold of the "loose end" of its next neighbor, showing crystal clear the way in which the outermost domain of GroEL (the part lining the rims of the barrel) can bind unfolded polypeptide chains.

Thus, in a sequence of events that came much quicker than anyone would have predicted before 1994, all of the important information about the function of the chaperone machine has been obtained. There are still some open questions and apparent contradictions between the results obtained by different methods, but a fairly complete picture of chaperone-assisted folding should turn up in the biochemistry textbooks quite soon.

Recycling Scheme in the Cell: Understanding How the Proteasome Works

Having considered examples of the jobs that proteins fulfill in Chapter 2, we can now, after this description of their production and maturation, directly proceed to the end of their life cycle, protein degradation. We will find out that there are surprising parallels between chaperones and the degradation machinery, and that the cell is quite economical with its resources. In fact, the concept of recycling materials is probably more than a billion years old. This can be concluded from the fact that the cells of nearly all life forms possess recycling systems that "deconstruct" proteins that have been damaged or are no longer needed. They dissect them into the amino acid building blocks, which can then be either reused for protein synthesis or further degraded in metabolism.

To degrade those and only those proteins that are damaged or no longer required, the cell needs a marking and a degradation system. The marker is a smaller protein, ubiquitin, which is attached to the protein to be degraded. And the degradation as such takes place in an extremely complex protein assembly system, the proteasome. In comparison with those protein-degrading enzymes that cells secrete (such as our digestive enzymes trypsin and chymotrypsin), intracellular proteases like the proteasome are a relatively recent research field with lots of open questions to answer.

As proteasomes are found in nearly all kinds of organisms, they have been discovered many times independently and given 20 different names, before a common concept was discovered. As early as 1968, cell biologists found cylindrical particles of unknown function in eukaryotic cells. On the other hand, enzymologists tried to identify a mysterious "multicatalytic proteinase" first described in 1980. It turned out that both groups of scientists were looking at the same thing—one at the shape and the other at the function of it. The cylinder is now known as the *20 S proteasome* (20 S is the sedimentation coefficient, which is an indirect measure of molecular size). In many kinds of cells the 20 S particle is the core of a bigger, irregularly shaped assembly, the 26 S proteasome.

The 20 S proteasome of higher organisms turned out to be a mix of 28 subunits that could be of as many as 14 different types—thus, it appeared to be a hopelessly complex system. Wolfgang Baumeister's group at the Max Planck Institute for Biochemistry near Munich, however, managed to identify an organism that builds the same structure from just two types of subunits arranged in a regular pattern. In the 20 S proteasome of the archaebacterium *Thermoplasma acidophilum*, two rings of seven beta subunits are sandwiched between two rings of seven alpha subunits. Cleavage of polypeptide bonds appeared to occur only at the beta subunits.

Baumeister's group made the best use of this relatively simple model system. In the years 1992–1994, they could describe the assembly process, the recognition of the substrates to be degraded, the enzymatic function, and finally the crystal structure of the *Thermoplasma* proteasome. The assembly is unusual in that the central beta rings cannot assemble on their own but need a finished alpha ring as a template. The substrate recognition of the proteasome is strictly controlled, because the protein digesting function is potentially dangerous for the cell. Proteins can only enter this

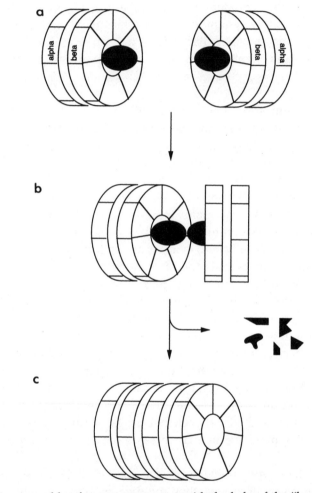

Figure 6:   Assembly of yeast proteasomes with the help of the "kamikaze chap-erone" Ump1p. (a) Assembly of beta subunits on a scaffold ring of alpha subunits results in an open half-proteasome with Ump1p bound. (b) When two halves pair up, two molecules of the chaperone are trapped in the proteasome cavity. (c) The fully assembled proteasome degrades Ump1p as its first substrate.

molecular shredder if they are (1) labeled with ubiquitin and (2) fully unfolded. Using a gold cluster attached to an unfolded protein, Baumeister and co-workers could show that it is the bulkiness of a folded protein that protects it from entering the proteasome by mistake.

Recently, a new twist involving both the assembly and the substrate recognition of the proteasome came up when the group of Jürger Dohmen at the University of Düseldorf (Germany) reported in 1998 that the yeast protein Ump1p acts as a chaperone in the assembly of the proteasome—and ends up being shredded to pieces by the machine it helped to build (Fig. 6). This finding again stresses how important it is that the potentially dangerous protein-degrading activity of the proteasome can only get started when it is enclosed in the cavity of the fully assembled protein complex. This is ensured by the kamikaze chaperone, which binds to the subunits and only gets eaten up when the assembly is completed.

The crystal structure worked out by the groups of Baumeister and Robert Huber (one of the trio who shared the 1988 Nobel Prize in chemistry for the crystal structure of the photosynthetic reaction center) at the Max Planck Institute revealed several new and surprising features. For instance, the enzyme has a new kind of active center (and hence a new enzymatic mechanism), which uses the amino acid threonine in its function, which in many proteinases is carried out by serine. This is why biochemists had earlier had trouble finding the active site. The researchers were also surprised to see that the folds of alpha and beta chains are nearly identical, although their amino acid sequences are very different. And finally, they were thrilled to find that this structure represented a new kind of fold, which is a bonus that has become rare as solved protein structures accumulate. Although complex organisms like ourselves can produce up to 100,000 different proteins, most structural biologists now believe that the number of fundamentally different folding patterns is quite small, possibly below 1000. Nature seems to have reused some basic design features again and again.

It is of special interest to compare the structure of the proteasome with that of the molecular chaperone GroEL discussed in the previous section. Both are barrels with a sevenfold symmetry, but while the molecular chaperone has as many windows as it has subunits, the "recycling bin" is tightly closed all around. The central tunnel (about 5 nm wide) is the only cavity of the proteasome. And there is no similarity whatsoever between the folds of the protein subunits, indicating that evolution has invented the barrel made of seven-membered rings at least twice.

This spectacular victory over the complexities of the proteasome gave the Max Planck researchers the courage to attack the even more complex eukaryotic system, using the 20 S proteasome from yeast as a model system. In 1996, they could indeed solve this structure as well. This is an important step toward the understanding of the proteasomes in higher organisms, which are known to play a crucial role in the immune response: They cut foreign proteins down into chunks that the immune cells then present on their surface to get the attack going. Thus, the proteasome is not only a degradation machine but also an important part of our immune system, and the remarkably good structural information that is available now will certainly help working out the details of this role.

4

Amazing Cells

From the nanomachines we shall now go one step upward in size and proceed to the nanofactories of the living world: cells. Maybe you are used to thinking of the cells that make up your body as specialized tools fulfilling their jobs in a specialized organ. This is one way of describing them, but it is also true that your cells are all part of an exceedingly clever plan set into action by that unicellular organism that was you on the day you were conceived. Think about it—in the moment of procreation, we are all unicellular organisms. And we owe all of our hereditary features to an information flow that goes from the nanoscale (DNA) to the macroscopic scale (body).

So, while the top-down view of the body using organs using cells makes sense for the medical doctor who eventually wants to find out why the body goes wrong, we shall prefer to stick with the bottom-up view that has taken us from atoms to molecules to protein systems, and go one step further and look at the amazing nanoworld of the cell. Cells can do really astonishing things to secure the survival of their descendants, and diversifying into a complex organism, like, for instance, a human being, is just one of these.

As with the proteins in Chapter 2, I shall present here a selection of cells and talk about the amazing things they can do, and I will try to explain how they manage to do them. The family tree comprising all life on Earth has three major branches characterized by three types of cells, as I will explain in the first section. Therefore, the following examples will cover all three types of cells. In addition, I will discuss the chemical weapons with which microbes fight each other, and which we can borrow to fight infectious diseases. Medicine is already being revolutionized by the structural knowledge we have obtained about the nanoworld of the cell, as drug designers are beginning to tailor their molecular tools to fit the target structures.

Three Kinds of Cells

The living beings that we would normally see in our everyday environment—people, pets, garden plants, insects, and so forth—represent only a very small fraction of the biological diversity found on our planet, and a very young one at that. All plants and animals are multicellular organisms, they all have cells of the most complex type, namely, eukaryotic cells (a definition that is based on the observation that they carry their DNA wrapped up in a cell nucleus). In the 4-billion-year history of our planet, eukaryotes only turned up at about halftime, and multicellular organisms less than a billion years ago.

So what are the alternatives? Traditionally, all cells without a nucleus were grouped together as "prokaryotes." However, when Carl Woese, working at the University of Illinois, set out in the early 1970s to investigate the family tree of these prokaryotes, he found that they fall into two very different groups, which have nothing more in common with each other than with eukaryotes. He placed those bacteria that produce methane, and those that like to live at extremely high temperature and/or in acidic solutions together in a new domain of life that he called the *archaebacteria* ("ancient bacteria"), or *archaea* in a more recent terminology (Fig. 1). In contrast, the common or garden bacteria have been labeled just *bacteria*, and more recently, *eubacteria* ("true bacteria").

Woese's new world-view was very slow to win ground among U.S. microbiologists, though it was enthusiastically embraced and confirmed

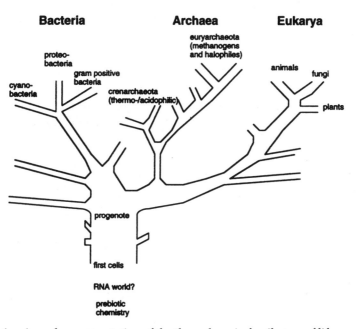

Figure 1: A crude representation of the three-domain family tree of life according to Woese.

by independent studies from researchers in Europe, including Kandler and Stetter in Germany. By 1996, when the first full genome sequence of an archaebacterium was published, the doubts had completely disappeared. It is still puzzling researchers, however, that they cannot clearly define the kinship between the three groups. That is, they don't know how the eukaryotic cell came into being. Presumably, both archae- and eubacteria played a role in the events that led to the first complex cells, but different ways of looking at this problem seem to yield different answers.

    The first hypothesis that shaped the way people think about the origin of the eukaryotic cell was proposed by Lynn Margulis 30 years ago. She suggested that a bigger than normal bacterium that may have developed a lifestyle of eating other bacteria by engulfing them within its membrane may at some time have engulfed but not digested a bacterium that was able to perform respiration, i.e., burning nutrients using oxygen. From this resulted an endosymbiosis ("living together within") between the two kinds of cells, during which the guest cell gradually lost the genes that were no longer required. While this hypothesis is widely accepted as a viable explanation for the origins of mitochondria, and can also be adapted for the chloroplasts of green plants, it does not per se explain why eukaryotic cells have a nucleus, and why they resemble archaebacteria in some kinds of genes and eubacteria in others. In fact, the whole archaebacterial domain was only discovered after Margulis put forward her endosymbiont hypothesis, so some revision of it was inevitable.

In 1998, William Martin, of the Technical University in Braunschweig, Germany, and Miklos Müller of the Rockefeller University in New York proposed the first radically new hypothesis on the origin of eukaryotes since Margulis. They suggested that a hydrogen-dependent archaebacterium was the host organism that engulfed a hydrogen-providing bacterium to form the first eukaryotic cell.

With the current bonanza of genome sequences from all three domains of life (see Chapter 3), a close inspection of the genome regions in charge of metabolic specialties should certainly provide the means of verifying or falsifying the new hypothesis in a matter of a few years. Thus, we may soon witness the removal of the embarrassing dilemma that we do not yet understand the most important step in the transition from the Earth inhabited only by bacteria to our current biotope teeming with numerous plant and animal species.

A Different Kind of Bug: *Methanococcus jannaschii*

If you are looking for weirdness in microbes, there is just one place to go in the family tree of life on Earth: the domain of the archaea. Some of them can live in water heated beyond the normal boiling point at temperatures as high as 113°C, others support both high temperatures and strongly acidic pH at the same time, and others still survive 1000-fold atmospheric pressure or temperatures below freezing. Apart from the fact that the electron microscope does not immediately reveal that they are different from normal bacteria, it may have also been their preference for hostile environments that delayed their recognition as a separate domain for so long.

As life under extreme conditions, including the extreme life of the archaea, is the topic of my other book, *Life on the Edge*, I will not indulge in my passion for this topic on these pages any longer. Instead, I am going to introduce you to the first archaebacterium that became a media star: *Methanococcus jannaschii*. When Woese published his revolutionary results in 1977, which basically implied that the classification of all life on Earth had to be changed on the most fundamental level, many scientific colleagues remained skeptical, and the general public failed to take notice. Nineteen years later, however, when Craig Venter announced that researchers at TIGR had completed the genome sequence of the first archaebacterium, and that it confirmed Woese's view of three domains of life, he made sure that the message got heard. As the novelty of the sequencing of an entire genome as such was beginning to wear off, the very weirdness of the archaebacterium and its importance for evolutionary considerations helped to make the achievement newsworthy. And Woese, the prophet ignored in his own country for almost two decades, was quoted all over America, from the *New York Times* to the *San Francisco Chronicle*.

But what about the most important if least visible star of this story? *Methanococcus jannaschii* (Fig. 2) was first isolated in 1983 from samples that the research submarine *Alvin* had retrieved from a hot spring on the ocean floor, 2600 m below sea level. As the first part of its name implies, it generates methane (the major component of natural gas), much the same way as its relatives who live inside cows or in the average compost heap. The second part refers to the Woods Hole microbiologist Holger W. Jannasch, one of the founding fathers of the biology of marine extremophiles.

A second remarkable property of *Methanococcus jannaschii* is that it does not require any organic nutrients—microbiologists say it's autotrophic. That means it can take up all of the chemical elements it needs in

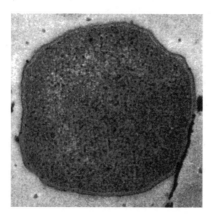

Figure 2:   *Methanococcus igneus*, a cousin of *Methanococcus jannaschii*.

the shape of simple inorganic molecules. For instance, it has its own system for nitrogen fixation, which presumably operates in a similar way as the one discussed in Chapter 2. Similarly, it can use hydrogen in its molecular (H_2) form, and it is happy with carbon dioxide as its only source of carbon atoms. Thus, all of the "food" it needs is contained in the seawater near volcanic sites on the seafloor. Because *M. jannaschii* is autotrophic, a description of its metabolic pathways, which one could eventually derive from the knowledge of the metabolic enzymes coded in the genome, would be of particular interest. It would indeed constitute the most complete map of the basic chemistry of life conceivable, as it would have to include the ways of making every molecule used by this cell from scratch.

As for its adaptation to extreme conditions, *M. jannaschii* is remarkable although not record breaking. It can be cultivated at temperatures between 48 and 94°C, and grows best at 85°C. It is happy with the pressures of around 250 atmospheres corresponding to the depth at which it was found. Apart from being the first archaebacterium and the first autotrophic organism, it was also the first extremophile to have its genome completely sequenced. There is an enormous and thus far grossly underused potential of biotechnology using proteins adapted to high temperatures or other extreme conditions. With the release of the *M. jannaschii* genome data, the sequences of more than 1700 extremely heat-stable proteins have been added to the general scientific knowledge—an invaluable resource for the future of biotechnology.

A surprisingly large proportion (56%) of these proteins turned out to be not related to anything known to science. Working out what they are will provide not only a scientific challenge, but also the opportunity of finding novel and potentially useful enzyme functions. But there are still hundreds that correspond to similar but nonthermophilic proteins of other organisms. Detailed investigation of these proteins will be useful for both the fundamental understanding of adaptation to extreme conditions and for the future application of heat-resistant proteins in biotechnology.

Knowing Where You're Going: Magnetotactic Bacteria Can Tell North from South

Like us, microbes have different preferences and inclinations. Some swim toward sources of light or heat, others away from them, and many of them are attracted or repelled by the concentration of certain chemicals in the water. The well-known gut bacterium *Escherichia coli*, for instance, has five separate systems for the specific recognition of chemicals, to which it responds by movement (chemotaxis). For all of these "behaviors" there are straightforward explanations in evolutionary terms (e.g., if the bacteria swim toward chemicals that might serve as food, and flee others that are toxic). Things get more tricky when we come across bacteria whose movements depend on the Earth's magnetic field.

In 1975, the microbiologist Richard P. Blakemore was the first to observe this strange kind of behavior, which he called *magnetotaxis*. The bacteria he studied were not to be distracted from their northward bound path by simple tricks such as turning the microscope slide they were on or altering the lighting. It turned out they had an inbuilt compass consisting of minute magnetite crystals, just a few tenths of a micrometer in length. These crystals are wrapped in membrane, resulting in a special cell compartment, the magnetosome (Fig. 3).

In the following years, further magnetotactic bacteria could be found in diverse environments. Given their characteristic property, catching and isolating them is certainly easier than for most other newly discovered breeds. Their widespread occurrence also set geologists thinking about possible biological origins of certain magnetite reservoirs that they had hitherto assumed to result from inorganic processes. Ironically, such bacteria could also be found in strictly anaerobic (oxygen-free) environments, although the magnetite is made up of iron and oxygen. This finding led to new questions as to how the bacteria produce their magnetite crystals.

Apart from the tricky question as to what evolutionary advantage a bacterium could get from an inbuilt compass, the well-oriented microbes point to a couple of other intriguing problems, including the magnetic orientation of higher organisms, the formation of magnetic sediment

Figure 3:   Electron micrograph of a magnetotactic bacterium. The dark oval structures are the magnetosomes containing small magnetite crystals.

rocks, and even the origin of life. The finding that the controlled formation of magnetite and other crystalline iron compounds is widespread among bacteria suggests that these may have played an important role in the early history of life on Earth. Long before molecular oxygen became available (remember oxygen is a waste product of photosynthesis and was not part of the atmosphere for the first 1.5 billion years!), iron sulfides and oxides could have played similar roles in the combustion of nutrients. Iron minerals are also very popular with people making theories about the origin of life. Witness the German patent attorney Günter Wächtershäuser, who built his much-talked-about theory around the properties of the iron sulfur compound pyrite, also known as *fool's gold*.

Alternatively, magnetites in ancestral bacteria could have simply served as storage devices for iron, a task that nowadays is fulfilled by a protein, ferritin. Thus, it may well be the case that there was no specific evolutionary reason for the bacteria to become magnetotactic. Maybe the bugs started building and keeping these minerals for other reasons and obtained their compass function as a free extra. Looking at it this way, we humans should be glad that biomineralization in our bodies uses a different metal ion as its main building block: the utterly nonmagnetic calcium.

Cells with a Vision: The Rods and Cones of the Retina

Signal conversion between different kind of carriers (chemical, optical, electrical) is one of the most important areas in which technology may profit from insights gained in biological systems. In Chapter 2 we have studied the molecular machinery of signal conversion in the cell, which is arranged around the G proteins as the central switchboard. Now we are talking about what cells can do, and I have—again—chosen an example from signal conversion, namely, the cells involved in vision.

At the back of your eyeballs is a layer of light-sensitive cells that—like the film in a camera—records an upside-down small scale image of what you are seeing. The retina is much cleverer than a conventional film, as it not only catches the light and the information it carries, but can also convert it into an electrical signal that then will be transmitted to your brain and create a visual perception. Strictly speaking, the retina is a part of the brain, as the light-sensitive cells have evolved from brain cells. There are two kinds of light-sensitive cells in the retina. The cones are mostly found nearer the middle, can distinguish colors, and are less sensitive than the rods, which are colorblind and more abundant near the edges of the retina. A human retina contains roughly 1 billion rods and 3 million cones.

As an example of how a biological cell can be completely devoted to a physical task, namely, converting a light signal into an electrical one, let us now consider the architecture of the rod cells (Fig. 4a). They are subdivided into two major segments. The outer segment (which ironically is turned inside, away from the light in the human retina for historical reasons) contains a pile of membrane "disks" into which the molecules of the light receptor, rhodopsin, are incorporated. Roughly speaking, the outer segment does the signal conversion job, while the inner segment keeps the cell alive and contains all of the compartments and structures that are needed for the life of any eukaryotic cell, including the nucleus, the mitochondria, and lots of ribosomes, as the rods are very active in protein synthesis. At the far end of the inner segment there is the synapse that provides the link to the nerves connecting to the brain.

One of the amazing things about rod cells is that each one can be stimulated to produce a nerve impulse by the arrival of a single photon (the smallest possible amount of light according to quantum mechanics). The primary chemical reaction triggered when a photon hits the cell happens in a molecule of retinal, which is a slightly modified version of vitamin A and has to be bound to the membrane protein opsin, which is called *rhodopsin* for as long as it carries retinal. Within a picosecond (10^{-12} sec) after the arrival of the photon, the kinked structure of the chainlike part of retinal changes to a stretched out version (Fig. 4b). In a reaction cascade very similar to the hormone response described in Chapter 2, the rhodopsin will now activate a specific G protein (transducin), from which the signal will be passed on and amplified by several orders of magnitude, until it eventually reaches certain ion channels that will briefly block the way for sodium ions. This results in a rapid change in the electrical potential across the membrane of the outer segment—in other words, a nerve impulse is born.

All of this happens within a second when just one photon arrives, and even faster for a more intense light pulse. For the record, I should note that the straightened-out retinal does not fit its binding site in the opsin protein any more and will be released from it in a slow reaction. It will have to undergo a chemical reaction that restores the kinked form before it can bind to an empty opsin molecule again.

However, the function of the rod cell is not only something that

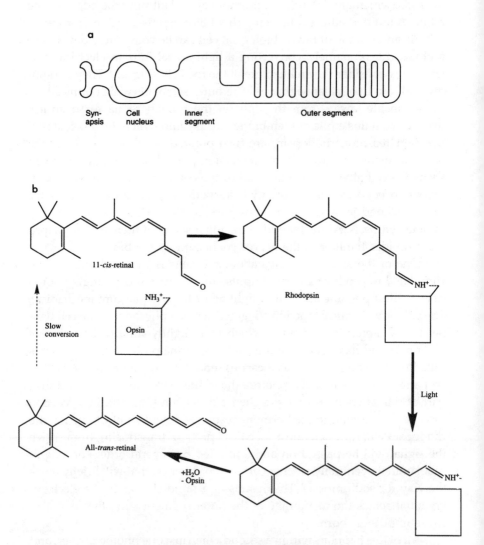

Figure 4:   (a) Schematic representation of a rod cell from the human retina. (b) The light-induced reaction by which "kinked" (11-*cis*) retinal is converted to the straight (all-*trans*) variant of the molecule. Chemists call this kind of reaction in which only the relative orientation of bonds changes, but no bonds are lost or added, an *isomerization*.

happens on the protein and chromophore level. Membranes play a very important part, too. The rhodopsin is actually incorporated into the peculiar membrane disks stacked up in the outer segment of the rod cell. The way it gets there is curious in that the membrane protein gets first incorporated into the plasma membrane of the cell, which then bulges inward to form the membrane bag that will flatten out to a disk. It can be shown that the sugar molecules attached to rhodopsin are at first on the outside of the cell and then end up inside the disk structure. From the distribution of the hydrophobic (water-avoiding) amino acid residues in the opsin sequence, researchers have derived hypothetical models of how the protein chain winds its way back and forth through the membrane in seven transmembrane helices. However, rhodopsin is among the most important proteins for which no high-resolution structure has been elucidated to date.

One intriguing aspect of the function and metabolism of the rod cell is that the energy required for restoring the active, kinked version of the retinal chromophore is not provided by a small molecule such as ATP (as one would expect) or GTP. Instead, the very molecules that make up the membrane into which the bacteriorhodopsin is embedded also provide the energy. As Robert R. Rando's group at Harvard has shown, the energetically more favorable stretched version reacts with a membrane component (lecithin) to form an energy-rich compound known as an *ester*. The enzyme that restores the kinked structure uses the chemical energy contained in the ester bond (which it cleaves) to introduce the kink.

Although the visual process is not yet understood in every molecular detail, it is very clear that this is an instance of natural information technology functioning to extremely high technical specifications. Understandably so, as any animal that fails to perceive the shadow of a predator as quickly as possible would certainly experience the negative side of natural selection soon enough. In summary, the cells of the retina are remarkable for detecting light impulse with

- Extremely high sensitivity—a single photon can be perceived and its arrival can be amplified to influence the movements of millions of atoms
- High speed with reactions on the millisecond time scale
- High capacity for adaptation to high or low background luminosity

And that's just the beginning of the pathway of visual perception.

Cell Wars (1): How Taxol Keeps Cancer Cells from Multiplying

One important reason why chemists keep creating novel molecules has to do with the fact that drugs against many diseases including cancer are difficult to develop in a rational way. The most common, irrational way of finding them is to generate thousands of new molecules, screen them for activity against all kinds of things, and then discard 99.9% of them. If one is lucky, the thousandth compound will be active against something. If one is even more lucky, one finds an interesting molecule in screens of natural substances. Bad luck, though, if the natural product is scarce and virtually impossible to make by chemical synthesis.

The Pacific yew tree (*Taxus brevifolia*), a coniferous tree mainly found in the northwestern United States, contains about 0.3 gram of the compound taxol in its bark. (Taxol is a registered trademark of Bristol-Myers Squibb, who would like the scientific community to use the term *paclitexel* instead.) Three hundred milligrams per fully grown tree, that is. This substance, which was discovered in 1964 and had its structure solved in 1971, has sent cancer specialists buzzing with excitement. They have labeled it the most promising new substance in decades. Clinical trials have proven its activity against leukemia as well as against tumors of the breast, ovaries, and lungs. The only trouble was that the treatment of each patient would require the sacrifice of six trees. And the trees are protected under nature conservation laws, because they are the preferred breeding places of a rare species of owls.

It was clear that an alternative way of getting this substance was required, and chemists in some 30 research groups around the globe rose to the formidable challenge of synthesizing the structure with four unusual merged molecular rings (Fig. 5). After a dramatic race, two groups finished the total synthesis of taxol almost simultaneously in the winter of 1993–1994. Robert Holten and his co-workers at Florida State University were the first to submit their manuscript, but they saw the paper of their competitors led by Kyriacos Nicolaou coming out in *Nature* a week before their work appeared in the *Journal of the American Chemical Society*. Each of them had required nearly 30 stepwise chemical reactions to build the structure from simple organic chemicals including single-ring compounds.

These synthetic procedures are certainly too complicated for industrial production of taxol—even if the yield on each of 30 steps was 90%, the overall yield would fall to $0.9^{30} = 4\%$. The substance is now being made by

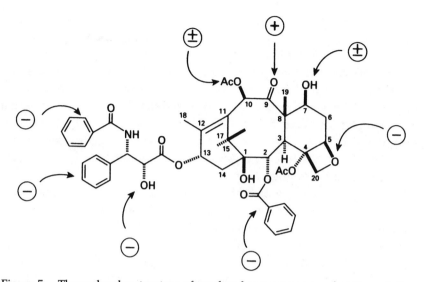

Figure 5:   The molecular structure of taxol and some structure–function relationships. ⊕, those parts of the molecule where modification can lead to enhanced activity; ⊖, those parts where modifications have resulted in decreased or total loss of activity; ⊕, structural elements that can be removed without obvious change in the pharmacological activity of the molecule.

chemical conversion of similar natural products that are available from renewable resources, like the leaves of other kinds of yew trees. In the long term, biotechnological approaches using cell cultures may evolve to outperform this semisynthetic strategy. Still, the total synthesis remains extremely important as it also shows up routes to the production of variants of the original structure, which can then be synthesized and searched through. After all, there may be a compound with an even better pharmacological profile. Chances of obtaining an even better taxol have also risen with the recent solution of the structural details of its targets in the cell: the microtubuli.

The cytoskeleton is the fibrous meshwork that stabilizes the cell like the poles of a tent, and its individual rods are the microtubuli, which we briefly met in Chapter 2 as the rails on which the kinesin motors move. These consist of 13 intertwined strings (the protofilaments), which are alternating rows of the protein subunits alpha- and beta-tubulin. While there are several kinds of cell poisons that act by stopping tubulin from forming microtubules, taxol was the first substance found to kill cells by enhancing the formation and stability of these tubes. The crucial difference is that the tubuli formed in the presence of taxol only contain 12 protofilaments, and have a smaller diameter. For the cell preparing for division, dynamical rearrangement of microtubuli involving both synthesis and dismantling is crucial. The wrong constructs with 12 strings are so stable that they will not easily redissolve. They tend to form useless bundles that in the long term remove most of the tubulin building blocks from the cell's supply and make cell division impossible. As cancer cells divide much more frequently than healthy cells in an adult, they are hit quite selectively by this kind of poisoning.

Up to this point, the behavior of microtubuli could be investigated using ordinary electron microscopy. However, for a complete understanding of the tubulin system, a key element was missing until quite recently: the high-resolution structure of the protein subunits. Because of the immense biological importance of this system, there have been numerous attempts to obtain crystals suitable for structure determination by X-ray crystallography, but for decades they all failed.

Considering this dilemma, Eva Nogales and Kenneth H. Downing at the Lawrence Berkeley National Laboratory in Berkeley, California, opted for an alternative method, which does not quite reach the resolution of a crystal structure, but has the major advantage of not requiring well-ordered crystals. Instead of crystallizing the proteins the traditional way, the Californians produced flat sheets of tubulin subunits by adding zinc ions to the solutions, with the goal of analyzing these sheets using advanced methods of electron microscopy. These "two-dimensional crystals" obviously contain the same protofilaments as the tubuli, but differ in the relative orientation of the strings. This is quite fortunate as it implies that each protein subunit is in an environment very similar to the one in the microtubuli.

Probing these sheets from different angles using a weak (i.e., not damaging) electron beam, Nogales and co-workers were able to determine an electron density map at a resolution of 0.37 nm. Although this does not quite reach the quality of good crystal structures (where individual atoms can be identified), it allowed the researchers to fit the chemical structure of the known amino acid sequence into their electron density map, resulting in unambiguous localization of each amino acid residue and identification of elements of secondary structure such as alpha helices and beta sheets.

The structure that they obtained, and published in *Nature* in January

1998, shows two very similar subunits. Although alpha- and beta-tubulin only share 40% of their amino acid sequences, both adopt essentially the same fold, in which numerous helices are arranged around a small central beta sheet. The structure also shows quite clearly the binding sites for the nucleotide GTP and for taxol.

Thus, with the structure and synthesis of taxol, access to its derivatives, and a reasonably well resolved structural model for its target protein tubulin, researchers are set to develop—rationally, at last!—new cancer therapeutics with improved specificity from the interesting group of the taxanes. Patients of the future will benefit from the finding that one can stop cells from dividing by keeping their cytoskeleton from dissolving.

Cell Wars (2): How Bacteria Get the Better of Antibiotics

There is a chemical warfare going on in nature between microbes of the eukaryotic kingdom and ordinary bacteria. The eukaryotes, mostly unicellular fungi (like yeasts or molds), have been especially inventive in producing substances that kill bacteria, but these have in turn evolved genetic traits that confer resistance against the attack. Among the chemical weapons from the fungal arsenal are the antibiotics that we humans have been applying for five decades to fight bacterial diseases. But in the 1990s it has become clear that earlier claims of victory have been precocious. More and more, scientists are beginning to realize that bacteria are fighting back.

The war against pathogenic bacteria has been one of the major hallmarks of medical progress in the twentieth century. As early as 1926, the microbiologist and writer Paul de Kruif celebrated this endeavor with his all-time classic *Microbe Hunters*, which remained in print for more than 50 years. Ironically, hunting down microbes and killing them efficiently only became possible 2 years after its publication, when Alexander Fleming (1881–1955) noticed that the mold *Penicillium notatum* produces a substance that appeared to kill bacteria in its surroundings. With the identification of penicillin and its clinical trials by Howard Walter Florey (1898–1968) and Ernst B. Chain (1906–1979) at Oxford in the early 1940s, the antibiotics age began. For the first time in human history, infectious diseases transmitted by bacteria could be fought with high efficiency. In the 1950s, prophecies of a victory over the plagues were heard, but four decades onwards, skepticism has taken over. In 1994, Bernard Dixon appropriately chose *Power*

Unseen—How Microbes Rule the World as the title for his collection of essays about microbial species. In the same year, the World Health Organization reported an alarming increase in the reported cases of tuberculosis—a disease caused by the bacterium *Mycobacterium tuberculosis*. Strains of this bacterium that are resistant to certain antibiotics are found all over the world. In April 1994, *Science* magazine devoted a special issue to the rising problem of antibiotics resistance.

At first, it looked like a fair race: Scientists had to develop novel antibiotics at least as quickly as resistance against the existing ones spread among bacterial populations. In recent years, however, researchers have felt reminded of the Red Queen in *Through the Looking Glass*, who has to run faster and faster to remain in the same place.

As Julian Davies of the University of British Columbia in Vancouver pointed out in the special issue of *Science*, a detailed investigation of the ways on which resistance spreads in nature is virtually impossible, because we only know a tiny fraction of the bacterial species on our planet. Therefore, ways and mechanisms by which resistance spreads can only be studied in simplified models. It becomes clear, however, that the antibiotics themselves favor the bacterial response in several ways.

One problem, which was obvious from the beginning, is that each application of antibiotics produces a new selection pressure. If among the millions of bacteria in the body of a patient there happens to be one that carries a mutation making it resistant to the antibiotic used in the treatment, this one bacterium has a major advantage over the others and will continue to multiply. Even if the immune system eventually gets the better of this new resistant strain, those bacteria that the patient has released into the world before the infection is over, will be more likely to be resistant, and they might infect other people on whom this antibiotic would then be completely inefficient from the beginning.

The second mechanism, which was initially thought to be extremely rare and therefore irrelevant for the clinical practice, has to do with the spread of resistance through the transfer of genetic material between bacteria. This can happen in different ways, but most efficiently with the help of ring-shaped DNA molecules, the so-called R-plasmids. Only in recent years has it become clear that this kind of transfer is much more common than was predicted earlier, and that barriers which were assumed to separate major groups of bacteria (like gram-positive and gram-negative) do not stop this process. But even worse news is still to come.

The third and most far-reaching piece of bad news for modern microbe hunters was the finding of Vera Webb and Julian Davies, who in 1993 discovered that pharmacists may have been handing out resistance genes with the prescribed antibiotic. It is difficult to ensure that antibiotics produced by fermentation are completely free from the DNA of the unicellular fungi that were used to make the drug. Analyzing the DNA impurities in antibiotic prescriptions, Webb and Davies also identified genes that can make their carrier resistant against the very same antibiotic they were found in. Since it has become known that the transfer of such genes between different organisms, while difficult, is not impossible, it can no longer be excluded that the spread of resistance genes has been favored both indirectly and directly by treatment involving antibiotics.

How do these genes make bacteria resistant? Roughly speaking, bacteria can defend themselves against the fungal (or human) chemical warfare by preventing the chemical from entering the cell, by destroying it, or by reducing the vulnerability of the target system (Fig. 6). All three mechanisms are found in bacteria, sometimes even in the same strain.

One of the most important—and most annoying—resistance genes belongs to the second class. It codes for the production of the enzyme beta-lactamase, which can cleave the crucial ring structure of an important class of antibiotics including penicillin. As researchers kept developing new derivatives of penicillin that would not be cleaved by the enzyme, the microbes kept evolving new variants of the enzyme to match the new antibiotics. Exchanging a single DNA base in the beta-lactamase gene may alter the substrate specificity of the resulting enzyme. Therefore, scientists have turned their attention to the possibility of using enzyme inhibitors that could be applied with the antibiotic and would protect it from being degraded by the enzyme. Although small molecule inhibitors have proven inefficient in preliminary tests, there is some hope that protein inhibitors like beta-lactamase inhibiting protein (BLIP) will do better. But even though beta-lactamase is one of the best studied proteins in the world, and although there may be no other enzyme for which so many inhibitors have been found and investigated, a final elimination of the resistance factor beta-lactamase is not yet in sight.

Therefore, some research groups are frantically searching for novel antimicrobial substances that may be able to replace the classical antibiotics, and may not induce resistance reactions quite as easily. A potential bonanza of this kind was discovered in the late 1980s by Michael Zasloff of the University of Pennsylvania in Philadelphia, when he isolated from the skin of the African clawed toad *Xenopus laevis* a peptide he called

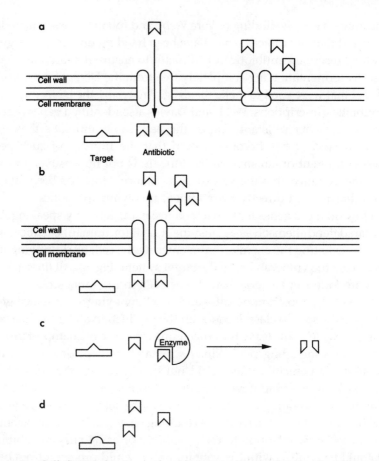

Figure 6: Cellular mechanisms of resistance against antibiotics. Bacteria can protect themselves from antibiotic activity by (a) blocking the access to the inside of the
cell, (b) actively pumping the antibiotics molecules out of the cell, (c) destroying the
molecules with the help of enzymes coded by resistance genes, or (d) varying the
target structure in a way that the antibiotic fails to recognize it.

magainin after the Hebrew word for shield. Before that, people had already
noticed that frog skin is somewhat of a poison cupboard, in which a whole
range of pharmacologically active compounds can be found. The medicine
men of both African and Native American tribes seem to have known this
from experience, as they traditionally used frog skin to prepare remedies.
But magainin was the first "broad-range antibiotic" to be isolated from this

source. Strictly speaking, there are two related peptides, magainin 1 and 2, each of which has 23 amino acid residues and no sequence similarity with any other known substance. Their activity against bacteria is comparable to that of traditional antibiotics. Zasloff, who has started a company developing salable antibiotics on the basis of the magainin peptides, is also keeping up the search for antimicrobial substances in sources that have thus far been neglected. One of his more recent discoveries, the steroid antibiotic squalamine, is found in the blood of sharks, and he also found antibiotics in human skin.

Apart from the development of new variants of the traditional antibiotics, the investigation of inhibitors for resistance-conferring enzymes, and the exploration of new classes of substances, there is one factor that is of paramount importance for the continuing fight against infectious diseases: the responsible application of the existing antibiotics. Each application of antibiotics that was not necessary or that was not carried through to completion will unnecessarily add to the gene pool of antibiotics resistance genes, and will increase the probability that long-forgotten plagues may return and microbes may become hunters instead of prey.

III

Toward the Nanoworld
Biology, Chemistry, and Physics Pave the Way for Nanotechnology

5

From Molecules to Supramolecules

The modular design principle (see Chapter 1) and a few billion years of evolution have enabled living cells to build an enormous variety of structures on the nanometer scale with relative ease. We have seen that these natural nanomachines can fulfill complex functions in a highly controlled fashion. Human engineers, in contrast, are still having problems in taking on this lesson from nature.

Partly, this difficulty may be related to the way in which we subdivide science into disciplines and subjects, leaving nanosystems without a proper place. For a chemist in the traditional sense, these systems are too big and even suspicious, because they are in part held together by non-covalent interactions rather than by proper "chemical" bonds. Biologists, on the other hand, have got enough to do describing all of the natural nanosystems and cannot be bothered making additional ones. And physicists as well as material scientists—while readily accepting responsibility for them—prefer to approach nanosystems in a "top-down" way, by etching smaller and smaller structures out of metal or semiconductor materials. Their progress toward the nanoworld depends on the limitations of miniaturization techniques.

What is really needed is an interdisciplinary strategy, one that would feed from all of these sources without being confined by the limits of any individual discipline; a strategy that would look at biology for inspiration, loot chemistry for building blocks, and borrow physical methods for novel ways of manipulating small things. Therefore, most of the research work presented in this third part of the book (Chapters 5–7) will be transgressing traditional boundaries. Nevertheless, I have sorted my selection into the categories of approaches rooted in organic and supramolecular chemistry (this chapter), in colloid chemistry, physical chemistry, or physics (Chapter 6), and in biology or biotechnology (Chapter 7). In other words, Chapter 5 is about molecular systems, Chapter 6 about all kinds of small things that are not molecules, and Chapter 7 about those nanoscale systems derived from living cells for some sort of useful function. While it is hoped this organization will help us to keep some sort of orientation, it should by no means be seen as a new set of boundaries. I am not claiming that this arrangement has any particular merit over other possibilities you may be able to think of. Readers should feel free to select the sections of Part III in whatever order they prefer. Personally, I will begin at the small end, that is, with the research based on chemistry, in the widest definition conceivable. Thus, the discussion will include associations made by weak interactions as well as covalently linked polymers, and biomimetic as well as purely synthetic approaches. In the spirit of the chapter title, we shall first deal with individual molecules, and later on with assemblies and associations between molecules.

The Neglected Dimension: Macromolecular Chemistry

Those molecules that most organic chemists would normally synthesize or manipulate only contain one or two dozen atoms. As we have seen in the previous chapter, the natural product taxol with less than 120 atoms is already an enormous challenge for synthetic chemistry. In contrast, the molecules of life, of which we met some representatives in Part II of this book, can easily contain thousands or even tens of thousands of atoms.

Only in the 1920s did scientists begin to realize that giant molecules are an important functional element in the living cell, and only then did the new scientific discipline of macromolecular chemistry (i.e., the chemistry of big molecules) come into being. This new branch of chemistry had its foundations largely laid by one person: the German chemist Hermann Staudinger (1881–1965). Beginning in 1921, he worked on both synthetic and natural macromolecules, and introduced the measurement of the viscosity of a solution ("Staudinger index") as a measure of the molecular weight of the dissolved macromolecules. He received the Nobel Prize in chemistry in 1953 (see Profile).

But how do macromolecular chemists obtain the objects of their studies? They could either isolate macromolecules from biological materials (apart from proteins and nucleic acids, there are also lots of sugary things like starch and glycogen on offer), or they could make their own. The simplest way of producing synthetic macromolecules is to line up small molecular building blocks to form long chains, a process that can make use of different kinds of chemical reactions between the building blocks ("monomers"), but which is generically called *polymerization*. This is the way most of the plastics we use in everyday life are made, as one can sometimes tell from their names. PVC, for instance, is poly(vinyl chloride), which means it is produced by polymerizing the building block vinyl chloride. Unlike the biological macromolecules we encountered in Chapters 2 and 3, the synthetic polymers used to make plastics and fibers normally contain only one or two kinds of building blocks, so they don't have an information content as proteins and nucleic acids have encoded in their sequences. Hence, they will not form any kind of well-ordered structure, but rather dangle around in fairly random conformations.

For the classical subdisciplines of chemistry (inorganic, organic, and physical chemistry), macromolecular chemistry has always remained a stepsister. The first polymers it came up with tended to be of ill-defined length and molecular weight, hence they were not "pure substances" in the eyes of other chemists. This led to the unfortunate development that the whole world of giant molecules, that is, the length range from 10 nm to 1 μm, remained "the neglected dimension" of chemistry.

Only in recent decades have various new developments and trends improved this situation. As far as the giant molecules of the cell are concerned, we have learned that they normally possess a well-defined structure that determines their function. While the foundations of macromolecular chemistry were laid in the face of doubts as to whether the small particles observed in substances like protein and cellulose were in fact individual giant molecules rather than noncovalent assemblies of ordinary

Profile

Hermann Staudinger

In the best academic tradition, the German chemist Hermann Staudinger attended six different universities during his *Wanderjahre* before homing in on the seventh, where he stayed. He was a student at Halle, Darmstadt, and Munich, and a lecturer or professor at Strasbourg, Karlsruhe, and Zurich. In 1926, at the age of 45, he finally settled down in Freiburg, a small university town in the southwest corner of Germany. At about the same time he chose a new research field, or rather, he invented one.

At the beginning of his research career, it looked as if he was going to become a classical organic chemist, someone who thinks of ways to make new substances consisting of small, well-defined molecules, synthesizes them, determines their melting point, and moves

small organic molecules, the explosive increase in detailed structural information about biomolecules that we have witnessed in the past decades has again and again demonstrated that macromolecules have well-defined structures and that they occur in an amazing natural variety. During the 1980s, novel synthetic approaches to big, well-defined molecules such as the football-shaped buckminsterfullerenes and the treelike dendrimers (see next section) have contributed to make this kind of chemistry socially acceptable. In particular, the realization that noncovalent interactions can be useful for the specific construction of highly complex structures has not only created the new discipline of supramolecular chemistry but also enabled chemists to venture into those areas of the length scale where biochemists used to be on their own.

on to the next compound. Thus, he published some 50 research papers and a monograph on the ketene group of molecules, before he moved on to a field that looked rather less promising at the time.

In the early 1920s, when Staudinger became interested in natural substances such as rubber and fibers, the prevailing view was that they consisted of ill-defined, noncovalent assemblies of small molecules. Against the odds, he could demonstrate that there are in fact long chains of chemically-linked units in natural fibers. What's more, he found ways of producing similar substances synthetically, by polymerization in the laboratory. The combination of new synthetic polymers and the beginning of a structural understanding of biological polymers resulted in a new concept: Staudinger called both of these substances *macromolecules*, and the study of their properties became known as *macromolecular chemistry*.

At Freiburg he founded an institute for macromolecular chemistry, and continued to contribute a huge body of work to the field that he founded, until his retirement in 1951, at the age of 70. Remarkably, most of his honors, including a bunch of honorary doctorates, and the Nobel Prize for chemistry, date from the 1950s. It took more than 30 years before his revolutionary work, which is the foundation of both molecular biology and the whole business of making things out of plastics, was recognized in the highest places.

The World's Smallest Tree: Dendrimers Are Not Just Pretty Molecules

Most people would prefer to look at a freestanding tree, a snowflake under the magnifying lens, or the coastline of Norway, rather than at a rectangular tower block, a round plastic button, or a straight highway. Presumably, this has to do with our visual experience telling us that structures that keep on subdividing into smaller, similar structural elements, like the stem, branches, and twigs of a tree, are typical of the natural world. In contrast, objects that are only structured on one scale, and uniform on all others, are most likely to be artifacts of the technologies developed by *Homo sapiens*.

Mathematicians have named these structures with self-similarity on different scales *fractals*, and they have discovered some interesting facts about them. For instance, fractal surfaces like coastlines get longer if they are measured more precisely. (If you added up the distances between the cities along the coast, you would get a much smaller value than if you walked along the beach with your measuring tape and took every little bay and peninsula into account.) In the 1980s, when chaos theory was widely popularized, colorful fractal graphics representing solutions to "chaotic" equations popped up almost everywhere—the best-known example being the Mandelbrot Set named after the mathematician Benoit Mandelbrot, best known for his colossal book *The Fractal Geometry of Nature*.

The beauty of fractals also struck the eyes of some organic chemists. In 1978, Fritz Vögtle's group at the University of Bonn, Germany, synthesized the first molecular tree from small organic molecules, and since 1984 the science of branched polymers called *dendrimers* or *arboroles* has kept branching out and growing at an ever-increasing pace, as manifested in an exponentially increasing number of publications about these molecules.

The principle that chemists use to grow these trees recalls the legendary fight of Hercules with the snake-headed monster, Hydra. They begin with a "double-headed" molecule. When they cleave off the heads, the necks will react with Y-shaped, double-headed branching pieces in a way that for each head cleaved off, two new ones will be installed. With the number of "heads" doubling in each reaction cycle, it only takes a couple of generations to create molecular hydras or trees—molecules of baffling size and complexity (Fig. 1).

These new kinds of molecules fill a gap in the length scale of synthetic chemistry—the gap that used to lie between the small molecules of organic chemistry and the uniform polymer chains. With the simple trick of using branched building blocks for polymerization, it has become possible to create well-defined, middle-sized molecules, which extend into three dimensions rather than just linearly. In fact, the main aspect that distinguishes dendrimers from ordinary polymers is their ball-like shape and symmetry. If one takes care to add the Y-shaped building blocks in layers (this is the purpose of the "heads" above, which in fact protect the reactive sites from reacting too early), dendrimers will naturally grow toward a highly symmetrical, globular shape. Therefore, dendrimers have some similarity with the water-soluble (globular) proteins. They attain the ball shape in a different way, however. While proteins have to fold up their linear chainlike structure to "become three-dimensional," dendrimers

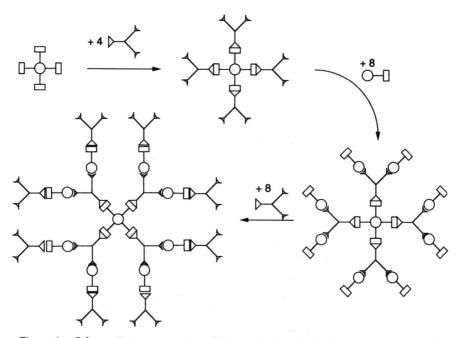

Figure 1: Schematic representation of the synthesis of a dendrimer. So as to avoid uncontrolled growth, each new layer is added in a sequence of two reactions, one introducing the branching (Y-shaped molecule), and the other providing the binding sites to which the next generation of branching units can be coupled.

grow from the center of the sphere into all directions. Unlike proteins, they are not at risk of losing their globular shape through unfolding events.

Mimicking biological nanoscale structures without having their weaknesses may be the strongest point for dendrimer applications. One could, for instance, grow molecular trees from long, water-avoiding hydrocarbon chains and attach water-soluble alcohol groups only to the outermost layer. This would result in a water-soluble bubble filled with oily molecular groups, resembling the so-called micelles that arise when lipids are in an aqueous environment and stick their oily tails together to keep them away from the water. Again, the dendrimer "micelle" would be much more stable than any comparable lipid structure could be. Similarly, one could construct dendrimers that would resemble biological membranes. In the first (at least to my knowledge) dendrimer product that has reached the market, the SuperFect reagent developed by Quiagen to facilitate the transfer of DNA into cells for genetic engineering purposes, the dendrimers appear to act like the histones in the nucleus of eukaryotic cells, in that DNA gets wrapped around the dendrimers for compactness and protection from mechanical damage.

It's not only the surface of the molecular balls that can be shaped during synthesis. Underneath it, dendrimers can have hidden qualities such as cavities that could accommodate guest molecules. Thus, dendrimers with programmed surface properties and cavities could serve as transporters for drugs, which might not be stable enough to survive on their own long enough to reach their target organ. Going one step further, one could make sure that an electrically-charged or a chemically-reactive molecular group protrudes into the cavity. This way, one could create a highly specific binding pocket similar to the ones used by enzymes to recognize their substrates. Model calculations have demonstrated that a dendrimer of six layers could take up 10 to 20 molecules of the drug dopamine and deliver it to the kidneys. Unwanted side effects that the drug could trigger in the brain can be excluded, as the bulky transporter (unlike the naked dopamine molecule) would not be able to penetrate into the central nervous system.

Although dendrimers appeared to be very useful in theory, it took a while before this could be matched in practice. Only in late 1994, after 10 years of speculation about their potential applications, hard data became available to confirm that dendrimers may be suitable for applications as catalysts or transporter molecules and may even outperform other substances. This development was enabled by rapid progress in the chemical manipulation of the fractal molecules, allowing chemists to incorporate functional groups in specific sites and to create well-defined and completely enclosed cavities underneath the surface of a dendrimer.

Egbert W. Meijer's group at the Technical University of Eindhoven in the Netherlands was the first to synthesize a dendrimer with guest molecules encapsulated in cavities. Starting from a "normal" dendrimer with 64 amino end groups, which a Dutch company sells by the kilogram, the scientists grafted chiral amino acids onto the tips of the branches, which turned out to form a massive shell with all of the characteristics of a solid-state material. From spectroscopical investigations on this substance, the researchers concluded that they had produced a molecule with a hard shell and a soft core, which should be able to incorporate guest molecules. And they could indeed encapsulate various kinds of molecules during the last step of the synthesis and then spectroscopically show that guest molecules were imprisoned in the cavities, which measured some 5 nm in diameter. Applications in drug targeting and in the analysis of isolated molecules will almost certainly be derived from this research.

Equally promising is the idea of using dendrimers in catalysis, i.e., to speed up reactions. The first step in this direction was taken by Gerard van Koten's group at the University of Utrecht in the Netherlands. Their work may help to find a way out of the old dilemma of choosing between homogeneous (i.e., dissolved) and heterogeneous (i.e., solid state) catalysts: The former are more efficient, but also more difficult to separate from the products than the latter. To find a third way, van Koten and co-workers bound their catalytic groups to different kinds of polymers. When they came to trying dendrimers, they found that these combined the advantages of homogeneous and heterogeneous catalysts. Being single dissolved molecules, dendrimers share the advantage of easy access for the reacting species with typical soluble catalysts. On the other hand, their high molecular weights and the persistent globular shape make it easy to separate them from the products of the catalyzed reaction using simple filtration methods. In contrast to ordinary linear polymers, which are known to get through filter membranes by snakelike movements called *reptation*, dendrimers have a particle diameter that is defined by chemical bonds and thus cannot change.

The catalytical group attached by the Dutch researchers to their dendrimers was a nickel atom activated by a wrapper of organic groups. This organometallic complex can catalyze the addition of halogenated hydrocarbons to a carbon–carbon double bond. (This means that the double bond becomes a single bond, while one of the carbon atoms binds the halogen, and the other one the remaining hydrocarbon compound.) Although the dendrimers carried up to 12 copies of the catalytic nickel compound, the efficiency of catalysis remained comparable to that of the unbound catalyst in free solution. Attachment to the dendrimer does not seem to hinder the access of the reacting species to the catalyst.

Linking organometallic compounds to dendrimers has been a general trend in dendrimer chemistry. The metal groups may be attached to the surface like the nickel discussed above, or within the core or even at the very center of the structure. In that case, the shielding of the core element will be the main consideration. A zinc–porphyrin complex protected in this way could, for example, act as a box to lock away electrons, keeping them safe from unwanted redox reaction with compounds in the solution.

In principle, there is probably no chemical compound that could not be incorporated into fractal molecules. Fullerenes, crown ethers, and many other types of molecules have already been used as stems for the construction of molecular trees. Furthermore, "biologically inspired" dendrimers have been made with nucleic acid and peptide building blocks. Such pseudo-biological macromolecules could find applications in biotechnology.

Obviously, most of these perspectives on potential applications are still highly speculative. However, the success in the field of catalysis and inclusion compounds has shown that the synthesis of useful dendrimers is possible. This is only the beginning of a whole new world of possibilities.

Writing the Amino Acid Code: The Surprising Success of Protein Design

Imagine you wanted to decipher the written language of an extinct culture. The only assistance comes from the sole survivor who cannot speak but can help in one of the following two ways. She can write down instructions in her language, which you would then decipher and try to follow. When you have acted according to the written instruction, the helper can confirm your success with a gesture. Alternatively, she could follow instructions that you try writing up, provided you have used the signs of her language in a grammatically correct and understandable way. Thus, you have the choice to learn the unknown language through either reading or writing.

Researchers face a similar problem when they try to decipher what has been dubbed "the second half of the genetic code," namely, the rules by which the one-dimensional sequence of amino acid building blocks folds up to form a complex three-dimensional structure (see Chapter 3). While the first half, i.e., the proper genetic code, unambiguously assigns one amino acid (or stop function) to each of the codon triplets of DNA, thus resembling a simple replacement coding such as the Morse signs replacing the letters of the alphabet, the "folding code" is more like a language, as the meaning of each element depends strongly on the environment, or, as linguists would say, on the context.

Much like in the case of the extinct language, the decoding of protein folding can be dissected into two partial problems. The difficulty of predicting the three-dimensional structure that a given sequence will adopt—that is, of "reading the instruction"—is known as the *folding problem* (see Chapter 3). And the task of designing a sequence that will adopt a desired structure—i.e., "writing instructions"—is called the *design problem*. Intuitively, one might think that reading a language should be the first step to achieve, before one can write it successfully. Nevertheless, and although there has been much more research on folding than on design, a series of advances reported in 1997 suggested that researchers are better at writing than at reading the language of proteins. A design challenge offered with a cash prize in 1994 was quickly met; protein designers have simplified amino acid sequences so that the majority of the polypeptide only contains five different amino acids; and one group has even let their computer do the design for them.

These developments suggest a major mood swing toward an optimistic view of the design problem. Only a decade ago, in contrast, most researchers would have been very skeptical about attempts at creating artificial protein sequences. The small number of pioneers found comfort in the thought that, after learning some essential rules of grammar, they would be able to use generously what little knowledge they had. To their advantage, the structures of natural proteins are only defined by roughly a quarter of the building blocks, and the others can be exchanged against certain other kinds, sometimes even against any other amino acid. By applying the few words and expressions they knew of the protein language to the whole of the sequence length rather than to just a quarter, they had the chance to shout where nature whispers and still get their message across despite their incomplete understanding.

In addition to this, the design pioneers used the modular design principle that is common in living systems as we have seen in Chapter 1. They started building a single helix, then a small protein with two helices, then a four-helix bundle. Some slow progress was made, but one was still far from understanding the grammar required to write new protein sequences. To draw some attention and more research efforts to this problem, George Rose and Trevor Creamer of the Washington University School of Medicine in St. Louis, Missouri, set out a cash prize for a design challenge. In an editorial published in the journal *Proteins* in 1994, they asked for the demonstration of two proteins that share 50% sequence identity and yet adopt different structures. As such a pair does not exist in nature, this challenge essentially posed the task of exchanging 50% or less of the amino acids in a given protein and thereby converting the protein into a differently folded state. In our linguistic metaphor, this would correspond to the task of converting this chapter into a report of a tennis match by exchanging less than 50% of the words.

Assuming that both the starting and the target structure are largely determined by a quarter of their sequences, one had to remove the appropriate 25% residues that determine the original structure, and introduce those 25% that would convert the protein into the target structure. In the worst case, if both sets did not overlap at all, this would require exactly 50% exchange, suggesting the task would be just about manageable, if one knew exactly the role and importance of each residue in a protein. This, however, was clearly beyond the state of the art, and this was why Rose and Creamer set out the cash prize of $1000, and even thought their money would be reasonably safe for some time.

However, protein designers made some significant progress more rapidly than anyone had anticipated, and thus the so-called Paracelsus prize was cashed in by Lynne Regan and her group at Yale University in 1997. They had managed to convert the beta sheet B1 domain of the immunoglobulin binding protein G into a variant of the all-helical DNA binding protein ROP (repressor of primer), which forms a four-helix bundle containing two identical molecules (Fig. 2). Massive experience in manipulating the sequences of both the B1 domain and ROP had enabled Regan and her co-workers to turn one into the other by exchanging only 28 of the 56 amino acids in the original sequence.

While this achievement was based on the experience, intuition, and creativity of scientists, the future of protein design may well happen without these ingredients. Only a few months after the solution of the Paracelsus challenge, the first protein designed by a computer program was presented by Bassil Dahiyat and Stephen Mayo at Caltech. As a design

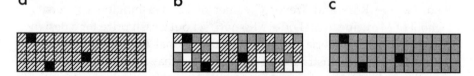

Figure 2:   How the Paracelsus challenge was met: To convert the structure of a beta-sheet protein (a) into that of an alpha-helical protein (c), half of the original 56 amino acids (striped) were replaced either by amino acids from the helical protein (gray) or by amino acids different from the corresponding position in both proteins (white). This resulted in the designed protein Janus (b), which has the structure of c although it shares half of the sequence of a. Black boxes indicate amino acid residues that are identical in all three proteins.

target, they used the structure of a finger-shaped protein domain known as the *zinc finger domain*, as it is normally stabilized by the presence of a zinc ion. The computer program, however, was instructed to create a sequence of 28 amino acid residues that would achieve a similar structure without using the stabilizing metal ion. Thus far, a zinc-free zinc finger had only been obtained with the help of two nonstandard amino acid building blocks by Barbara Imperiali's group at Caltech.

Using the insight from earlier works on zinc fingers along with the general experience the small community of protein designers has accumulated so far, Dahiyat and Mayo created an algorithm that was able to check through the 2×10^{27} different sequences and various side chain conformations of each, whether the target structure would be favorable for them or not. The protein sequence filtered out of this astronomical number of possibilities was named *FSD-1* (for "full sequence design"). It showed little similarity with any known natural sequences. Only in six positions did it agree with the sequence of the zinc finger used as the starting point. Thus, it can be plausibly called a "new" protein, rather than a variant of the natural zinc finger domains. Using NMR spectroscopy, the researchers determined its three-dimensional structure in solution and proved that it does indeed fold up to a zinc-finger-like structure without a metal binding site.

In fact, FSD-1 is the smallest protein known thus far—natural or designed—to adopt a complex structure with all of the typical secondary structure elements without the help of metal ions or disulfide bonds. This suggests that computer-aided protein design will indeed make important contributions in the future (the follow-up paper in June 1998 described a protein variant designed to be extremely heat-stable)—even though the enormous computational effort will limit this approach to very small proteins for the time being.

One possible way out of this dilemma was investigated by David Baker's group at the University of Washington in Seattle. Manipulating the sequence of the SH3 domain, which is a unit quite commonly found in many complex proteins involved in the signaling between cells of higher organisms, they started simplifying the protein so that it could be made of less than the usual 20 different amino acids. Like Dahiyat and Mayo, they selected from a large number of sequences. However, as their target was a much simpler sequence, in which as many positions as possible would be filled with just five kinds of building blocks (isoleucine, lysine, aspartic acid, alanine, glycine), they managed without supercomputers and could perform the selection experimentally.

They used the ability of the correctly folded SH3 domain to bind certain peptides as a selection criterion, to pull only molecules with the correct structure out of a pool with many different sequences. They discovered that—apart from the peptide binding site, which had to be maintained for the selection to work—95% of the amino acids could be replaced by those from the set of five. The resulting protein only contained 14 different amino acids, but both its binding capacity and its folding speed were at least as good as those of the natural domain.

Like the solution of the Paracelsus challenge, this work demonstrates that protein designers have learned to use the language of proteins quite efficiently. They know which words are important, and which ones are exchangeable. Even though they do not yet command all of the subtleties of the protein grammar, their current knowledge enables them to tackle the remaining problems systematically. The surprisingly rapid progress made between 1994 and 1997 also provides a solid foundation for future applications of protein design in drug development. And it may also help those researchers who are dealing with the inverse problem and trying to read protein sequences. With all of those genome sequences flowing in at an ever-increasing rate, it becomes more and more important to learn to read this information properly.

A Tunnel through the Cell Membrane: Self-Assembling Nanotubes

Although they may be seen as only nothingness, holes can cause many interesting and useful properties in natural and synthetic materials. Holes of molecular dimensions (i.e., measuring a few nanometers) allow us to separate different kinds of molecules—the smaller one may enter the hole and spend some time inside, while the bigger one will float past it. Holes provide an additional surface that could serve to bind molecules or even to catalyze reactions. Holes piercing through (cell) walls could serve as doors, windows, valves, and the like.

During the 1990s, various kinds of holes and hollows became very fashionable in chemistry. With the epidemic spread of the football-shaped fullerene molecules (see Chapter 6), another hollow molecular shape gained a lot of attention in the 1990s: tubes with inner diameters on the nanometer scale, so-called nanotubes. In Chapter 6, I will show how the carbon layers found in natural graphite can be rolled up to form tubes.

Here, however, we shall look at an alternative way of producing cylinders: by stacking rings.

Peptides (amino acid polymers too short to fold up like proteins) are readily synthesized and can have all sorts of interesting properties depending on the natural or nonnatural amino acid building blocks used. Making use of this potential, M. Reza Ghadiri and his co-workers at the Scripps Research Institute in La Jolla, California, created a ring-shaped peptide containing eight amino acids, including two units of glutamic acid on opposite sides of the ring. In alkaline or neutral environments, the side chain of this particular amino acid would carry a negative charge, and the repulsion of equal charges would therefore prevent the rings from interacting. If the pH is shifted to the acidic range, however, the charge will be neutralized and there will be no repulsion left. Then, the possibility of forming hydrogen bonds between the peptide backbones of the rings will favor the stacking of rings to form tubes (Fig. 3). (Designing the rings to fit together has mainly involved using the natural L-amino acids in alternation with their mirror images, the D-amino acids.) Additional hydrogen bonds can be formed between the glutamine side chains, which will define the orientation of the rings in the stacks and provide additional stabilization for the tube.

Thus far, the behavior I have described might have been a theoretical prediction based on computer-assisted molecular simulations. But what happens in an actual experiment, when a solution of the ring-shaped peptides is shifted to acidic pH? Although others had predicted ring stacking before, Ghadiri and co-workers were the first to do the experiment. After the pH shift, they observed the growth of crystal needles several micrometers long within a few hours. Using a combination of methods including electron microscopy and spectroscopies, the researchers could prove that these needles actually consist of aligned nanotubes. Additional computer modeling showed that among the various conformations that the peptide might adopt, only the one forming the predicted hydrogen bonds would fit into the experimentally confirmed dimensions of the crystal unit cell. The tubes were found to have an inner diameter of 0.7–0.8 nm and to grow to several hundred nanometers in length.

Having accumulated convincing evidence for the formation of tubes from stacked rings and even calculated a model structure, the group still managed to go one step further. They succeeded in incorporating the nanotubes into a membrane and showed that it forms a tunnel through which ions can flow to the other side—as they do through a certain class of

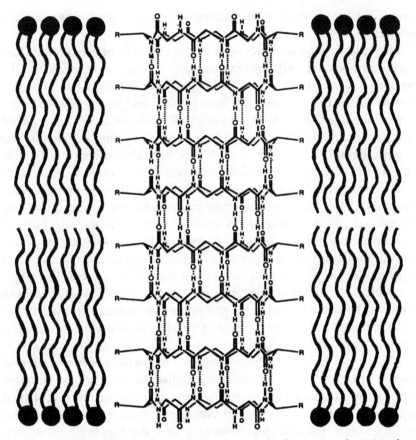

Figure 3:   A pile consisting of eight cyclic octapeptides forms a synthetic ion channel in a membrane. The hydrogen bonds (dotted lines) between the rings correspond to the binding pattern between the strands of a beta-pleated sheet. Thus, one could also describe this structure as an eight-stranded beta sheet rolled up and closed to a cylinder by formation of peptide bonds between the ends of the strands.

natural membrane proteins, the so-called ion channels. A simple way to demonstrate such an effect would be to form small globules of membranes ("vesicles") and then change the pH of the surrounding medium. If the membranes contain ion channels, the pH difference between the liquids inside and outside the vesicles should rapidly disappear (as one could demonstrate using an indicator dye). Intact membranes with no channels, in contrast, should preserve the difference. The peptide nanotubes passed this test too, but there was one final challenge left for them.

The ultimate and most sophisticated test for ion channels or transmembrane transporters is the patch clamp recording technique developed by the German scientists Erwin Neher and Bert Sakman, who shared the Nobel Prize for physiology or medicine in 1991. If one puts a very slim glass pipette onto a membrane and slightly reduces the pressure inside it, the glass rim will insulate this membrane patch from the rest of the membrane, and one can measure selectively any current flowing through the pores or channels within the patch.

As expected, the presence of the cyclic octapeptide enabled the flow of charged particles, such as potassium ions, through membranes that had not allowed anything through before the peptide was added. The synthetic peptide turned out to be three times more efficient than a natural ion channel formed by the peptide gramicidin A. Other cyclic peptides that lacked one of the design features thought to be essential for the stacking interaction had no capacity to act as ion channels.

Others had tried before to construct synthetic ion channels. Mostly, they designed very long molecules that spanned through the entire width of the membrane or at least half of it. Ring-shaped molecular building blocks were already in use to ensure there was a rigid opening that wouldn't collapse. The prototype of all synthetic ion transporters was the class of molecules known as *crown ethers*, which the industrial chemist Charles Pedersen discovered in 1967 by serendipity, when analyzing an unwanted byproduct of a failed reaction. (He is probably the only chemist who received a Nobel Prize for research he published just before his retirement, at the age of 63.) Crown ethers are flat, ring-shaped molecules with oxygen atoms pointing inward, which can bind metal ions. Their outer rim is sufficiently water-avoiding to be able to dive through membranes and transport the bound ions in a shuttlelike manner.

In the 1980s, a group at the University of Kyoto went one step further, when they coupled a different ring molecule (a cyclodextrin formed by six sugar units) with four long, hydrophobic tails. Two of these "half-channels" are meant to combine to form a proper tunnel, with the cyclodextrins guarding the entrance and exit. While these channels were not very efficient, they still allowed the passage of cobalt or copper ions at rates significantly above the control experiments.

Jean-Marie Lehn, one of the founding fathers of supramolecular chemistry and joint Nobel Prize winner with the above-mentioned Pedersen and Donald J. Cram, turned the idea of the Japanese group around and put the ring in the middle of the membrane. His group at the College de France in Paris developed so-called bouquet molecules, which have a crown ether in the middle and long threads of polyethers sticking out of it.

Hydrophilic groups at the ends of the threads provide the motivation for the molecules to stretch out and form a tunnel. They do indeed allow lithium and sodium ions to pass membranes, and there is good evidence indicating that they act as channels rather than as shuttles.

However, none of the constructs based on the idea of a ring with threads attached was nearly as efficient as the peptide nanotubes. With regard to potential applications, the latter have the additional advantage that their structures should be easily modified. Varying the geometry of the peptide rings, one could produce tunnels of different diameters. And varying the chemical composition, specific channels could be created for specific applications, e.g., for the targeting of a given drug. This way, one could not only drill holes into the cell membrane, but even build tightly controllable valves into it.

Tying the Knot: Topological Chemistry

Topology is a very useful scientific discipline as it allows women to remove their bras without opening their blouses—provided the former are sufficiently elastic. For topological analysis, one can stretch and deform objects at leisure, as long as the connectivity is maintained (that is, scissors are not allowed for the bra problem or in any other topological transformation). Topologically speaking, the bra is not really "under" the blouse, and indeed, neither piece of clothing is topologically connected with the body.

Two interlocked rings of a chain, for instance, would constitute a nontrivial topological object, which could occur in innumerable different forms (including molecular ones) while maintaining the constraints and freedoms defined by the interlocking. Topology, which could also be defined as the science of "spatial relationships," is a subdivision of mathematics, and it is also the basis of many apparently magic tricks and riddles.

Chemists, and supramolecular chemists in particular, have developed a strong interest in topological objects such as interlocked rings, pearls on a thread, or complicated knots. The resulting, noncovalent assemblies are generally called *supramolecules*, which bypasses the tricky question as to whether such a thing should be regarded as one or as several molecules. One reason for their increasing popularity is that the topological interlocking is an elegant method of coupling molecules to one another in a noncovalent fashion while keeping different options open as to in which way they may interact chemically. If, for instance, the interlocked molecules contain different binding sites for specific parts of their partner molecule, the system could act as a molecular switch. Such systems, which could respond to an electron transfer or to a pH shift, were developed in different laboratories during the 1990s. They are regarded as potential functional elements for nanoscale machines of the future.

Much of the pioneering work in the field came from J. Fraser Stoddart's group at the University of Birmingham (England). Stoddart seems to derive inspirations for his nanoscale constructs from macroscopic toys, as more than thirty of his research papers have come out as a numbered series entitled "Molecular Meccano." His playful topological molecules have included a molecular train set, in which a small ring compound circles on a larger one and can be stopped at different stations. Even more complicated in terms of synthesis was the supramolecular complex that was meant to mimic the Olympic rings, and therefore called *olympiadane*. Systematically, it is called a [5]catenane, indicating it has five interlocked rings (Fig. 4a).

However, one doesn't even need several rings to create a topologically complex molecule. As Jean-Pierre Sauvage's group demonstrated in 1990 at the Université Louis Pasteur in Strasbourg, France, one can construct ring molecules that form an indissoluble knot in themselves. The first example was the trefoil knot, whose synthesis is schematically shown in Fig. 4b. As a scaffold for the construction work, Sauvage used two copper ions, around which two molecules formed a full turn of a double helix. Linking each end to the opposite end of the other reactant molecule, he then created a closed knotted ring which can be shown to be equivalent to the trefoil knot.

Like the double helix in the intermediate, the trefoil knot possesses a handedness (chirality), which implies that the structure shown here could not be interconverted with its own mirror image by any topologically allowed means. The result of the synthesis is a mixture of left- and right-handed knots. Crystallization of the material, however, leads to a perfect separation, as each crystal only contains one kind of molecule.

Back in the 1960s, the first attempts to make interlocking molecules were essentially a gamble. Starting from a solution where the open-chain variant of the molecules is present in high concentration and then closing the rings, one can expect that a small percentage of the rings will be interlocked by pure chance. Because of their higher molecular weight, these catenanes can be easily separated from the single ring molecules. The latter can be reopened and used for another attempt.

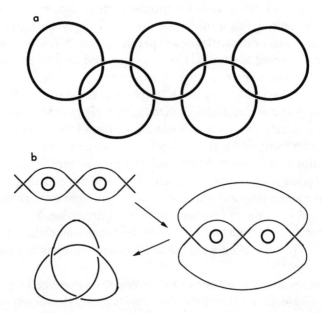

Figure 4: Topologically complex molecules. (a) Olympiadane, a molecule of five interlocked rings. (b) A trefoil knot can be obtained from a double helix wrapped around two metal centers (circles), if the ends of the helix-forming strands are connected in the way shown and the metal ions are removed. Note that the resulting knot structure is chiral, which means that it cannot be superimposed with its mirror image.

The recent renaissance of topological chemistry, in contrast, had nothing to do with gambling. The newly developed methods of organometallic chemistry make a systematic and much more elegant approach possible. Using metal ions as scaffolds, the target molecules can be deliberately bent into the desired shape, and then linked up to form the rings or knots desired. The challenge for the chemist consists in designing the right organometallic intermediate, fixing the molecular building blocks in a conformation that can be converted to the final product. Once the knot is tied or the rings are interlocked, the metal centers that were only bound noncovalently, can be easily removed.

In some cases, however, and especially for molecular switches and similar devices, the metal will not be removed, as it may play an important role even after the end of the synthesis. The affinity of a metal ion toward its organic partner tends to depend strongly on the chemical conditions and can be controlled specifically by offering or removing electrons. This possibility of switching on a molecular scale suggests that topological molecules, apart from being fascinating toys, may one day become really useful.

A Few Useful Things to Do with DNA

We have seen in Part II that the cell normally confers the tasks of building complex structures and realizing subtle chemical manipulations to specialized proteins. DNA, in comparison, may appear as a rather dull molecule, which has only four different building blocks, and whose higher-order structures mainly serve the purpose of saving packing space.

Even though DNA in the cell serves a single purpose only, this does not rule out the use of its building blocks and design principles for the construction of other things. One important advantage of this biopolymer is that it can nowadays be edited with great ease. The polymerase chain reaction provides a means of rapidly copying any DNA sequence, while restriction enzymes allow highly specific editing of the molecules and automated sequencing allows reading the information contained in a DNA sample (see Ways & Means on pp. 64 and 65).

Nadrian Seeman at New York University realized that these were ideal conditions for using DNA as a construction material. Thus, in 1990, he and his co-worker Junghuei Chen set out to design and make a nanoscale cube from DNA. Each of the six surfaces of the cube would be enclosed by a ring-shaped molecule of DNA containing 80 nucleotides, i.e., 20 on each side. Thus, each of the 12 edges of the cube would consist of a double helix with 20 base pairs, corresponding to exactly two helical turns. At each of the eight corners, three double helices would meet to swap partners (Fig. 5).

Starting from ten open-chain, single-stranded DNA molecules, the researchers needed essentially five steps involving cyclization, formation of double strands, coupling, and purification, to obtain the final product. Using analytical methods based on the accessibility of the strands for DNA cutting enzymes, they could prove that the construct has the right topology required for a DNA cube of their specific design. That means the strands are wound around each other and the rings interlock exactly in the topological way required. To prove that the structure actually had right

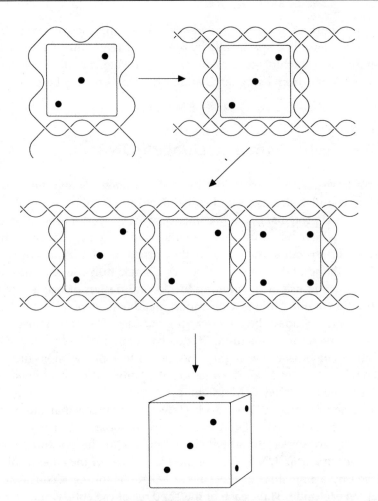

Figure 5:   How to make a cube out of DNA. Each face of the cube is surrounded by a ring of DNA, which interlocks with the rings defining neighboring faces. Strands designed to pair up in double helices forming the "edges" of the cube are linked together by enzymatic ligation. The cube object can be distinguished from the earlier states of the assembly by gel electrophoresis.

angles and equal sides like a cube, they would have to await the formal structure determination. That would require several orders of magnitude more of the material than was produced in the first demonstration—Chen and Seeman used radioactive tracer methods to analyze their DNA constructs.

This problem, however, did not stop Seeman from marching on to produce even more complex structures from DNA. With Y. W. Zhang, he published in 1994 the construction of a truncated octahedron (the shape you get when you combine two pyramids base to base and then cut off each of the six corners, resulting in six square and eight hexagonal surfaces). As with the cube, each of the 24 edges of this new construct also consisted of 20 base pairs. In total, this new DNA creation contained 1440 nucleotides, with a molecular mass of 800 kDa. This corresponds to large natural protein complexes, such as the molecular chaperone GroEL and the proteasome, which we met in Chapter 3. This supermolecule even contains loose ends, which may in the future serve the construction of endless porous lattices similar to the inorganic zeolites.

Later on, Seeman became also interested in molecular knots like the ones discussed in the previous section. Approaching this challenge his way, he also managed to get a trefoil knot from DNA, and more recently (1997) Borromean rings, that is, a set of three or more rings interlocked in such a way that cutting open one of them would release all. In August 1998 (just minutes before I started the final editing of this chapter), Seeman and colleagues from both New York University and Caltech reported the successful design of two-dimensional crystals made of either two or four different kinds of DNA "tiles." The assemblies, which were between 1 and 2 nm thick and several micrometers wide, were analyzed in detail by atomic force microscopy (see Chapter 6). This work could prove an important breakthrough both for building nanostructures with DNA and for DNA computation (see below).

Apart from being fascinating toys for chemists, the DNA constructs from Seeman's laboratory may well find applications in future technologies. Although DNA is a rather expensive material, and the structural details and stability have as yet to be confirmed, the unrivaled access to specific nanoscale hollow shapes and meshworks will ensure DNA a place on the short list when it comes to selecting the building blocks for the technology of the future. Possible applications could include transporter, scaffold, and even catalytical functions.

But it's not just the mechanical construction kit properties of DNA that have aroused the interest of chemists during the 1990s. It has also emerged that the interior of the double helix is a remarkably efficient wire for electrons. In 1993, Jackie Barton and her group at Caltech found that the speed of electron transfers through the aromatic DNA bases stacked in the middle of the double helix like a spiral staircase is extremely fast in comparison with other biological systems. The velocities she quoted were in fact so high that most people didn't believe her. In 1995, however, Thomas Meade and Jon Kayyem, also working at Caltech, but using different approaches, arrived at a qualitatively similar result with slightly lower numbers, and managed to convince the disbelievers.

In their experiment, organometallic complexes involving the heavy metal ruthenium were used for both the emitter and the receiver of the fast current (see illustration on the front cover). The emitter can be activated by a flash of laser light, and the arrival of the electron at the receiver can be conveniently observed as it changes the spectroscopic properties of the molecule. Conceivably, the complex architecture of the first ruthenium complex, which the electrons have to pass through before they reach the "electron highway" in the middle of the double helix, could be the reason why the transfer is slower than in Barton's experiment. Jackie Barton believes that her experiments, in which the electron was released directly on the "highway," measured the true speed of electron transfer in DNA.

An important outcome of these studies was the finding that the DNA "wire" only works in double helices. Even when emitter and receiver are bound to the same DNA strand, the presence of the exactly complementary second strand is absolutely essential for the electron flow. This opens up possibilities for the development of highly sensitive and specific probes for the detection of certain DNA sequences. To investigate the presence of a known DNA sequence, one could synthesize the complementary strand, couple it with the appropriate complexes, and then use the spectroscopic assay of fast electron transfer to detect the presence of the sequence of interest.

In 1995, Kayyem founded a company, Clinical Micro Sensors, Inc., with the aim to develop DNA analysis systems based on this idea. In these devices, the specific probe strands complementary to the sequence of interest will be attached to a disposable DNA microchip, onto which a very small amount of the sample of interest could be applied. Virtually any biological, medical, or environmental sample could be used with little or no preparation, and without the need to amplify the DNA by PCR procedures. The spectroscopic readout of the electron transfer signal could then be carried out by anybody using a hand-held or bench-top device. At the time of writing, prototypes of both the DNA chip and the hand-held reading device have been presented.

Not only can DNA replace wires, it could also one day outperform electronic computers. In November 1994, Leonard Adleman of the University of Southern California at Los Angeles reported that he had built a kind of "chemical computer" using DNA. The first problem he solved with it was a simple instance of the "traveling salesman" problem consisting in finding the shortest route linking a number of cities. Like a conventional silicon-based computer, DNA can store information in a code. Using methods of molecular biology, one can read, copy, or sort these coded data sets. Of course, each of these steps takes much longer in the DNA system than in a silicon chip. This can be compensated, however with the advantage that a reaction tube can easily contain 10^{19} different strands of DNA, which represent as many different data sets. Richard Lipton of Princeton University suggested in 1995 that this massive parallelism should allow the DNA computer to solve problems that are "intractable" for conventional computers.

This prognosis has managed to wake up the computer scientists who were only moderately impressed by Adleman's molecular biology computer. Parallelism is the big issue for the future of computation, and unconventional methods to achieve it may well spell the end of the silicon chip one day. We shall revisit the future of computation in the last part of this book (Chapter 9).

Be Fruitful and Multiply: Self-Replicating Peptides

All of the amazing things that living cells can do with the help of their protein and nucleic acid machinery are dwarfed by one achievement that is at the heart of the very definition of life: They can make copies of themselves—without anybody's help. They have the complete know-how of how to make more cells of the same kind, which sometimes may require long and complicated pathways, such as the production of a whole organism. This is what sets them apart from other biological entities such as viruses, which need the (involuntary) assistance of a living cell to replicate.

Now can this achievement of self-replication be mimicked in molecular systems simpler than a living cell, with just a few components? Both chemists and biologists have been asking this question for very different reasons. For chemists, there is the challenge of designing molecules that can perform certain tricks, and self-replication is a particularly intriguing one. In a distant future, nanotechnology may require self-replicating systems so as to be able to manufacture large numbers of artificial nanomachines, as we will discuss in Chapter 9. Biologists, on the other hand, are at a loss over a question that has puzzled them ever since Darwin came up with evolution. It is well established that all life on Earth descends from one type of microbe, which lived a couple of billion years ago and already had DNA, a cell membrane, ribosomes, and dozens of enzymes that most cells have today. But what was before then? From which simpler forms did this ancestral cell evolve? In 1953, the classic experiment of Stanley Miller and Harold Urey established that the simple building blocks of life can arise in a completely sterile "primordial soup." However, the path from the first amino acids to the first cells is still littered with question marks.

Among all of the many theories and speculations in this field, there is one hypothesis that has increased in popularity ever since the groups of Thomas Cech and Sidney Altman demonstrated that RNA can have catalytic function like enzymes. If RNA can be both an information molecule (like DNA) and an action molecule (like proteins), so the hypothesis goes, the modern DNA–RNA–protein biology could have been preceded by an RNA-only system, the "RNA world." Although there are problems at the joints, where one cannot as yet explain how the RNA organisms started recruiting proteins for their enzyme jobs, nor how the RNA world came into being in the first place, the hypothesis has the major advantage that it can span a considerable range on the complexity scale from early one- or two-molecule systems to fairly complex "metabolic" networks with dozens of different, specialized RNA molecules. Thus, a fair proportion of the time gap between the first macromolecule and the first cell could possibly be covered by Darwinian evolution acting on assemblies of RNA molecules.

This hypothesis has motivated a lot of research on catalytic RNA molecules (ribozymes), for which such an "evolution in the test tube" could indeed be demonstrated primarily by Gerald Joyce and his co-workers at the Scripps Research Institute in La Jolla. I have discussed the RNA world, ribozymes, and the origin of life in some detail in my book *Life on the Edge*. For the present context, however, I will address self-replication from the perspective of chemistry and nanotechnology. In this respect, a development that only started very recently could become highly important, namely, the finding that peptides can self-replicate, too.

In 1996, M. Reza Ghadiri's group at Scripps surprised the ribozyme world (and everybody else) by demonstrating that a relatively simple polypeptide made of 32 amino acid residues and designed to adopt a helical structure that can again curl around a second molecule of its kind in a so-called coiled coil structure could catalyze the formation of its equals from two complementary fragments containing 15 and 17 residues, respectively. Although the researchers had chemically activated the ends of the fragments in a way that they can react to form the 32-residue product, the reaction was found to occur very slowly at the beginning. Then, as the concentration of the full-length product in the mixture increased, so did the speed of the reaction. From the characteristic change in the reaction rate, it could be shown that the peptide indeed catalyzes the formation of more molecules of its own kind. This happens through a scaffolding effect in which the longer peptide helps the two shorter ones meet in the right position and orientation for the formation of the chemical bond to occur rapidly.

While this result was surprising and important, it was only the first step toward putting peptides on the map in the field of replicators. As the theoretician Stuart Kauffman has pointed out, there is not a single molecule in the living world that replicates itself. While organisms and, in many cases, cells, replicate themselves, it is important to note that biomolecules replicate *each other* in a complex network of interactions. Sure enough, Ghadiri and co-workers could follow this lead and demonstrate the mutual replication of two peptides that differ in one of the two constituent fragments (Fig. 6). In a more recent piece of work, the group could also mimic the occurrence and "repair" of random mutations in the replicating peptide system.

While these findings are not very likely to convince the RNA world fanatics that they should from now on believe in a "peptide world," they represent an important achievement in molecular design toward an ambitious functional goal. Chapter 9 will consider the potential roles of replicating systems for nanotechnology.

Toward Artificial Enzymes: Synthetic Supramolecules Compete with Catalytic Antibodies

More than a century ago, a concept was born that is still very topical today: molecular recognition. It happened when a very serious professor of chemistry at the University of Berlin apparently lost his self-control for a second and, in the penultimate paragraph of a research paper, ventured a little bit into the field of speculation. The interaction between an enzyme and its substrate, he thought, would only work out when both contain complementary structures. "Figuratively speaking," he wrote, "I would

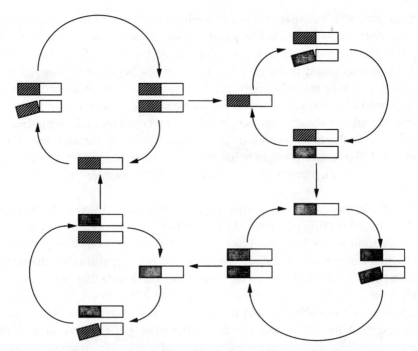

Figure 6: Self-replicating peptides can form networks of replication cycles, if each product can assist the formation both of its own kind (top left and bottom right) and of a different kind (top right and bottom left).

say that the enzyme and the glucoside [substrate] must fit together like a key and a lock, before they can interact chemically." Then he controlled himself again—as he thought more highly of experiments than of hypotheses, and as structural investigations concerning enzymes were nowhere near the feasible in 1894, he did not follow this idea any further. Only once more did he quote this analogy to refine it a little bit. The second Nobel laureate in chemistry, Emil Fischer (1852–1919), owed his fame not at all to this hypothesis, but mostly to his fundamental contributions to the chemistry of sugars.

The proponents of the emerging new discipline of physiological chemistry, however, were quick to adopt the lock and key hypothesis. Nowadays, a century after its first airing, the hypothesis is much more alive and kicking than the whole syllabus of Fischer's sugar chemistry, which today mainly serves the purpose of torturing second-year chemistry students. Locks and keys even survived the onslaught of Daniel Koshland, who in 1958 showed that many enzymes are not as rigid as a metal lock, but rather adapt to the shape of the key, that is, the substrate. His "induced fit" model seemed to replace the lock and key hypothesis.

But far from it. In an astonishing instance of parallelism between ideas in applied technology and biochemistry, the real locks and keys evolved along with the knowledge about enzymes. In every safety lock, there are moving cones that will enact a kind of "induced fit" to the shape of the key. The main reason for the surprising longevity and continuing popularity of Fischer's metaphor, however, may lie in the fact that recognition between molecules is no longer a specialty of enzymologists. The new science of supramolecular chemistry is mainly concerned with pairs of molecules that fit together as keys and locks (or host and guests) without forming stable covalent bonds. And in these artificial systems, the shapes of the recognition partners are often more rigid than enzymes and their substrates. Thus, they fit the centenarian metaphor better than most enzymes would. Other scientific disciplines, including polymer chemistry, surface and colloid chemistry, are concerned with similar problems, aiming at the development of "intelligent" materials.

Nevertheless, enzymes and their substrates—nature's locks and keys, so to speak—play an important role in the work on molecular recognition, be it as a starting point for variation or as a target for synthetic efforts, the role model against which the efficiency of an artificial catalyst will be judged. Artificial or novel enzymes can be made either way. If one wants to start from natural systems, protein engineering can change existing enzymes and redefine their substrate specificity. If, however, one looks for catalytically active giant molecules that have nothing in common with natural enzymes, there are two different possibilities:

1. Selection of active components from a large pool of suitable starting materials, like antibodies or nucleic acids, or
2. Design and synthesis of a new molecular system

Some design is also involved in the first approach, the selection of catalytic antibodies. This concept, which was developed in the 1980s by Peter G. Schultz and co-workers at the University of California at Berkeley, is based on the simple idea of bringing the energy of the transition state (see Fig. 5 in Chapter 1) down by designing a molecule that can bind to it. As the transition state is by its very definition a futile arrangement of molecules that cannot be filled into bottles or injected into rabbits, the tricky design part in this approach consists in making molecules that are sufficiently similar to the transition state of the reaction to be catalyzed, and sufficiently different from the reacting species to trigger the induction of an antibody that selectively binds the transition state and thus brings the energy barrier of the reaction down. Using this strategy, catalytic antibodies have been developed for various reactions, even including some for which no natural enzyme is known so far.

Strategies based purely on design have not been quite as successful thus far, but have demonstrated their merits. One way is to design novel amino acid sequences to form novel enzymes—unnatural but still made up of amino acids—as was discussed above. Alternatively, one could argue that most of the structure of the natural enzymes is just a complicated way of building a scaffold to protect and stabilize the important bit, the active site. Thus, one might try to design simpler molecules, which would provide this protection with a much smaller number of atoms, and still provide a similarly efficient active site. In particular, the recent advances in supramolecular chemistry and molecular recognition have opened up entirely new and interesting perspectives for this approach. While early work from the 1980s often featured cyclodextrins (rings of sugar molecules with a hydrophobic binding pocket in the middle), the use of porphyrins as building blocks has revealed completely new ways of binding and catalysis. Porphyrins are relatively large but flat natural ring compounds that carry out crucial functions both in plants (chlorophyll, with a magnesium ion in the middle) and in animals (heme group in hemoglobin, with an iron ion in the middle). Even bacteria have heme groups in their redox enzymes (cytochromes).

Using porphyrin rings with a zinc ion in the center as building blocks, Jeremy Sanders's group at the University of Cambridge, England, constructed a superwheel containing three such units (Fig. 7). Within the large open space in the middle, molecular groups can bind to the zinc ions of the individual porphyrins. Testing the influence of this compound on standard chemical reactions, they found that it actually catalyzes the well-known Diels–Alder reaction (an elegant and efficient way of making six-membered carbon rings by using the spare electrons contained in the double bonds of the reacting molecules). Moreover, it enables the reaction to attain the more stable conformation of the product, whereas in the uncatalyzed reaction most molecules get stuck in a conformation that is less stable but reached more rapidly. (Chemists would say the "artificial

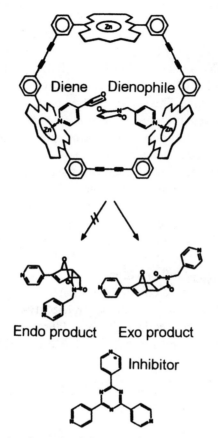

Figure 7:   A host molecule made of three porphyrins linked by rigid spacers. This construct can act as an organic "enzyme" in that it speeds up the Diels–Alder reaction between the diene and the dienophile, and directs it specifically toward the more stable *exo* product, while in the absence of the complex, the reaction would result in a mixture of *exo* and *endo* products. The inhibitor (bottom) acts like a typical enzyme inhibitor.

enzyme" switched the reaction from kinetic control, where speed counts, to thermodynamic control, where stability counts.)

One problem with enzymes is that they are difficult to switch off. Therefore, nature has come up with inhibitors for those enzymes whose activity needs to be stopped at some time or in certain situations. Taking this lead from nature, Sanders and co-workers designed a compound that can block all three zinc ions simultaneously. When tested experimentally, it turned out to be a very efficient inhibitor indeed, displaying all of the characteristic features of a natural enzyme inhibitor competing with the substrate for access to the binding site. Sadly, the product of the catalyzed reaction first studied was an inhibitor as well. Unlike a good enzyme, the triporphyrin complex refused to let go of the product and start again with a new set of reactants. This problem, however, can most probably be overcome by changes in the design of the system.

Potential applications for nonnatural catalysts with the substrate specificity typical of enzymes can be sought wherever natural enzymes are either not existent or not stable enough for the technological requirements. Thus, the difficulties in targeting a therapeutic enzyme to a given organ or cell type in the body without loss of activity on the way, or the problems with conducting a biotechnological process at very high temperatures could be bypassed. In organic synthesis, novel catalysts might help direct the creation of only one of the two mirror-imaged structures of chiral compounds—which is still one of the main difficulties in the synthesis of natural products. It was exactly this remarkable discovery—that enzymes can distinguish mirror images with 100% reliability where synthetic chemists are fighting for every single digit beyond the statistical 50%—that had led Fischer to the lock and key hypothesis more than a century ago.

6

From Quantum Dots to Micromachines

Most of the time, common sense allows us to predict how our physical (macroscopic) environment will respond to our actions. If you drop an apple, it will always fall. If you spill liquid, it will spread out. Common sense also tells us that many characteristic properties of matter are independent of the amount present. Thus, 2 liters of water will boil at the same temperature as 1 liter. Some properties follow simple rules of proportionality, e.g., 2 liters of water weigh twice as much as 1 liter. Whether a wire made of iron is thick or thin, short or long, will not change its color, melting point, or the load it can carry per cross section area.

For the world of small things, however, common sense rapidly hits its limits. A small drop of water will not spread out but will remain round. A dust particle will not fall but float. Friction and surface tension, those marginal effects normally neglected in high school physics, will suddenly dominate over the scale-independent forces like gravity. And further down, when one approaches the atomic scale, quantum mechanics come into the equation, and just about anything can happen. For instance, splitting a particle into smaller bits may change its color, as I will explain below.

When considering macroscopic (visible) amounts of a substance, scientists often make the generous assumption that the size of their sample is infinite in comparison with the atomic scale. They assume that the very few atoms that happen to be near a surface are outnumbered by the bulk atoms (whose behavior is unaffected by any surface effects) by so many orders of magnitude that they can be safely ignored. However, when the layers get really thin, or the grains of dust get really small, a substantial fraction of the molecules or atoms are close enough to the surface to experience the difference from the bulk phase. This can then lead to interesting and often counterintuitive properties, which shall be outlined in this chapter.

Similarly, miniaturization of chemical and mechanical equipment meets limitations that are not only determined by manufacturing methods but also by microscopic forces such as surface tension. Nevertheless, amazing things have been achieved with micromanufacturing methods that are just passing the micrometer threshold into the nanoworld, as we will see in the last section of this chapter.

Overall, this chapter will present a wide variety of nanoscale systems having in common that they are synthetic but not molecular in a strict sense. We shall follow a line of increasing complexity, beginning with "dots," passing "bars," "tubes," and thin films, and finally arriving at complex two- and three-dimensional micromachines.

Divide and Discolor: Q Particles Are Different

If one were to split a red particle into halves, one would expect to get two red particles—normally. For Q particles, however, things aren't quite as simple. These minute grains of semiconductor materials measuring only a few nanometers across can be black, brown, red, or yellow, depending on their size. The "Q" is to be read as a warning that weird quantum-mechanical effects have got something to do with this strangeness.

To understand these color changes and a few other remarkable properties of Q particles, we should first recapitulate why semiconductors are semiconducting, and why they are different from both conducting and insulating materials. Solid metal and semiconductors are not made up of molecules but rather of vast arrays of atoms. The electrons are no longer found in well-defined clouds (orbitals) surrounding each atom, but smear out over the whole solid body in so-called bands. The special thing about semiconductors is that among the two bands, in which the electrons of any solid-state material can reside, the one with the lower energy (the valence band) is fully occupied, while the one with the higher energy (the excited state or conducting band) remains empty (Fig. 1). In this situation, neither of the two bands can transport any charges. They only become conducting when electrons from the lower band are catapulted into the upper one, by some kind of excitation energy, which might come from light, heat, or

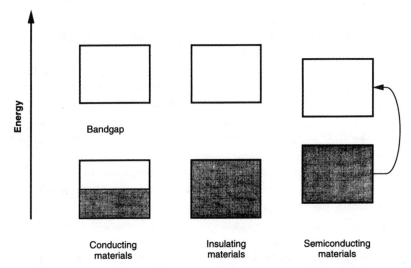

Figure 1: What makes semiconductors special? The energy levels that electrons can occupy in solid-state materials can be described as a low-energy "valence band" and a high-energy conductance band. In metals or metallic conductors there are empty spaces in the valence band, such that electrons can move easily. In nonmetallic, insulating materials, however, the lower level is filled up so there are no empty spaces that an electron could move to, while the higher level is so high up that it can't be reached. The special property of semiconductors is that they are basically insulators with a very small gap between the two levels. Thus, a small amount of energy provided as general thermal motion, or as light, could transfer electrons to the higher level and enable conductivity in both bands. If unsure whether a given material is metallic or semiconducting, heat it. Semiconductors should get more conductive at higher temperatures (more electrons getting pumped up to the higher level), while metals will lose part of their conductivity, because the thermal vibration hinders the flow of electrons.

electromagnetic fields. If this excitation is triggered by light waves, certain wavelengths of the light are absorbed in the process, depending on the width of the energy gap between the bands (the "band gap"). This selective absorption of some parts of the continuous spectrum of visible light is the reason why these materials appear to be colored—we see the color of the remaining light that is scattered but not absorbed.

Q particles, then, are halfway between the "infinite" semiconductor material, and a molecule made of only a few atoms. This unique position explains their weird properties. On the nanometer scale, the band gap—which is a characteristic and unchangeable property in bulk semiconductor materials—widens as the particle size shrinks. Accordingly, both the color and the electronic responsiveness of the particles become size-dependent.

How can these particles be made? Making Q particles of just any size is not that difficult. In fact, it can inadvertently happen to chemistry students in their first year. They sometimes have to produce cadmium sulfide—a substance that was used in exposure meters back in those times when these were separate from and almost as big as the camera—by bubbling hydrogen sulfide gas through a solution containing cadmium ions. Depending on the exact conditions, they may obtain particles just a few nanometers wide, which will readily flow through filter paper. This intriguing effect will usually result in dissatisfaction of the students who wanted to separate cadmium from other dissolved substances for analytical reasons. For the chemical preparation of Q particles, however, this route provides the easiest access to nanosize systems. Chemists exploring the marvels of the nanoworld, like Horst Weller at the University of Hamburg, Germany, routinely use this approach to make Q particles.

Physicists, in contrast, approach the investigation of quantum-mechanical effects in small particles from a different direction. They would profit from the continuing miniaturization of microfabrication methods (which I will explain in the last section of this chapter), defining nanometer-sized areas on microchips either by etching away the surroundings or by applying minute electrical fields. The resulting "quantum dots" can be incorporated into electronic devices.

By careful manipulation with very small voltages, quantum dots can be made to behave like "artificial atoms." If one moves just one electron from the valence band to the conductance band, the former will retain a positive charge, and the latter a negative one. Thus, a pair of charges corresponding to the simplest atom (hydrogen) is obtained. Artificial atoms have the advantage that the number of charges can be chosen at liberty, so that researchers can conduct investigations right across the periodic table using only one model system. They are particularly useful for testing the predictions of quantum-mechanical theories in simple experiments.

A third field that is related to both the physical and the chemical approaches to semiconductor nanoparticles, is the chemistry of metal clusters. These chemical entities, which may contain up to a few dozen metal atoms (like the iron clusters in the nitrogenase enzymes in Chapter 2), also display quantum effects, albeit in an even smaller size range than the semiconductors. One interesting kind of gold cluster will be the subject of the following section. While these three research fields have been developing independently for more than a decade, recent developments suggest that they converge on a new and deeper understanding of the quantum effects in nanosize particles.

The united forces and creativity of all researchers involved will be required to lead these interesting materials to the realm of useful applications. Although they have remained a topic of basic science thus far, numerous applications can be imagined. They could be used, for instance, for the development of better solar panels, involving porous materials coated with Q particles. By varying the particle sizes appropriately, one could adapt the absorbance of the panel to the properties of the sunlight and thus make better use of its energy content.

In chemical reactions, the high proportion of surface-exposed atoms in these materials suggests they would be suitable for catalysis. Titanium dioxide nanoparticles, for instance, have been considered for the catalytical clearing of wastewater.

The biggest potential, however, is in the fields of electronics and photoelectronics. Using semiconductor Q particles, one not only can selectively convert light of a chosen wavelength into a current, but one can also make the particles shine by applying a voltage to them. In physical applications, one would certainly wish to exploit the fact that Q particles make it possible to "handle" single electrons or photons. Physicists are already discussing single-electron transistors, and optical switches. These may become elements of tomorrow's supercomputers.

Gold Clusters Shine Brightly

From small semiconductor clusters, we now proceed to equally amazing metal clusters which emerged from research into the chemistry of gold.

Yes, although gold is known to be the noblest of all metals, it can in fact form chemical compounds. For instance, if chemists heat finely powdered gold with chlorine gas, they obtain a salt (gold chloride), which they can dissolve in water, crystallize, and convert to numerous other gold compounds with different oxidation levels. Thus, it might almost be mistaken for a normal chemical element, had there not been the historical equivalence of gold with wealth and power, leading to the obsessive attempts of alchemists to "make" gold. This obsession drove the development that eventually led to the science of chemistry, but also burdened it with a dubious heritage.

Nowadays, as gold no longer builds or destroys empires, and its power has faded next to the importance of other resources such as oil and uranium, chemists can return to the interesting chemistry of this metal without being suspected of secretly practicing alchemy. Nevertheless, there are only a few researchers who study gold compounds. But what they find is often surprising and intriguing.

Copper, silver, and gold are meant to be similar, as they share the same group in the periodic table. Gold, however, being the heaviest member of the group and having a very complex electronic structure, remains a bit of an outsider. One incarnation that has proven particularly interesting is the monovalent gold ion (Au^+ to the chemist), which is analogous to silver in the usual compounds like silver nitrate or silver bromide, but behaves very differently. For instance, it is not stable in solutions where it is on its own, but it can be stabilized with small organic molecules (ligands) that serve to shield it. The resulting gold compounds often contain several Au^+ ions in a kind of supramolecular unit, and tend to form weak bonds between the metal ions. Quite a few of these compounds, including the phosphane gold complexes, can be made to fluoresce when excited by UV light. (That is, they emit light of a longer wavelength than that used for excitation, which enables them to "convert" invisible UV to visible light.) Intensive investigation of these phenomena during the 1980s has shown that most gold compounds can only shine in the crystalline form. In rare cases discovered only recently, solutions of the compound may be luminescent, too. And then there is a third way, which was only reported in 1997. When Ella Fung, working with Allen Balch at the University of California at Davis, tried washing crystals of a gold compound she had prepared with chloroform, they began to shine, although neither the dry crystals nor the solution of that substance was luminescent.

Although those crystals had not been deliberately irradiated with UV light, the researchers soon came up with the hypothesis that an inadvertent exposure to UV, e.g., from the room lights, could have stimulated this effect. Systematic investigation using a UV lamp confirmed that UV light can bring the crystals into an excited state, which is stable for hours and only starts releasing the energy in the form of yellow light when the crystals are at least partially dissolved. Although the luminescence fades quite rapidly, it can be reactivated by a renewed irradiation with UV light. And if one evaporates the solvent used for washing the crystals and irradiates the solid, this will luminesce on contact with chloroform as well. Different solvents can trigger this effect, but its intensity increases with the solubility of the gold compound in the solvent. These findings, along with the observation that neither chemical reactions nor mechanical stress can make the compound shine, lead to the conclusion that the process of dissolving the crystalline material is crucial.

It remains unknown, however, what the excited state looks like and how the luminescence phenomenon arises. Structural investigations carried out by Balch's group revealed a stacking of the ring-shaped gold complexes (Fig. 2) with the triangle of gold atoms always in the same orientation. As this crystal lattice with its unusually short distances between the metal centers is as unique as the solvent-induced luminescence, researchers are wondering whether the former might be the cause of the latter. The lengthy columns with their core made up of nanoscale "toblerone bars" of pure gold might be the key for understanding the phenomenon. According to one hypothesis, the UV light might induce a charge separation resulting in electrons migrating along the toblerone bar, which may act like a nanoscopic gold wire. Electrons may then get stuck at irregularities of the crystal, where they would store the energy corresponding to the charge separation, until they are released by the dissolution of the crystal. The reunification of electrons and positively charged metal centers would result in the luminescence phenomenon.

Thus far, this is only speculation, and the same holds for the potential applications that have been discussed in the literature and include sensors for solvent vapors, energy storage, and photochemical switches. These dreams will only materialize when the phenomenon is understood and directed into technically defined pathways. And, of course, only if there are no other materials that can fulfill the same function at less expense. Nevertheless, these findings have thrown up intriguing questions, and they have demonstrated that noble elements don't have to be boring elements.

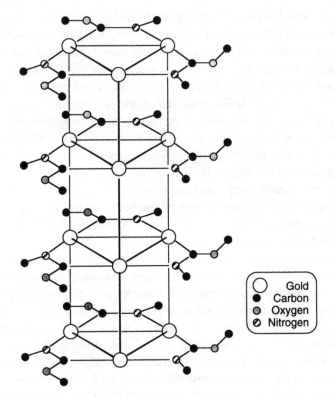

Figure 2: Schematic representation of the triangular prismatic structure of the gold cluster found to emit light on contact with solvents. Hydrogen atoms are not shown.

Carbon Nanotubes as Electronic Devices

Back in the stone age of electronics, that is, at the beginning of the twentieth century, engineers used big evacuated tubes to get electrons going. Amplifiers based on vacuum tubes made the development of radio technology possible. Later on, these were replaced by much smaller and smarter electronic components, the semiconductor transistors, which made the explosive progress of computers possible. And now, at the end of the century, it looks as if one day transistors could be replaced by tubes again. Not by big old tubes, but by smart new ones, namely, by tubes made of rolled-up graphite. In 1998, it was demonstrated for the first time that such a carbon nanotube can be used as a transistor.

Historically, carbon nanotubes are a byproduct of the phenomenon that became known as the *fullerene fever*. After Wolfgang Krätschmer's group at the Max Planck Institute for Nuclear Physics in Heidelberg had described a recipe suitable for the mass production of these soccer ball-shaped molecules, fullerene chemistry spread epidemically (quite literally, as the increase in publications and citations was successfully modeled using the mathematical descriptions developed for epidemics).

One of the many scientists infected was Sumio Ijima, who worked in the research laboratories of NEC in Tsukuba, Japan. While trying to optimize his procedures to produce fullerenes, he slightly changed the technical parameters in his discharge apparatus (see Ways & Means, pp. 154 and 155), and was surprised to find that instead of soccer balls he obtained long and thin fibrils. Electron microscopy revealed these fibers to consist of concentrically stacked graphite cylinders, whose ends were capped with fullerenelike hemispheres. Like the fullerenes, these tubes represented a novel modification of carbon. As their diameters typically measured a few nanometers, they became generally known as *carbon nanotubes*, or less formally, as *buckytubes*.

Theoreticians predicted that individual tubes of rolled-up graphite should have intriguing properties. Ordinary graphite is a conductor in the directions parallel to its carbon layers, and an insulator in the direction vertical to them. Naively, one could assume that rolling up the layers would result in a one-dimensional conductor along the axis of the tube, while the orthogonal direction (the plane cutting the tube at a right angle) has electrons running around in circles and not getting anywhere, like a hamster on a treadmill (or a scientist on the career ladder). Unlike scientists and hamsters, however, electrons are so small that most of their actions are governed by the weird laws of quantum mechanics, especially if they are confined to a narrow space such as the cross section of a nanotube. And to make things even more complicated, there are lots of different ways of rolling up a graphite layer. Of all of the different tubes with a given radius, only two will be symmetrical with respect to rotation around their axis. Based on the appearance that the rim of such tubes takes along orthogonal cuts, they are called *zigzag* and *armchair* tubes (Fig. 3). All other kinds of tubes have screwlike patterns, resulting in a chirality. They are normally characterized by the angle (theta) at which their rolling vector is positioned to the zigzag line. Theoretical calculations have predicted that because of quantum-mechanical effects, the electronic properties of carbon nanotubes will depend not only on their radius, but also and

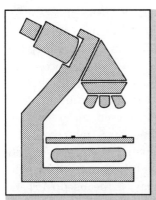

Ways and Means

How to Make Fullerenes and Nanotubes

One of the major breakthroughs that chemistry witnessed over the past few decades was the realization that pure carbon not only can occur in the forms of the three-dimensional lattice of diamond (where each atom has four neighbors) and the layer-cake structure of graphite (where each layer is tiled with hexagons), but also in a variety of molecular or clusterlike forms, which can be described as graphite layers rolled up to balls or cylinders.

The most symmetrical species, buckminsterfullerene, has the shape of a soccer ball and the formula C_{60}. (In case you haven't got a soccer ball at hand, it's made of 12 pentagons and 20 hexagons. Each of the 60 corners is surrounded by 2 hexagons and 1 pentagon—see diagram.) It had been observed as a prominent peak in mass spectra of soot particles obtained by vaporizing graphite and then condensing the carbon vapor, but failed to be recognized as a well-defined molecular species. Things only got rolling in 1985, when Harry Kroto of the University of Sussex in Brighton, England, persuaded Richard Smalley at Rice University into allowing him to use his molecular beam apparatus for a couple of weeks. Kroto wanted to create carbon clusters resembling those that he had observed indirectly in outer space. During this collaborative research, C_{60} emerged as a substantial peak in mass spectra, and the soccer-ball structure was put forward as a hypothesis. There are entire books written about this discovery and the ensuing fullerene fever. Suffice it to say that one more step was needed to convince the last skeptics and to trigger the epidemic spread of fullerene research: the method for bulk synthesis

of these molecules, which was developed by Wolfgang Krätschmer and Donald Huffman at the Max Planck Institute for Nuclear Physics in Heidelberg, Germany.

Their simple apparatus, which they had developed in 1983 in an attempt to re-create interstellar dust particles in the lab, consisted of a vacuum chamber containing two graphite rods touching in a sharp point, which can be heated by passing current through them, a smoke catcher on which any evaporated carbon would condense, and a variable amount of inert helium gas—because helium is the second most common element in space. When the current is switched on, the point where the graphite electrodes touch will have the highest resistance and will therefore be heated to temperatures up to 3000°C. Next to this point there will be hot vapor, which will turn to smoke further on, rise by thermal convection, and eventually deposit on the smoke catcher. Studying the spectroscopic properties of carbon deposits created at different pressures of helium gas, Krätschmer and co-workers discovered that the higher vacuum (less than 40 mbar) led to particles behaving like graphite, while a helium pressure of around 150 mbar (15% of atmospheric pressure) created materials with different properties.

Infrared spectra suggested that there were only four different vibrations in these molecules, which suggested to Krätschmer that he might be on the way to a large-scale synthesis of fullerenes. When the chemist W. Schmidt suggested extracting the product with benzene, the protocol was complete—C_{60} was obtained in preparative amounts and the soccer-ball structure that had thus far been a hypothesis could be proven rigorously. Variations on the method yielded C_{70} and other higher fullerenes, along with the carbon nanotubes, and the rest, as they say, is history.

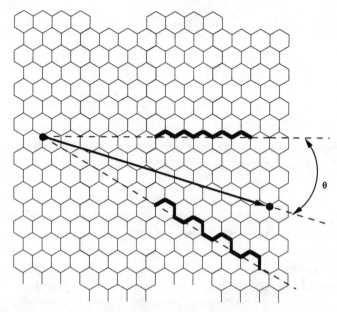

Figure 3:   The conversion of a graphite layer (honeycomb pattern) into a nanotube can be characterized by the wrapping vector, which can point from one corner to any other analogous one (solid circles). When the sheet is rolled up, the base and point of this vector will meet and it will form a circle. The wrapping direction shown as a horizontal in this figure is special in that the resulting tubes will be symmetrical with respect to the long axis of the cylinder. Cutting such a tube at a right angle to its axis will result in a "zigzag" edge like the line drawn more thickly. A similar kind of symmetry, with an "armchair" edge, is obtained with wrapping vectors rotated by 60° or multiples thereof. For any other directions, however, there is no rotational symmetry, and no smooth cut. In these nanotubes, the "zigzag" lines will wind around the axis of the cylinder in a screwlike fashion. Therefore, these tubes possess a handedness (chirality). Their structures are defined by the angle theta between the nearest zigzag line and the actual wrapping vector.

very sensitively, on this angle theta. That is, one could make both one-dimensional metal wires and semiconductors from the same material—the same atoms in the same pattern—just by changing this angle.

   This intriguing prediction was not particularly easy to verify. One has to get single nanotubes (nonstacked) with a known angle theta and then measure their electronic properties. In 1997, two research teams managed to do this—one led by Charles M. Lieber at Harvard, the other by Cees Dekker at the Technical University of Delft in the Netherlands and

Richard Smalley of Rice University. Both teams used scanning tunneling microscopy to relate the electronic properties of single nanotubes to their structural parameters. Both found that theta can adopt a variety of values, and that the width of the band gap (see Fig. 1), which determines whether a material is a conductor or a semiconductor, was indeed very sensitive to changes in theta.

Only five months later, the Dutch group had already made the next step: from the semiconductor to the first transistor. Dekker and his co-workers placed semiconducting nanotubes across an arrangement of three parallel platinum electrodes, resulting in a carbon-based field-effect transistor (FET). In FETs, the conductivity between two electrodes (source and drain) is controlled by the voltage applied to a third contact (gate). Conductivity measurements on the nanotube FET resulted in exactly the kind of nonlinear functions typical for transistors. When they performed a control experiment with "metallic" nanotubes, the researchers obtained the linear current–voltage relationship expected for metallic conductors, independent of the gate voltage.

Thus far, the electronic characteristics of this new transistor are not understood in detail. There are only qualitative models based on the similarity with conventional transistors. A deeper understanding, along with better means to incorporate nanotubes into circuits, will be required before they can become really useful at the applications front. When these targets are met, however, there will also be great promise of improved and even novel electronic components that could be built using only one sort of atom.

The big question, of course, is: Will the molecular transistor one day outperform the conventional silicon devices? As yet, we only have a demonstration that a nanotube transistor is working in principle. The prototype is a few hundred nanometers long and thus falls within a size range accessible to silicon technology, which has the advantage of providing integrated small-scale solutions including both the electronic components and the circuitry. Hence, if the nanotube transistor is to succeed, it will need molecular circuitry that beats the microchips in size and speed. In a distant future, such molecular nanochip devices may become the standard in electronics. Although silicon technology has been the major technological revolution of the second half of the this century, it is approaching fundamental limitations already. If a new electronics based on nanotubes can bypass this limit, the silicon chip may be replaced by tubes in the next century.

Carbon Nanotubes as AFM Tips

The methods of scanning tunneling microscopy (STM) and atomic force microscopy (AFM) developed by IBM scientists in the late 1970s and 1980s (see Ways & Means, pp. 160 and 161) are in principle suitable for "feeling" the fine structure of a surface atom by atom. What is limiting the performance of these instruments, however, is the quality of the thin tip acting as a probe that either touches or exchanges electrons with the surface. Ideally, these tips should end in a single atom, possess a well-defined geometry, be conductive and chemically inert. It may sound like a joke, but it is absolutely true that until recently, the best method to create tips that performed reasonably well (yet came nowhere near the criteria listed above) consisted in cutting through a metal wire with an ordinary pair of scissors. Alternative (and more difficult) methods like etching the wire tips or building up pyramids of atoms failed to provide better probes. In the best case, the diameter at the tip still measured a few hundred nanometers, which means that the outermost layer contains thousands of atoms.

Researchers in the lab of the 1996 Nobel laureate Richard Smalley at Rice University could drastically improve this situation by literally gluing a molecular antenna onto a conventional probe. This antenna consisted of a single carbon nanotube, some 10 nm wide and between 100 nm and 1 μm long, capped with a fullerene-like hemisphere. The researchers had simply coated the tip with a suitable glue and dipped it into a bundle of such nanotubes. In most cases, this resulted in just one tube glued to the tip.

This new kind of probe fulfills the abovementioned requirements almost perfectly. It has a well-defined and well-known molecular structure, is conductive, chemically inert, and as thin as anybody could wish for. Surprisingly, the thin and fragile-looking tube structure provided additional advantages in force microscopy, where the surface is tapped by mechanical movements. The tubes are stable enough to withstand the forces applied to the tip, and yet they are elastic enough to avoid unwanted collisions with the surface. Moreover, the new probes are relatively easy to make, although one does need a bit more equipment than just a piece of wire and a pair of scissors.

Wafer-Thin Patchwork: A Rubber-Stamp Trick Combines Nano- and Biotechnology

Gold is a very remarkable material for reasons much deeper than its glitter and market value. Having already dealt with the intriguing properties of bar-shaped gold clusters, we will now require the services (and surfaces) of thin layers made of this metal. If you roll it out carefully, you can get a foil as thin as a thousandth of a millimeter. In 1911, Ernest Rutherford bombarded such a foil with alpha particles, and made precise observations as to how most of them went straight through the sheet and only a few were deflected in peculiar ways. This classic experiment laid one of the foundation stones of modern physics in demonstrating clearly that most of the space in an atom is actually empty, as the majority of the mass is concentrated in the very compact nucleus.

Equally thin sheets of gold are nowadays back in the limelight of scientists' interest, though this time they only serve as a foundation for even thinner layers. Gold is chemically inert, and if you use it in a layer only 200 nm thick, it is practically transparent and not that expensive. These are some of the reasons why George Whitesides of Harvard University found thin gold sheets the ideal foundation for the construction of novel layer structures composed of chain molecules stacked vertically in parallel like the woolen threads in a North African carpet, and densely packed. These molecular carpets are called *monolayers*, as they are just as thick as one molecule is long, i.e., 1–2 nm.

Whitesides and his group also struck gold with their decision to use sulfur-containing thiol groups to couple the organic molecules to the noble metal. The thiols not only provided the desired coupling reaction, they also swept all impurities off the gold surface, sparing the scientists the trouble of using conditions of extreme purity. At the other end, the threads of this carpet can be coupled with various chemical compounds, producing a variety of different surface properties.

Moreover, Whitesides and his co-workers developed a new method that allowed them to produce molecular carpets with nanoscale patterns in them. Using a microfabricated "rubber stamp" to apply a certain sort of thread (a hydrocarbon that is sticky for proteins) to some parts of the surface but not to others (see Fig. 4 for details), and then filling in the blanks with a different, protein-avoiding kind of molecule, they could produce a monomolecular layer with a well-defined pattern of different binding properties.

To test the efficiency of the protein-binding islands in the pattern, the researchers spread out living cells on their molecular carpet, hoping that the proteins contained in the cell membranes would selectively bind to the designed binding regions. Surpassing all expectations, the cells not only stuck to the pattern, they even adapted their outer shape to square or rectangular geometry according to the borderlines given in the pattern. In this way, living cells can be cultivated at well-defined positions of a nano-

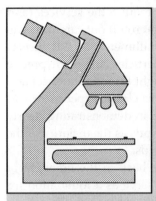

Ways and Means

Scanning Probe Microscopies
(STM and AFM)

Walking through walls is one of the things which don't work in our everyday environment, but may work in the crazy world of quantum mechanics. Consider, for instance, as a nanoscale equivalent of a brick wall, an energy barrier that an electron following prequantum physics would not be able to overcome. Quantum mechanics tells us that there is still a certain probability of finding the electron on the other side—as if someone with the habit of walking against a brick wall every day would get through once or twice per year. Physicists explain this effect on the assumption that the electron is not only a particle, but in this case more of a wave, and they call it *tunneling*.

This effect is the basis of a method of structural analysis developed by Gerd Binnig and Heinrich Rohrer in the IBM research laboratories in Zurich in the late 1970s. The wall that an electron will not normally but occasionally pass is the empty space between the surface to be studied and the probe, whose tip should ideally be just one atom wide. The next layer can contain more atoms. As the probability of tunneling decreases by a factor of ten for each 0.1 nm of additional distance, the second layer has virtually no importance. By suspending this one-atom tip just a few atomic radii above the object to be investigated, and readjusting this distance using the measured tunneling current, one can "feel" the structure of the surface and fathom its peaks and troughs without ever touching it. Once it became possible to control tip placement with sufficient accuracy, this technique [scanning tunneling microscopy (STM)] quickly established itself as a standard method of analysis in materials science. In fact, the technique is surprisingly robust and easy to handle as witnessed by the reports of a hobby engineer who built a high-quality STM instrument in his garage.

Atomic force microscopy (AFM) is a variation on this theme, presented in 1986 by Binnig, C. F. Quate, and C. Gerber. In this case, the probe will actually touch the surface, and its vertical movement will be controlled by the repulsive force measured when the surface is touched. Further analogous developments involve magnetic interactions and ion conductivity.

Both AFM and STM have increasingly been harnessed for the investigation of biological molecules in the early 1990s. Initially, researchers were already flowing over with enthusiasm when they could picture individual biomolecules, such as double-stranded DNA. This was special, because other structural methods, such as X-ray crystallography or NMR spectroscopy, would only give information derived from averages over many molecules. More recently, biological applications of AFM and STM open the prospect of observing individual molecules in action—which is difficult by conventional methods, as we saw in Chapter 2. Thus, a group at the University of California at Santa Barbara coupled molecules of the enzyme lysozyme to a surface before feeding them substrate. While the enzyme was busy cleaving its substrate molecule, the researchers literally tapped all across its surface, and recorded height fluctuations of about 1 nm, which lasted for up to 50 msec. This effect they interpreted as a conformational change related to the activity of the enzyme.

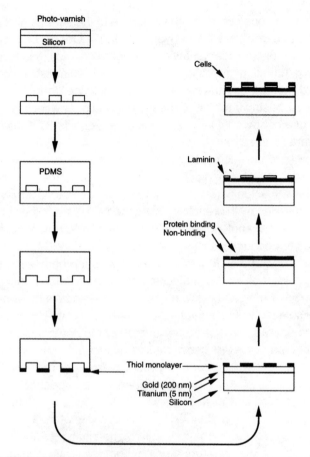

Figure 4: How to make a patterned monomolecular layer using the "rubber stamp" technique developed by Whitesides and co-workers. A negative of the desired pattern is produced by photolithography, one of the conventional methods of microelectronics (see Ways & Means, pp. 170 and 171). This involves illuminating a silicon surface covered with a light-sensitive coating through a mask to produce the pattern. At the places exposed to light, the coating peels off. The resulting negative then serves as a mold in which the "rubber stamp" is cast using polydimethylsiloxane (PDMS). Once this rubber stamp has been produced, it can be "colored in" with various kinds of molecules many different times. The molecular layer can then be transferred onto a gold surface. In the example shown here and mentioned in the text, a monomolecular layer of a thioalcohol is stamped onto a gold layer. The gaps are filled with a protein-avoiding substance (a thioalcohol coupled with polyethylene glycol). When the resulting chemically-patterned surface is exposed to laminin (a protein of the extracellular matrix), only the binding areas of the pattern get coated with protein. When cultured rat liver cells are spread out on this pattern, the cells will only bind to the protein-coated patterns, and they will even adapt their outer shape to fit the contours of this pattern.

scale grid, in a well-defined shape, and in an unusually high density, but without touching each other. This suggests that researchers using this approach will be able to follow the fates of many individual cells, each of which can be identified even by fully automated analysis systems through its position on the grid like a house on a city map. Thus, the new method may have far-reaching consequences for several areas of biomedical research that involve testing the reaction of cells to changes in conditions. Potential fields of application include screening for new pharmaceuticals, toxicity testing, and genetic engineering.

Binding cells to the patterned monolayers is just one of many applications of the "rubber stamp method." As Stephen M. Edgington pointed out in the journal *Bio/technology*, the relatively simple handling of this method makes nanotechnology with biomolecules accessible for almost every laboratory. For each kind of biologically relevant molecule a specific binding site can be designed. Central institutions such as Cornell's National Nanofabrication Facility in New York State can help inexperienced researchers to get started with the technology of the future.

Monolayers on solid substrates not only have a promising future, they even have a history reaching back some 60 years. When Irving Langmuir (1881–1957) and his co-worker Katharine Blodgett first succeeded in transferring such films from the liquid–gas boundary (where they cause the foaming of beer, for instance) onto solid substrates, no one really knew what to do with them. This situation changed radically during the early 1990s. The thin layers, which are also known as *Langmuir-Blodgett films*, have become almost fashionable. This is not only because the physics-oriented nanotechnology efforts have yielded potential applications that the chemically variable "soft" approach using thin layers may be more likely to realize. Another reason relates to the new methods for characterizing and visualizing these materials, including AFM (see previous Ways & Means, pp. 160 and 161). These methods have been refined to a degree that they can detect even small irregularities in the thin films.

Meanwhile, several groups are busy creating monolayers of biologically active or chemically interesting molecules on solid surfaces. Like Whitesides, James K. Whitesell of the University of Texas at Austin uses the affinity of thiol groups to gold surfaces for this purpose. His group has arranged peptides to a densely packed layer of helically coiled molecules. If the peptide helices are of different length, one can use enzymes to cut them down to a uniform length—the first implementation of a molecular lawnmower, so to speak. In this case, too, the variability of peptide chemistry promises a variety of novel, "pseudobiological" surfaces.

However, it doesn't always have to be soft layers that are coated onto hard foundations. Ceramic-coated plastics, if one could make them, would find a wide range of applications from light, wear-resistant machine parts, to sensors and magnetic storage media, and even to entirely new, "intelligent" materials. As the common methods for producing ceramic coatings require high temperatures (800°C), which most plastics would not withstand, the task seems to be impossible.

However, a group working at the company Battelle in Richland, Washington, has turned to natural systems for a solution. After all, the production of eggshells, bones, and teeth involves the production of hard mineral coatings on sensitive organic foundations and without using high temperatures or any aggressive conditions (see Chapter 4). As the group reported in *Science* in 1994, the biological membranes serving as foundations for these biomineralization processes contain special functional groups that direct the crystallization of the inorganic compounds from the oversaturated solution in such a way that it preferentially happens at the surface. If one attaches these very same molecular groups (e.g., sulfonic acids) to plastic surfaces (e.g., polystyrene or polycarbonate), one can mimic the mechanism of biomineralization and coat the plastic material with ceramic surface layers at temperatures well below 100°C. One of the potential applications of this method is biomimetic in every way: Bone implants made of porous titanium could be coated with a thin film of calcium phosphate, which is the natural precursor of the bone mineral apatite, without blocking the pores, which are important for the linkage between the natural bone and the implant.

Peptides on gold, ceramics on plastics—the close connection of thin films of organic or inorganic materials with inorganic, biological, or metal foundations is almost a metaphor for the way in which the scientific disciplines are beginning to merge when it comes to dealing with the nanoworld. Biologists may use nanotechnology, electronics compounds may contain biomolecules, advanced materials may combine the durability of (inorganic) granite with the chemical variability of organic synthesis and the optimized structural properties of biomolecules. And between all of these thin layers, there may well be a gold mine or two hidden for the intrepid explorer to find.

"Organic Metals" as Novel Protective Coatings

The 1970s are widely known as a decade that the survivors love to hate—for the shallow music, the horrible fashions, not to mention hair styles, but perhaps most of all for the invasion of everyday life by a flood of cheap things made of plastic. Wood, glass, metals, nearly all other materials lost ground to polymers. The poly-somethings came in all shapes and sizes, they could be hard or soft, transparent or colored in whatever dreadful hues fashion came up with, they could be almost anything— except conductors for electricity.

Not that nobody tried to make plastic wires. Following a chance discovery by Hideki Shirakawa in Tokyo, the quest for intrinsically conductive polymers was widespread in the late 1970s, and led to molecular chains that did the trick in principle. However, they proved hard to handle in practice. Dreams of TV screens that roll up like a blind evaporated as quickly as they had sprung up, and most companies and researchers involved lost interest in the 1980s. One of the few who persisted was the German chemist Bernhard Wessling. In 1981 he joined the middle-sized company Zipperling Kessler & Co., a supplier of vinyl plastics for the good old black LPs, which had been struck hard by the success of audio cassettes and later of the compact disk. He brought the company back into business with the production of specialized compound plastics. His cherished long-term goal, however, was and still is the development of conductive polymers, which he prefers to call *organic metals*. To focus on this goal, he founded the subsidiary firm Ormecon and sold part of the production facilities of the mother company.

The name *organic metals* points to the fact that these novel materials not only share the conductivity of metals, but they are also metal-like in more complex physical properties such as the dependence of conductivity on temperature. Furthermore, the term emphasizes that the immediate applications of these new materials will not be in transparent circuitry or roll-down computer monitors, but in rather down-to-earth fields like protective coatings. After more than 15 years of research and development, the first product containing organic metal reached the market in 1996. It is Corrpassiv™, a heavy-duty anticorrosion primer suitable for metal surfaces exposed to seawater or other strongly corrosive media, and it was confirmed by independent studies to be remarkably efficient in protecting these.

The reason for this high efficiency against corrosion is directly related to the metallic properties of the active ingredient, namely, nanometer-sized grains of the polymer polyaniline, which has electrons that are as mobile as in a metal. If ranked with other metals according to its electrochemical potential (which, roughly speaking, determines how hard it is to tear away electrons from the solid metal and convert the neutral atoms into pos-

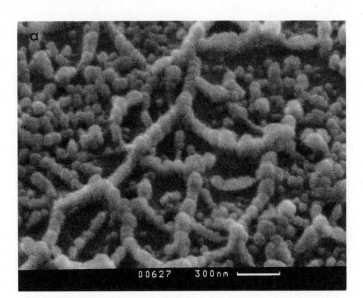

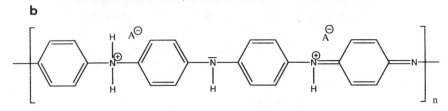

Figure 5: "Organic metals." (a) Electron micrograph of a dispersion of polyaniline. (b) Chemical structure of a basic unit of the polyaniline chain.

itively charged ions that will dissolve in water), polyaniline is somewhat
nobler than copper, and slightly less so than silver.

One of the intriguing properties of polyaniline is that it is even more
"metallic" if it is blended with other polymers, in a so-called dispersion, in
which the conductive polymer contributes only one-quarter by weight.
Wessling insists that true conductive polymers cannot be soluble in any
kind of solvent, and that therefore the dispersion method, involving small
grains of substance suspended in a liquid, is the only way to handle them.
Having such a dispersion with only one-quarter or less taken up by the
active ingredient leaves plenty of room for playing around with the other
ingredients, so as to optimize the other properties of the blend. For the

anticorrosion primer, for instance, only 1% of the organic metal is needed, and a lot of research and development work at Ormecon was invested into the optimization of its adhesion to the metal to be protected, and of its compatibility with various kinds of paint to be applied above the primer.

Soon after the primer became commercially available, a second poly-aniline product followed: a new surface finish for printed circuit boards. It can be applied from an aqueous dispersion onto copper in a wafer-thin layer (80 nm), and has advantages both in the nontoxic production processes and in the quality and durability of the finish. Future potential applications include transparent conductive coatings, "intelligent windows," sensors, and displays. Although these will be macroscale devices, they contain some degree of nanotechnology in the sense that they owe their crucial advantages to the efficient control of material structures on the nanometer scale.

Small Wonders: The Era of the Micromachines Has Begun

Whatever you may have read in fairy tales or in *Gulliver's Travels*, size does matter, and scaling things up or down does not usually work—neither in nature nor in engineering. This is a consequence of the same principle that allows grasshoppers to jump multiples of their body height, while elephants could only manage a small fraction. The trouble with scaling is that different properties change in different ways. If your body was scaled up by a factor of two in all dimensions, you would be twice as tall, but eight times as heavy as before. The increased weight would have to be supported by bones and tendons with only the fourfold cross section, and be moved by muscles with only four times the original power. Chances are you would collapse under your own weight sooner rather than later.

Well, the human example is purely fictional, as nature normally sticks with the scale on which certain types of organisms have proven to be functional and fit for survival. But in prescientific engineering, there must have been many who thought they could build a ship just like the one that worked so nicely, but double the size. And if you look at the nutshells with which Columbus crossed the Atlantic, you come to the conclusion that all efforts of scaling ships up to a more accommodating size must have failed dismally. Engineers call this problem the *cube–square law*, because the weight and thus the stress on the structure increases with the cube of the linear size, while the cross sections of the elements and thus their strength only increase like the square of it.

While the cube–square law is extremely bad news for people who want to build big things, it is in fact good news for the engineers who are interested in developing extremely small machines. It implies that the power is going down less rapidly than the weight, hence a large number of miniature machines would be more powerful than their equivalent weight cast into one big engine. Although other effects such as friction and surface tension may affect small machines more than big ones, it has been calculated that millimeter-sized engines could be ten times more efficient than the state-of-the-art aircraft jet engines of today. Which again reminds us that lots of small insects can fly, but elephants can't, even if they have ears as big as Dumbo's.

While pollen-sized aircraft may be only relevant to the Secret Service, other submillimeter machinery has recently reached the mass market. So-called microelectromechanical systems (MEMS) can be manufactured very cheaply and in high copy numbers using the technologies developed for computer chip production (see Ways & Means, pp. 170 and 171). Most probably there was a MEMS right in front of you the last time you sat in a car. That sensor (accelerometer), which detects abnormally high accelerations in accidents and then gives a signal for the air bag to be inflated, is typically etched out of a silicon chip measuring less than 2 mm across. Needless to say the same speck of silicon also contains all of the electronics that the device needs. Launched in 1995, the micro-accelerometer was an instant success, as it is not only smaller and smarter but also 100 times less expensive than the devices available before (see Fig. 6 for an explanation of how it works).

The air bag accelerometer as an example nicely illustrates a major strength of the silicon-based micromachines. As they are made essentially the same way as computer chips, they can be coupled seemlessly with whatever electronic devices you want them to interact with. Looking at it from the other end, one could say that the computer chip is now growing hands and tools and sensors. However, there are limits to what one can etch out of silicon. If one is interested in truly three-dimensional machinery, the silicon technology, which goes only a couple of micrometers deep, is far from perfect. And some applications specifically require other materials such as polymers or ceramics.

One of the alternative methods that could be used to solve these problems is the LIGA method, which has been developed in Karlsruhe,

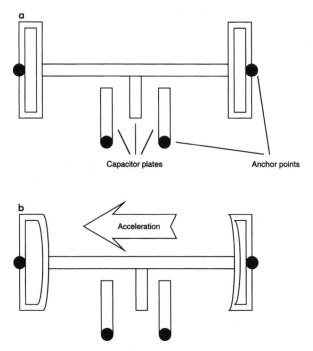

Figure 6:   Design principle used in microfabricated accelerometers for air bags. When the movement changes abruptly (i.e., because of an accident), the inertia moves the beam out of its resting position (top). With this movement, the middle capacitor plate will also be shifted (bottom). While the capacitances measured between the mobile middle plate and the fixed outer plates are normally equal, their difference on movement of the beam indicates acceleration and electronically triggers the mechanism inflating the air bag.

Germany, since the late 1970s. Basically, the method involves cutting the required structure out of a suitable substrate using highly focused X-rays as can be obtained from synchrotrons. Then, a metal can be deposited in the hollow and the original cast can be dissolved. In a third step, the metal shape can be used as a cast for structures to made of ceramics or polymers. While the structural features produced must be at least 1 μm across, the resolution of the method extends beyond the threshold of 1 μm—into the nanoworld. The first commercial application of LIGA is possibly going to be an extrafine nozzle for inkjet printers, which would produce a resolution of 2400 dots per inch.

The general trend observed in recent years is that microfabrication has grown out of the nursery era—instead of making very small toys, micro-

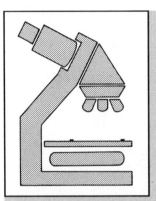

Ways and Means
Photolithography

Microchips are popping up everywhere, and after 30 years of computer revolution they are set to revolutionize other kinds of machinery as well. Microsensors can be built into chips; laboratory processes can be miniaturized to an extent that they can be run on a chip; and tomorrow's microchips will probably perform tasks that we haven't even dreamt of as yet. But how on Earth is all this achieved? How can people produce these steadily shrinking structures?

The incredible success story of the computer chip relies on the equally amazing success story of a manufacturing process that was invented in 1959, namely, photolithography. If that's all Greek to you, the literal meaning is something like "writing on stone using light." The "stone" is a wafer made of layers of silicon (semiconducting), silicon dioxide (insulating), and silicon doped with impurities (conducting). And the writing does not happen in a line-by-line fashion, but rather in the way in which photographic prints are made from negatives. Only that in this process the negative, called a *mask*, is bigger than the print. By shining light through the mask, a miniaturized version of its pattern is transferred onto the light-sensitive layer (the photoresist), which covers the silicon wafer in much the same way as the light-sensitive layer of photographic paper. In those places that have been exposed to the light, the photoresist can be removed with a solvent, and the silicon/silicon dioxide can be etched away with an ion plasma (a gas consisting mostly of charged particles), leaving isolated islands of semiconductor material from which the photoresist is also removed in the end.

Pushing forward the limits of miniaturization in this method has meant that the wavelength of the light used had to become shorter, and its energy higher. Thus far, this has worked very successfully, as the amazing fulfillment of G. Moore's prophecy shows. As the Intel cofounder had predicted in the late 1960s, the number of electronic elements that can be squeezed onto a microchip has doubled every 18 months—for the past 30 years. However, as the size of the smallest features that can be used in mass-produced chips approaches the critical "point one," namely, 0.1 μm or 100 nm, the limitations of photolithography become obvious.

For one, the feature size is limited approximately by the wavelength of the light used. Near-UV light is common standard now, but beyond 180 nm the quartz optics used for the mask and for focusing the image to a smaller size will absorb the light. Researchers are investigating the use of mirrors instead of lenses, but thus far, they lose most of their UV light on the way. Furthermore, the high energy of short-wavelength radiation means that the photoresist will heat up and the pattern may be distorted as a consequence.

Among the alternatives that are being investigated is the use of X-rays, which are electromagnetic radiation like light but with a wavelength that is typically 100-fold shorter. The problems with this lie in the fundamentally different techniques needed to focus X-rays. It is generally believed that the computer industry will not switch to X-rays before it has squeezed the last bit of potential improvement out of the UV photolithography. Another alternative might be direct (line-by-line) writing using an electron beam. This, however, is too slow to be able to compete for mass production. Thus, it appears that photolithography will stay with us for a few more years, until it finally hits the wall of physical laws barring further improvement.

engineers are busy filing patents and writing business plans. As the air bag story has shown, a very small sensor can become very big business fairly quickly. Other devices that could follow that track might be pressure sensors—both for blood pressure and for flat tires. And, eventually, albeit more slowly, the sensors will also be joined by micromachines that not only "feel" something but move or shake something, so-called actuators. Because of their small size, micromachines may be hard to spot, but one should definitely watch out for them.

7

Biotechnology

In the last two chapters, you may have gotten the impression that many of the nanoscale technologies described in this book will only find practical application in the distant future. However, one way of handling very small things has been (unknowingly) practiced for millennia, namely, fermentation. Since prehistorical times humans have used both living cells (the yeast in brewing and baking, bacteria in yogurt) and enzyme preparations (rennet in cheesemaking), even though they hardly knew what they were doing until Louis Pasteur discovered that brewing, winemaking, and other kinds of fermentation involved specific microbes. After Pasteur had provided a scientific foundation for the study and application of fermentation processes, these evolved into the wider endeavor now known as *biotechnology*. Today, this includes a wide variety of technical processes involving either cells or cell extracts. They supply food, drugs, insecticides, and the range of products is growing fast.

Considering how troublesome it is for scientists and engineers to build novel nanoscale technologies from scratch, harnessing the existing nanotechnology of the living cell for the desired purpose appears to be an attractive option. Today, this approach is still stronger than true nanotechnology, and it will remain the strongest competitor for some time. In some cases, such as the rubber stamp method discussed in the last chapter, nano- and biotechnology may merge to result in something more powerful than each individually.

While the use of cells and enzymes has a long history, the direct and controlled manipulation of genes (unlike the semicontrolled manipulation in breeding) is a recent addition to biotechnology, and one that is perceived as both promising and potentially risky. Gene technology can make impossible things possible, like blue roses or frost-hardy potato plants, but it also has its limits. Detecting and addressing single copies of individual genes is a technical problem very similar to those involved in manipulating other nanoscale materials. Using specific molecular responses to light is a good way of tracking down such small things. With genes, this can be done with the help of a protein from jellyfish, as we shall see below.

Earlier on, we saw that weak interactions are particularly important for the assembly of complex systems within the living cell. Now there are occasions when one wishes to disrupt these weak interactions, but not to change the chemical bonds. One way of doing this is by using high pressures. As I will explain below, there is a significant—and thus far underused—potential for the application of high pressure in biotechnology and particularly in food processing.

Finally, I shall not try to cover up one fundamental weakness of biological materials: They tend to decay quite readily. While this can be an advantage in the environmental context (when biodegradable materials are desired), this poses problems for the shelf life of products derived from biological substances. Pharmaceuticals, which are rapidly shifting from simple chemicals toward complex biological molecules, are a case in point, and I shall discuss the merits of different preservation methods in the last section of this chapter. Among other things, the last two sections will also show that biotechnology as a discipline also shares some overlapping interests with physical chemistry, as exemplified here in the use of pressure and other extreme conditions in biotechnology.

As a final warning I should mention that this chapter cannot give anything like a complete overview of this very wide and diverse field. Such an endeavor would indeed fill a volume on its own. Instead, I hope that the random samples I have drawn from it will give an impression of its variety.

How to Tell Right from Wrong in Genetic Engineering

One of the biggest issues in modern biotechnology is genetic engineering, that is, changing the genetic blueprint of an organism (and its descendants) by either manipulating its genes or transferring different genes from other organisms to the species to be engineered. In this way, microbes can be coaxed into making foreign proteins, like human insulin (Chapter 3), or food plants can be made to become resistant against frost, or pests. While this section will focus on genetic engineering aimed at the large-scale production of specific proteins, the following one will deal with the genetic manipulation of plants.

Genetic engineering relies on one very important assumption, namely, the universality of the genetic code. If you transfer a gene that codes for insulin in humans into a bacterium to express what is called *recombinant human insulin*, you want the bacterium to read the words of the DNA message exactly the same way as the human cells do. From Chapter 3, this assumption, which was held as a dogma for two decades, has been found to be untrue in several cases. Hence, when genetic engineers choose their systems, they should make sure the genetic information is read the same way in both donor and recipient of the gene to be transferred.

Even when this requirement is met, however, they may still be bound for trouble. One of the potential problems arises from the fact that the code has several different codons for one and the same amino acid. Within these sets of equivalent codons, one specific letter combination may be very common in one organism, but rare in others. These differences are particularly drastic between the three domains of life, for instance, between higher organisms and bacteria.

What can go wrong when a human gene gets smuggled into a bacterium? If the codon usage of the foreign gene is different from that of the host bacterium, i.e., if the gene contains a particular codon with high frequency, which the host would regard as rare, the bacterium may run out of the molecules (tRNAs) that are meant to specifically recognize this codon and present the corresponding amino acid to the ribosome for incorporation into the emerging protein. The ribosome will not wait for the right molecule forever. Rather, it will bypass the problem in one of the two following ways. It will either incorporate a wrong amino acid and then carry on with the correct sequence, or it will slide one letter forward or backward on the messenger RNA and thus read a codon that is no longer in the correct reading frame. The latter case is more catastrophic for the resulting protein, as the ribosome will stick with the frameshift and continue to read wrong codons until it hits a stop codon. (As a linguistic analogy, try to read the following frameshifted sentence: T hec ats ato nt hem at.) The protein will have little in common with the desired product, and will be easily found out and separated from it. In contrast, the former case in which just one amino acid was exchanged, is much more difficult to detect.

Help may be at hand, if one can identify the problem in time. If misreadings are found to occur regularly at a certain "hungry codon," this can be "fed" by adding the corresponding amino acid to the growth medium. It is more difficult to detect errors that only occur with a frequency of less than 1%. Methods commonly used in purification and analysis may fail to discover such small impurities, which in medical applications might trigger side effects, such as unwanted immune reactions. To make recombinant proteins safe for pharmaceutical applications, the most up-to-date varieties of mass spectroscopy, liquid chromatography, and microsequencing will have to be applied in routine assays.

There may be an alternative approach, however, which would bypass the codon problem altogether and is based on an invention by the Russian biochemist Alexander Spirin. His group at the Institute for Protein Research in Pushkino near Moscow developed a cell-free protein bioreactor, in which the genetic information can be translated into proteins in the absence of living cells. One only has to feed the appropriate cell components, like ribosomes or tRNAs, into the reactor and supply them with messenger RNA and amino acids. As Spirin reported in *Science* magazine in 1988, this technique can keep a cell-free protein synthesis going for more than 20 hours, producing several hundred molecules of very pure protein product per molecule of messenger RNA.

One advantage of this method over the genetic engineering approach is that the reactor only produces one kind of protein, while the bacteria used in production of recombinant proteins will make the desired protein along with more than 1000 undesired ones, which requires laborious separation and purification procedures. Furthermore, it would be easy to select the components in a way that could exclude any problems of incompatibility or codon misreading. And finally, the bioreactor could also produce proteins that would be short-lived in or even toxic to a living cell. While scientists agree that this invention could be potentially useful, there have been discussions regarding its realization, after attempts to establish the method in other laboratories failed. Although the future of the protein bioreactor is looking a bit uncertain right now, it would definitely be a useful thing to have.

The Quest for the Blue Rose: Trying to Make a Fashion of "Blue Genes"

Red roses are for love, white for death, and both colors along with the intermediate pinkish hues are as old as the history of the Old World. New colors only arrived in Europe at the beginning of the nineteenth century, when yellow roses were imported from the Far East. Since then, plant breeders have come up with some 50,000 varieties in nearly all of the colors of the rainbow, including green and purple, but with one exception: You can't have blue roses. Even those varieties that have the word *blue* in their name are purple at most, but never true blue.

Researchers have isolated thousands of pigments from the petals of different varieties of roses, characterized them, tracked down the enzymes involved in their synthesis, and the physiological conditions required for the proper coloring. After all of this, it dawned on them that blue roses cannot be bred as a matter of principle. All roses known lack the enzyme that would convert the common intermediate dihydrokaempferol to the blue delphinidine-3-glucoside (Fig. 1). The only way out of this dilemma is to transfer "blue genes" from different plant species. The DNA sequence encoding the enzyme in petunias could be identified and transferred to petunia mutants whose enzyme was deficient. In principle, it should be possible to transfer the gene into roses as well, and provide them with blue petals. There may be problems with the subtle details of the physiological conditions, as the resulting color could be sensitive to slight differences in the pH of the plant sap.

With an eye on the billion-dollar market for cut flowers where novelty is a major incentive for buyers, the companies Calgene Pacific in Australia and Suntory in Japan have embarked on the quest for the blue rose, trying to use the genetic approach outlined above. The companies anticipate significant commercial interest, especially in Japan, without fearing any problems of acceptance. Genetically engineered plants may indeed cause less worries to a skeptic public as long as they are not destined to be eaten. In a similar quest that probably addresses even bigger market values,

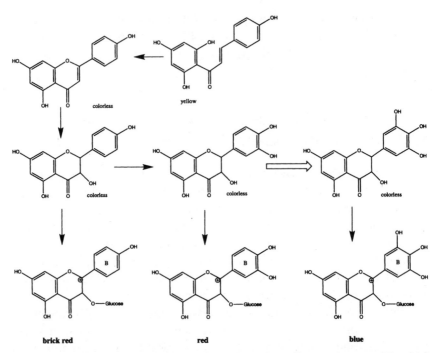

Figure 1:   Biosynthesis pathways of the anthocyanine flower pigments. The thick light arrow indicates the deviation that is anticipated to lead to blue roses. Note that for each of the three pigments shown at the bottom of the figure, the final biosynthesis step is identical (attachment of glucose) and can be carried out by the same enzyme. The difference in color is only brought about by the different number of hydroxyl (OH) groups on the ring labeled B.

scientists are also trying to produce blue cotton by genetic engineering, to save the trouble and cost of dyeing it chemically. Thus far, however, no sightings of roses with blue genes or of genetically engineered blue jeans have been reported—at least to my knowledge.

The Green Spark: A Fluorescent Protein Helps Tracing Gene Expression

Bioluminescence, that is, creating light from metabolic energy, is a fascinating phenomenon, and more common than you may have thought. Intriguingly, evolution reinvented bioluminescence more than 30 times in independent lineages. Apart from the well-known fireflies and glow-worms, there are also a wide variety of fish, jellyfish, bacteria, and even mushrooms that glow in the dark. Although much of the fundamental work on bioluminescence was based on the light organs of insects, the greenish glow you are most likely to see around a biology lab these days comes from the molecular systems of the jellyfish, *Aequorea victoria*.

Why is it that the luminescence system of these wobbly creatures has become so useful? This has to do with the fact that the jellyfish has two separate steps leading from the perception of a chemical stimulus to the production of green light. In the first step, the protein aequorin responds to a signal (carried by calcium ions) by sending out light. As one can verify by exposing the purified protein to calcium ions in the test tube, this light is not green, but blue. In the jellyfish, however, you will never see the blue light, as it is immediately absorbed by a second protein, which converts the energy into green light. This latter molecule has become universally known as the *green fluorescent protein* (GFP). To produce its characteristic green glow, it needs no other molecules. It will be activated by blue or UV light alone, even if it has been produced by genetic engineering and has never been anywhere near a jellyfish.

This remarkable property of GFP directly leads to an important application, which was first suggested by Martin Chalfie and co-workers from Columbia University in 1994 and became general laboratory practice in a matter of months. If one wants to transfer a gene into a different organism, so that the latter starts producing the protein encoded by the gene, one can simply couple the gene for GFP with the gene of interest. After the gene transfer, one places the transformed cells underneath a UV lamp (available in any molecular biology lab). If the cells produce green light, the transfer was successful. It's as simple as that. There have been other luminescence assays before, but they all required additional chemicals, which would have to be transported into the cell through the membrane. If the cells refused to take up the required substrate, this would have led to a false negative result.

Thus, GFP was recognized as a gene marker of unique potential, and within a year after publication of the first paper on its application, its gene was commercially available as a molecular biology kit. Biophysicists, too, enjoyed playing around with this protein. They tried to make it even more useful by making it shine in different colors, and they can even make it blink rhythmically, as we will find out below.

Basic research into the structure and mechanism of GFP had trouble keeping up with the pace of the progress in molecular biology. Only in 1996 could the molecular structure of the protein be revealed. It was found to be a novel and unusual protein architecture, which can be admired on the cover of this book. The outer coat of the protein is a completely symmetrical and remarkably large barrel made up from 11 strands of a beta-pleated sheet. The ends of the barrel are covered with lids made of short helical segments. Within the cavity of the barrel, there is a much longer helix, whose axis coincides with that of the barrel. And bang in the middle of that helix we find the luminescent part of the molecule—the chromophore. It is formed by an unusual chemical reaction taking place between neighboring amino acid residues within the protein chain (Fig. 2), as the protein folds for the first time.

Knowing the three-dimensional structure of this protein is particularly important, as this structure is thought to catalyze the very unusual process by which the chromophore is formed. As the formation of the chromophore has worked nicely in every host organism that was ever tried, researchers suspected that it was an autocatalytic reaction, that is, a reaction catalyzed by the same molecule rather than by some other, as yet unknown enzyme. However, the direct proof of this hypothesis was only accomplished in 1997 by Brian Reid and Greg Flynn at the University of Oregon. They produced the protein in the form of not yet folded polypeptide chains clumped up to so-called inclusion bodies in *Escherichia coli*. After purification and denaturation of the inclusion bodies they could observe GFP molecules that had never been folded, let alone active, fold up and carry out the chemical modifications that lead to the formation of the chromophore—a process lasting several hours.

The known structure also allows us to understand or predict how mutations, i.e., the exchange of individual amino acids in the sequence, will affect the luminescence of the protein. Although the green light that is produced is essentially monochromatic (i.e., all photons have roughly the same wavelength), the energy intake can occur in two different ranges of the spectrum. The natural protein from jellyfish absorbs best violet to near-UV light (around 396 nm), but it can also use bluish-green light with wavelengths around 476 nm. Researchers have worked out that the former is related to the electrically neutral state of the chromophore, while the latter requires a negative charge in this part of the molecule. By introducing subtle changes in those regions of the protein known to be close to the chromophore, they can now influence its charge state and thus produce GFP variants with tailor-made optical properties. Practical reasons would,

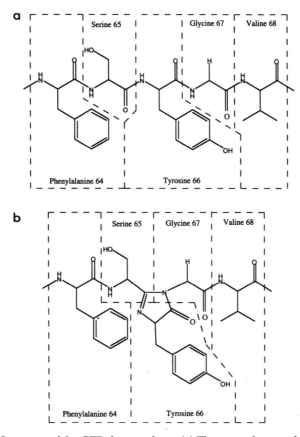

Figure 2: Structure of the GFP chromophore. (a) The normal, open chain arrangement of the residues that form the chromophore. This is how the polypeptide chain is synthesized on the ribosome. (b) The ring structure that GFP adopts autocatalytically during the first few hours after synthesis and folding. Only this structure shows the green fluorescence.

for instance, speak in favor of a stronger absorbance at 480 nm because there are lasers with this specific wavelength, which could be used to illuminate protein molecules with very high precision of both space and time.

Two of these variants also led to the discovery of blinking in GFP, made in 1997 by W. E. Moerner's group at the University of California at San Diego. To observe individual molecules of GFP separately, the scientists had brought the protein molecules into a porous jelly, so that they could not move around but could still be accessed by light and chemicals. They irradiated the trapped molecules with light of the appropriate wavelength, and filmed the luminescence through a microscope. Provided that the molecules are separated by a distance longer than the resolution of the microscope, the light emission of individual molecules can be recorded separately.

In this way, Moerner and his co-workers could establish that each molecule fluoresces for a few seconds, then goes dark for a few seconds, and then starts to shine again. This "blinking" lasted for a couple of minutes, and ended when the molecules had sent out around 1 million photons, at which time they "retired" and remained permanently inactive. However, even this "retired" state could be reactivated by irradiation with light of a shorter wavelength (higher energy) than that used in the original experiment.

Obviously, the protein can occur in three different states: the active one, the permanent dark state, and the intermittent dark state. While physicists are confident they can explain the first two states, it is the dark state between light pulses that made them scratch their heads. Current theories are still rather hypothetical, and I won't go into any further details here.

Apart from the novelty and intellectual challenge, this experiment also has practical importance. It is probably the first molecular optical system that can be switched at room temperature between two different states that can be read out from individual molecules. Thus, a molecule that responds to a short illumination with blinking would code for a binary 1, while one that is in the dark state would code for 0. While similar switching can be performed on the protein bacteriorhodopsin, reading out the information stored in the molecules would require a measurement of absorbance in that case. The advantage of GFP being luminescent and detectable on a single molecule level suggests possible applications in many areas of future optoelectronic devices, through to the elusive protein-based computer.

Closer to the present-day reality, however, application of GFP and its variants has become common practice in many laboratories. And it is not only unicellular microbes that glow in the dark to reveal the presence of a transferred gene. In some places, whole plants and animals will light up, in others just certain parts of them, like tumors, for instance. Karl J. Oparka and his co-workers at the Scottish Crop Research Institute in Dundee have coupled plant viruses with the GFP marker to study how the virus spreads through infected plants, and which factors may influence its progress. Plant physiologists in Japan have used GFP to study the heat shock reaction in rice plants.

GFP shines in animals as brightly as in plants. Pioneering studies involved GFP expression in fruit flies (1994) and in zebrafish (1995). Using a GFP variant with an increased luminescence intensity, Masaru Okabe and his co-workers at the University of Osaka, Japan, could for the first time produce mice that under the UV lamp shone in bright green through and through. The researchers had smuggled the gene into fertilized eggs, and it had indeed been passed on to all mature cells of the body. Moreover, it was passed on to a new generation of green fluorescent mice.

Such studies, of course, are not meant to address the problems you may face when you have lost your lab mouse in the dark. Mainly, they promise to deliver new insight into the development of mammalian embryos, along with new diagnostic tools for medical applications. GFP could be used to track the spread of metastases. More generally, wherever cells of different origin are observed together, fluorescence labeling would provide a convenient way of distinguishing them. And gene therapy methods of the future will certainly benefit from the option of controlling and targeting the therapeutic gene using a GFP marker. In a pioneering experiment, GFP could be introduced into and kept stable in a cell culture derived from human melanoma cells.

More and more complex tools will be built with and around GFP. In one recent example, Atsushi Miyawaki and his co-workers at the University of California in San Diego have combined two differently colored variants of the protein in one construct. They surround a calcium binding unit made of the protein calmodulin and the peptide M13. As soon as the calmodulin binds a calcium ion, the geometry of the construct changes in such a way so that the variant that absorbs and fluoresces at shorter wavelengths can pass on the energy to the other GFP moiety, which then will emit light of a characteristic wavelength. Depending on the binding efficiency of the calmodulin variant used, this method can measure calcium concentrations ranging from a 100th down to 10 billionths of a mole per liter, with a spatial resolution that allows researchers to compare the concentrations between different compartments of one cell.

Biophysics, medicine, developmental biology, molecular biology, . . .— there seems hardly an area in the wide field of the life sciences left in which the green spark has not yet lit up. GFP serves as a model substrate for molecular chaperones, as a probe for measuring biophysical parameters within cells, and as a luminescent trace to follow the transport pathways in cells or organisms. While a few other molecules have had similarly explosive careers, none has spanned so many different aspects and found practical applications in so many different areas. The green light seems to say "go" in more than one sense.

Squeezed Eggs for Breakfast: Why Pressure Cooks Better Than Heat

Domestic arguments about eggs that were boiled just 1 minute too short or too long may finally become history in the twenty-first century. Pioneering food biochemists, like Rikimaru Hayashi of Kyoto University, say that the best would be not to boil the egg at all, but rather to use pressure. Such a "hard-pressurized" egg would adopt the same material qualities as a cooked egg, but there would be no chemical alterations of amino acids and vitamins, such as can lead to a sulfury taste in overcooked eggs.

While the stiffening of egg white and yolk under pressure is a consequence of pressure-induced unfolding of the proteins, pressure treatment of food can also bring other beneficial effects, such as killing microorganisms (i.e., improving the shelf life of the product), gelatination (formation of a jellylike state) of starch, and the inactivation of enzymes that might catalyze unwanted reactions during storage and processing of the food. Biochemically, all of these effects are based on the fact that pressure disrupts the weak interactions (see Chapter 1) that stabilize the soluble and biologically active structures of the biomolecules, and thus convert them to a state that is insoluble and/or inactive. Thus, pressure changes can be a convenient tool to shift around the weak interactions that are so important for functional nanosystems, while leaving the chemical bonds unharmed.

As pressure treatment can gelatinize and sterilize at the same time, it can be used to good effect in jam production. In Japan, several kinds of pressure-produced jam (which has never experienced any heat treatment) have been in the shops since 1990. Color and taste of this jam correspond exactly to the unprocessed fruit—again because of the advantage that pressure, unlike heat, does not favor unwanted reactions. The next pressure-processed food products to reach consumers in Japan were a grapefruit juice that tasted less bitter and a tangerine juice that had a longer shelf life than the usual product. Many other applications are currently being developed and tested in Japan.

In the rest of the world, however, the gentle, ambient temperature food technology has not yet found much backing. One of the few experts outside Japan is Dietrich Knorr, of the Technical University of Berlin, Germany. His group studies the effects of high hydrostatic pressures on food characteristics like foaming, gelatination, texture, and enzyme activities—especially with a view on potential applications in the food industry. He has followed the Japanese lead from early on. At one stage, he even hired a graduate student with knowledge of Japanese, with the specific task of translating research papers published only in that language.

In principle, however, there is no reason why high-pressure food technology should not be applied in other countries as well. In the industrialized world, high pressures have been handled for decades, in many branches of industry. The existing know-how would only have to be adapted to the specific requirements of food processing. Therefore, experts are hardly worried about safety aspects of the new technology. As Bart Mertens of the Belgian company FMC Corporation likes to point out, the analysis of material strain has been improved to perfection over many years, so that pressure equipment today can be absolutely safe. Moreover, food technology would only require compressed liquids rather than gases. As the volume differences are much smaller for liquids, even a sudden unwanted decompression of a pressure container would not release very much energy.

Uncertainty, however, persists with respect to the consumer's reaction to pressure-processed food. The thought of food processed in bulky steel autoclaves may leave an aftertaste of unnaturalness with some people, although in fact the food products will be more natural than comparable products were before. Marketing arguments will be based on the more gentle treatment of flavors and vitamins guaranteed by nonheat processing.

Sleeping Beauty in the Glass State: How to Preserve Biochemicals

Peas, beans, and broccoli can be kept frozen for months. It is thought that the vitamins will be better preserved by this method than in canned vegetables. However, if you try the freezing method with cucumbers or strawberries, you will be reminded that freezing and thawing can be quite devastating for biological materials. When ice crystals form or get moved around, they can break cell walls and other biological nanoscale structures. The plant tissue will be unable to keep the liquid back and will thus become wobbly.

As in food science and technology, preservation of biological and hence sensitive substances is also an important issue in pharmacology, even though the neatly sealed tablets or vials do not always betray their highly sensitive contents, which may include proteins like insulin, inter- leukins, or other biomolecules. To exclude the risk factor of spoiled prod- ucts, drug companies must ensure that at least those prescriptions that the patient would take home and apply without medical supervision are stable at ambient temperatures for years at least. Biomolecules in aqueous solution would not fulfill this requirement. In contrast, they would pro- vide good growth conditions for unwanted microbes and thus be very sensitive to rapid decay.

To avoid these problems, one tends to withdraw the water from the solutions, after they have been frozen. Freeze-drying (lyophilization) in- volves rapid freezing of the sample, followed by slow evaporation of the frozen solvent in high vacuum. The solutes will remain in the vial as a dry, porous, and very light mass. You will know at least one example of such a product: instant coffee. The assumption that this method is gentle for biomaterials relies on the long-established fact that chemical reactions proceed more slowly at lower temperatures.

This hope, however, could be treacherous in the case of freeze-drying. As Felix Franks, director of the biopreservation division of the company Pafra in Cambridge, England, found out, unwanted things may happen even during very rapid freezing. As most of the water freezes, the dis- solved substances will become enriched within the last pockets of liquid. Their extremely high concentration can make chemical reactions happen quickly even though the reaction rates as such are slow at the low tempera- ture. Furthermore, the pH of these liquids can be shifted dramatically by up to four units—enough to knock out a protein. Another problem that may arise is the formation of small and irregular crystals.

Franks and his colleagues are therefore investigating alternative methods. One of their favorites is to cool liquids below their freezing point but without allowing them to take on the ordered structure of the solid state. The best-known example for such a material is glass, and scientists speak of a "glass state," or of "glasses" in a general sense, even if the material involved is not what windows are made of. The extremely high

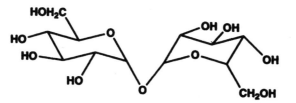

Figure 3:   Chemical formula of the carbohydrate trehalose, which yeast cells produce in large amounts as a protection against heat stress.

viscosity of materials in the glass state slows chemical reactions down very
efficiently. Similarly, the conversion to the proper, crystalline solid state
can take millenia. If you come across a tumbler with sparks of crystalline
material scattered through the glass, it will most likely date from the
Roman Empire.

To convert the aqueous solution of a biological substance into such a
long-term stable glass, one gently evaporates the water until the solution
has turned into a syrup, which will eventually harden to a glass. Adding
carbohydrates (sugars) to the solution will both stabilize the protein and
facilitate the glass transition (you could try this with a glass of honey). The
first practical applications have been found in the food industry already.
Ready-to-bake products can easily be manufactured in such a way that
they only awake from their sleep in the glass state when they get heated to
at least 20°C above the normal storage temperature. Similarly, ice cream
manufacturers are interested in suppressing crystallization to ensure their
products are creamy rather than crunchy.

Applications in pharmacology are developing more slowly. Although
the molecular biology company Pharmacia has been using a sugar mix
from Pafra to stabilize their DNA manipulation products since 1990, very
few pharmaceutical companies are trying the new method. Researchers at
Eli Lilly, for one, have shown that the natural sugar trehalose (Fig. 3),
which yeast cells use to protect themselves from heat stress, can also
protect preparations of human growth hormone from damage during
freeze drying. Thus, the hormone, which is routinely prescribed to children whose growth is retarded because their bodies aren't producing
enough of it, may well become the first "glassy" prescription drug.

IV

A Big Future for Tiny Machines?

8

Which Ingredients Are Needed for a Technological Revolution?

Roaming through the nanoworld in the previous chapters we have gained an impression of what the nanoscale systems in the living cell can achieve, and what rewards and barriers scientists encounter when they try to understand or even to imitate this natural machinery. The architecture and mode of action of many "simple" proteins have been described in great detail. In particular, the mechanisms and structures of enzymes that degrade biomolecules (proteinases, nucleases, lysozyme) and those of the oxygen carriers myoglobin and hemoglobin have been in textbooks for more than a decade.

The cell's constructive processes, in contrast, are not nearly as well understood. To this day, the molecular details of the workings of the cell's protein factory, the ribosome, have remained one of the hardest problems in biology. Similarly, the language in which the amino acid sequence of a protein describes the functional, three-dimensional structure of the folded molecule is being deciphered only very slowly. Although many chemical and mechanical functions are understood on a molecular level, we should remain aware that we only know and understand a small part of the processes going on in a living cell.

There is even the risk that the partial information that we possess may not be representative. For instance, all known molecular structures of proteins refer to molecules that can either be crystallized (and therefore solved by X-ray crystallography) or have a relatively small molecular weight (which would allow for structure determination by NMR spectroscopy). Thus, we cannot strictly rule out that some large proteins may contain structural features that inhibit crystallization of the molecules and thus cannot be found by either of these methods.

When we now proceed to an assessment of the prognoses and prophecies for a "nanotechnological revolution" it will be useful to keep ground contact by remembering that

- We have learned a lot about natural nanosystems from the explosive increase in structural data, but
- We still know only a small part of the machinery of life really well, and that
- Many processes that appear to work effortlessly in living cells optimized by more than 3 billion years of evolution cannot easily be mimicked by engineers who don't have quite as much time at their disposal.

With these caveats in mind, we will have a closer look at the promises of nanotechnology, which are quite generous. According to the nano buffs, machines that can handle individual molecules, even atoms, and combine them in a desired way will revolutionalize our everyday technology within the first half of the twenty-first century. A world population of more than 10 billion people will then leave all limits to growth behind and live in unbelievable wealth (Chapter 9). Our current "high-tech" tools will then be found in museums next to Stone Age axes. However, before we indulge more in these promises—and shiver at the matching worries about what could go wrong—let us first try to understand what exactly makes a technological revolution.

How to Start a Technological Revolution

Right now, as you are reading this book, you are benefiting (I hope) from a revolution that started some five and a half centuries ago. Sadly, we don't know exactly how Johannes Gensfleisch (ca. 1397–1468, better known under the name of his house, "zum Gutenberg") conceived the idea of printing books with movable type, or how he developed it to a working technology. Achieving letter type of sufficiently uniform dimensions such as to warrant a flat printing surface and smooth lines must have been the major difficulty. He eventually overcame this problem by making the type from metal and casting all of them in the same mold, which could be combined with different letter shapes and adjusted in its width. It is known that this development took him several years of work and considerable amounts of borrowed money. It would have certainly failed had he not possessed a sound knowledge of metallurgy. His research and development phase is thought to have begun in 1436 and ended around 1455 with the first ever print run: 160 to 170 copies of the 42-line Gutenberg Bible, of which 47 have survived.

It is difficult to overestimate the importance of this development. It broke the information monopoly of the church and its army of monastic scribes and put an end to the Dark Ages; it made the Reformation, the Enlightenment, and the rise of modern science possible. Arising while the first European universities were still in their infancy, book printing was set to become *the* information technology for education for five centuries. It is estimated that within the 50 years after the Gutenberg Bible, more books were produced than in the 1000 years before. And the technique he developed lasted for more than 500 years, until light reprography finally replaced the Gutenberg style lead cast letters, as a new information revolution began, that of the personal computer.

Like book printing, other inventions including steam engines, cars, synthetic fertilizers, and computers have also had profound impacts on the everyday lives of many people and could similarly be described as revolutionary. Others, from the paper clip to the diesel engine, have established themselves as useful parts of our lives, but without creating the kind of upheaval that one would associate with a revolution.

Whether a potentially revolutionary invention will in fact trigger a revolution is something almost impossible to predict—although it sometimes appears perfectly obvious with hindsight. Some great minds have exposed themselves to eternal ridicule with predictions such as "Flying machines heavier than air will never work" and similar. In fact, finding retrospect explanations of why we are traveling on subsonic jet airplanes—rather than zeppelins, supersonic jets, or rockets—and similar questions can become quite tricky.

Three ingredients, however, have a proven potential to trigger technological revolutions: new materials, improved production techniques, and—especially in recent history—miniaturization.

Materials

From the Stone Age to the Iron Age, the early history of our species and its technology is classified by the materials that started new eras by opening up new technical opportunities (Fig. 1). Progress can be seen in the change from materials that are simply found or gathered from the natural environment (bones, stones), to metals that had to be retrieved from ores using fire, but that had the advantage of being more versatile in their applications. Continuing this line of thought into our time (which others will perhaps call the Polymer Age one day), metals, glass, and the like are now being replaced by substances that are chemically assembled from smaller molecules. Again, polymers have the advantage of being more versatile than metals.

Still, polymers are far from being the culmination of technological development, as they cannot fulfill all demands we may have for "advanced materials." Their production uses up valuable resources and energy, and their widespread use in disposable products has led to pollution problems, as they are neither biodegradable like paper or wood, nor as easy to recycle as iron.

A common property of the materials from the Stone Age to this day is that they normally come in macroscopic (grams to tons) amounts, with rather uniform or statistically distributed structures on the nanoscale. From our nanoworld perspective, even a small piece of granulated plastic is still a mass product. And in comparison with the corresponding amount of biological material, this piece of matter is utterly stupid. It does not contain a significant amount of information, and it cannot act in any "intelligent" manner.

Hence, the expectations for the materials of the next technological revolution are clear: They should be more like biological materials in the sense that they make use of self-assembly, of molecular information, and of sophisticated nanoscale structures. They should become "intelligent" in that they should be adaptive and functional on a molecular scale. In fact, the difference between nanomaterials and nanomachines may become meaningless. (In the same way as you could call muscle tissue a material or

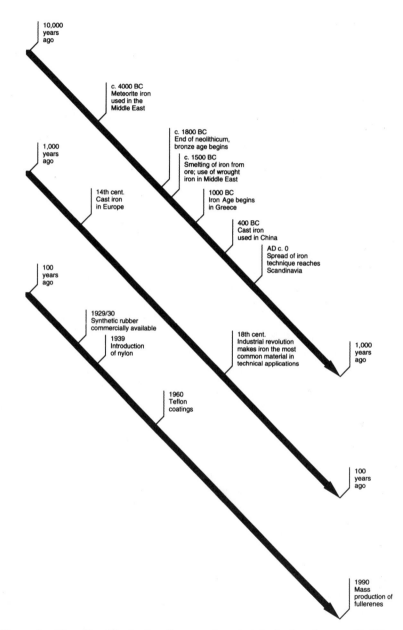

Figure 1:   Time line illustrating the use of materials during the past 10,000 years. Note that the time axis is logarithmic, with the length of each arrow corresponding to a factor of ten.

a collection of machines.) For practical reasons, of course, they should be inexpensive to produce and either degradable or recyclable.

Somehow, the classification of eras associated with materials has fallen from fashion after the end of the Iron Age—perhaps it was too embarrassing that iron was still the lead material of the nineteenth century and one of the major materials of the twentieth. Strictly speaking, the Iron Age may not have ended just yet. More recent history will use production methods as milestones of development, as we do when we speak of the industrial era.

Production Methods

To turn materials into usable products, one has to work on them, using the hands, cutting or drilling tools, or processes like melting, casting, or forging. Combination of simple products results in complex machines, including more sophisticated tools which can then be used to produce still more complex machines. Such "feedback loops" have occurred in history, resulting in rapid change, as, for instance, during the Industrial Revolution of the eighteenth century, mainly in England. New and better materials come hand in hand with new methods of processing them and shaping them into products. Metals can be melted and cast, but stones cannot. Polymers can be foamed, but metals cannot. Furthermore, new materials can lead to new tools, which in turn allow new production methods. And new production methods can open access to new materials. This cyclic interdependence of causes and effects can behave like a chemical reaction that produces its own catalyst, thus accelerating on its own.

Apart from the change of the starting materials and the growing complexity of the products, the major trend in the recent history of production technologies was the introduction of machine production, gradually proceeding from improved tools in the early textile industry toward largely automatic production lines of the twentieth century. While products for everyday use were made manually for millennia, we are now familiar with the notion that most of them are made by machines, leaving only those processes where decision-making is involved to human operators, designers, or controllers.

One important consequence of the machine production is that the length scale is no longer limited to such parts that human workers could grasp with their hands (or tweezers). The mechanization of production has thus paved the way for the miniaturization of the products.

Miniaturization

Brought about by the introduction of powerful yet affordable computers and the explosive growth of the Internet, the one technological revolution you are probably most familiar with happened over the past two decades. While materials and production techniques were important triggers for the information revolution, it would not have happened without a spectacular progress in the miniaturization of electronic elements and circuits. In this case, miniaturization is not only an issue of saving space or materials. Making electronic circuits smaller also makes them faster, more efficient, and less expensive. From the early 1980s to the early 1990s, memory capacities and calculation speed have increased 1000-fold. Since 1973, the number of transistors in typical microchips (and many other parameters as well) has kept growing exponentially with a doubling time of 18 months, which nicely matched a prediction made by Intel founder Gorden Moore. A single electronic element for a memory device cost roughly $10 in the 1950s—now this unit is approaching a millionth of a cent.

As for the impact on society, everyone who has witnessed the way computers spread through all areas of society and economy will not need any further explanations to understand what impact the miniaturization of one technical device (the microchip) can have on the quality of the final product and on the daily life of a large number of people. For the benefit of younger readers who have never known a world without computers, I should—at the risk of sounding like a grandfather—mention that I hadn't seen such a thing before 1981, and I have only had a private PC since 1990. Nowadays, I find it hard to believe that I—or anybody else—should ever have written anything without one.

And yet this revolution remained invisible for the normal citizen in the sense that the electronic circuits and elements in question can no longer be seen with the naked eye and can hardly be imagined by lay people. Their accomplishments, counted in gigabytes and teraflops, remain abstract numbers for the nonspecialist, and even with the knowledge that small and affordable computers would have the power they have today one wouldn't necessarily have predicted that every other household in the industrialized nations would have one.

Nanotechnology, if it is going to be the next technological revolution, will be still more abstract and even more difficult to predict. Direct control of single molecules or atoms, molecular manufacturing, and nanostructured materials may lead to highly complex systems on the nanometer scale. These could be much more complex than a present-day computer—but probably not more complex than a plant or an animal.

A Definition of the Buzzword *Nanotechnology*

Like the generations before us, we tend to regard our present technology as advanced, modern, and accomplished. We may be thinking that it can only be improved in minor details, and that there is little space for major technical innovations. People who start a career or buy a house will not normally consider the possibility that housing or work life may change radically in a matter of two or three decades.

But there is, of course, an enormous potential for change. To see this potential and the direction it could take, one only has to compare our production methods with those of the molecular machinery of living beings.

Production methods of our industrial era rely on

- Macroscopic manufacturing, in which countless atoms or molecules are handled in bulk amounts
- Materials whose properties can be controlled within limits, but that are not adaptive or intelligent
- Machines, which can carry out simple processes automatically, but mainly operate on the macroscopic scale

In the living cell, in contrast, even the most complex structures assemble in specific, programmed ways from simple molecular building blocks. Living beings can even control the structures of "inorganic" building materials, using molecular interactions to guide the precipitation of the mineral from solution. And even the most complex machines of the cell are no bigger than 25 to 50 nm.

Thus, nature has been the inspiration for those people who want to base a fundamentally different kind of technology on small-scale design.

According to the prognoses of K. Eric Drexler, which will be discussed in some detail in the next chapter, the nanotechnology era will be different from our current industries in the following respects:

- Molecular manufacturing, that is, products can be assembled on the nanometer scale with extreme precision allowing the rearrangement of individual atoms and molecules
- Materials with novel and/or adaptable properties, controllable by molecular manufacturing
- Miniaturization of electronic and mechanical parts down to the atomic scale, leading to nanomachines, whose compactness and efficiency could even outperform the cellular systems

Let us regard these three points as a preliminary definition of "nanotechnology," and proceed to meet the prophets of nanotechnology, their fans, and their opponents in the next chapter.

9

Visions of the Future

Dramatic events are happening on the moon. Having liberated a sample of nanomachines designed to build a new temporary shelter from the raw materials of the moon rock, three men are attacked by a bunch of gobblers— nanomachines that can break down biomolecules—and eventually killed. Only a few people know that this was murder, committed by mixing self-replicating destructive nanomachines with the assemblers. The general public believes it was an accident and sees it as an indication that nanotechnology is generally unsafe. During the following years, public opinion swings to a wholesale and worldwide condemnation of nano-technology, and its last proponents seek asylum on the moon . . .

The promises, risks, and fears surrounding nanotechnology become quite drastically clear from the plot of Ben Bova's recent novel *Moonrise*, in which some lives are saved, and others destroyed by "nanobugs." Today (1998), nanotechnology may still be science fiction, but when it does arrive, we should be prepared, to make sure it does not end in violence and public disapproval, as in Bova's novel. Therefore, it is important that we try to anticipate what revolutionary changes in technology may be ahead of us.

Profile

Richard P. Feynman

The species of genial physicists, I mean the world-famous geniuses who turn physics upside down with one or two equations scribbled down at the age of 21, seems to have gone more or less extinct in the second half of the twentieth century. Somehow, the Einsteins, Fermis, Heisenbergs and Paulis of this world seem to have come upon us more or less at one time (presumably when physics was in need of being revolutionized by a few geniuses).

There is, however, one notable exception to this rash observation—everybody's darling postwar genius, Richard Phillips Feynman (1918–1988). As the anecdotes from his life have filled two best-selling tomes (*Surely You're Joking, Mr. Feynman* and *What Do You Care What Other People Think?*), and several excellent biographies have been written about him, I can here restrict myself to some basic biographical facts that will only serve to provide some background to his 1959 speech about the "room at the bottom" discussed in the main text.

After a youth spent tinkering with radios and student years at MIT and Princeton, Feynman graduated just in time to get involved in the Manhattan Project, although his memoirs concerning this time are

Although scientists are generally reluctant to make predictions, there are a few who have ventured into this insecure field and thought about the coming impact of very small things. I will present these "prophets" and their ideas, including the very detailed predictions that K. Eric Drexler has made about the development and impact of nanotechnology. I will also relate the criticism that has been raised against these predictions. As a slightly less controversial case study, I will finally discuss the anticipated future of computation.

mainly about how he kept cracking the security codes at Los Alamos. After the war, he spent four years at Cornell, laying the foundations of his quantum electrodynamics (QED), which would earn him the Nobel Prize in 1965.

In 1949, he came to Caltech (via Brazil, where he spent a sabbatical), where he remained for the rest of his professional life. The first topics he addressed there were the intriguing deep-temperature phenomena of superfluidity and superconductivity. While he managed to develop a successful theory to explain the former, he openly admitted that he failed with the latter.

In 1959, when he was asked to give the after-dinner speech at the annual meeting of the American Physical Society, miniaturization was already a popular word, but unlike today, it meant reducing the size of things to cupboard or bench-top size. Feynman, as a theoretical physicist concerned with things that are a lot smaller than atoms, must have felt the gap between this "miniaturization" that engineers were achieving on the meter scale, and the nanometer scale with which physicists and also the emerging molecular biologists were familiar.

He slightly overestimated this gap when he offered two prizes of $1000 each for an electric motor of a 1/64th inch cube (0.4 mm in each dimension) and for a book page shrunk by a factor of 25,000 in each direction (corresponding to a font height of approximately 100 nm). While the prize for the book page was only claimed in 1985, the miniature motor was just about doable with conventional technology available at the time of the talk. An engineer who had read a reprint of Feynman's talk built the motor in his spare time and presented it to Feynman less than a year after the speech.

The Prophets of Nanotechnology

On the 29th of December, 1959, Richard P. Feynman (see accompanying Profile) held an after-dinner speech at the annual meeting of the American Physical Society, announced under the now-famous title: "There's Plenty of Room at the Bottom." The physicist, whose genius and quick wit

Profile

K. Eric Drexler

Although Eric Drexler is now known as "Mr. Nano," the original interest that drove him toward small things was rather big: space. When he came to MIT as an undergraduate in 1973, he was obsessed with the idea of making human settlements in space possible. In his very first year he began giving informal lectures on this topic, organizing study groups, and so forth. Soon, however, he began to realize that with the existing technology, space settlements would not be economically viable.

Being among the few scientists who acquire knowledge beyond the boundaries of their chosen field, Drexler also learned about genetic engineering, and how, in the 1970s, it became possible to reprogram living cells to produce biological structures that they did not normally make. He realized that genetic engineering could have consequences beyond the scope of biology, beyond bacteria making

were at the time only known to his colleagues in quantum physics, amazed his audience by predicting things that seemed out of this world. At a time when the word *computer* stood for a room filled with wiring, he said computers of the future should be made of wires that would only be 10 or 100 atoms in diameter. What would happen, he asked his audience, if we were able to arrange individual atoms the way we want them to be? Could we write the entire *Encyclopaedia Britannica* onto the point of a needle? To show that such things must be possible in principle, Feynman mentioned the living cell as a shining example, as it not only stores an enormous amount of information in a very small volume, but also possesses the hardware to read out the information and put it into action.

human insulin or growth hormone. He had this idea of getting cells to make a molecular computer, and generalized it later to the concept of molecular machines, even before he graduated from MIT, in 1977. Intriguingly, he developed these ideas without knowing of Feynman's 1959 speech, on which he only stumbled in 1979.

Only when he realized that others had had similar ideas, did he start thinking about publishing his ideas, which resulted in the paper in the *Proceedings of the National Academy of Science* entitled "Molecular engineering—an approach to the development of general capabilities for molecular manipulation," which came out in September 1981. Although the paper did not exactly trigger the nanotechnology revolution right away, it did secure Drexler a place in history as the first person to point out that the design of novel proteins is a problem that can be solved independently from the inverse question, the folding problem, as I explained in Chapter 5.

In 1985, Drexler moved to California with his partner, Chris Peterson, a growing clan of followers, and the manuscript for *Engines of Creation* (his first popular science book), which would be published in 1986. At Palo Alto, they set up the Foresight Institute, as a "non-profit, educational organization founded to help society prepare for nanotechnology." Each November, the institute organizes a "Foresight Conference on Molecular Nanotechnology", where an annual continuation of the Feynman Prize is awarded. The sixth conference took place November 12 to 15, 1998.

Reports say that the physicists were amused rather than enlightened. Most people thought that Feynman was joking. Although Feynman is now credited for this remarkable piece of foresight, which made him the first prophet of nanotechnology, his talk was a false start in that it did not convince the assembled physicists that manipulations on the atomic scale would one day become reality. And while Feynman only played with this thought on a few occasions, our second prophet dedicated his life, heart, and soul to the job of telling people about the potential benefits of nanotechnology.

Since 1981, the theoretician K. Eric Drexler (see the Profile for biographical details) has been publicizing his views on what a wonderful new world could be created with the help of nanotechnology (see Further Reading chapter for details). The foundation of his vision is that the analytical methods of AFM and STM (see Ways & Means on pp. 160 and 161) could be developed further into synthetic methods allowing scientists to manipulate individual atoms. Since the 1980s, researchers have used AFM and STM to probe surface structures with not-quite atomic resolution. Then, in 1990, a research team of an IBM laboratory made one of Drexler's predictions come true. They used an AFM-like instrument to position 35 xenon atoms on the surface of a nickel crystal in such a way that the atoms—if read with an STM—spelled the letters "IBM." As Feynman had pointed out in his 1959 lecture, this ultimate degree of miniaturization would provide a grain of sand with the capacity to store all of the information contained in all of the books in the world.

Extrapolating this thought even further, Drexler predicts that one day nanoscopic machines, which he calls *assemblers*, will be used to manipulate

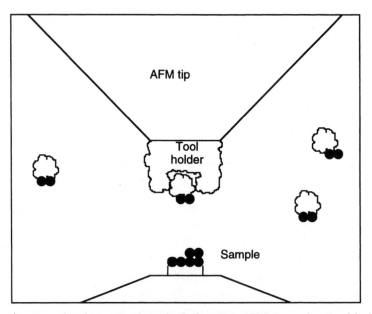

Figure 1:   A molecule manipulator built from an AFM tip and a "tool holder" designed to carry molecular tools that position the molecules in such a way as to build up a sample molecule by molecule. According to Drexler, such instruments should become the precursors of the assemblers.

atoms and molecules at will. For instance, they could be made to undergo certain chemical reactions, which in bulk chemistry may be unlikely because of the requirement of the molecules to meet in a certain arrangement and with the necessary energy. A postulated intermediate on the way from the present day AFM to the hypothetical "assemblers" is the molecule manipulator shown in Fig. 1.

One assembler building up a desired product molecule by molecule wouldn't be much help, of course, as it would need astronomical time scales to complete its task. Remember that the number of atoms in a single gram of carbon is a 5 with 22 zeros, and even for very heavy atoms like uranium, there is just one zero less in this number. Therefore, one needs billions of billions of these nanomachines. How do we get that many assemblers? Well, just use assemblers to build more assemblers. Nanomachines that can make copies of themselves are called *replicators* in Drexler's concept of nanotechnology.

The combination of these two basic elements—assemblers, which can create any desired structure by molecular manipulation, and replicators, which can provide us with large numbers of assemblers—led Drexler to his prognosis of a technical revolution, which may cause more upheaval than all of the inventions of the twentieth century rolled in one. In the next section we shall have a short time-travel into the future as he sees it. Enjoy the ride—for harsh criticism will bring us back to reality afterward.

Drexler's Brave New World—A Guided Tour

In his books, Drexler likes to indulge in glowing visions of what tomorrow's world would look like if the potential of nanotechnology were applied for the benefit of all humanity. According to him, a world population of more than 10 billion people could live in unprecedented wealth without harming the natural environment or exploiting part of the population.

For one thing, the option to arrange atoms and molecules at will would free us from the need of using raw materials with a certain chemical structure. Every kind of waste could be recycled on the level of atoms or small molecules. No natural resources would have to be used up for materials any more. Nor for fuel, as nanomachines collecting solar energy much more efficiently than today's solar panels will then be so robust that they can be painted onto the surfaces of roads and houses, converting solar energy at virtually no cost.

These achievements would of course wipe out the twentieth-century-style industrial production that is presently gobbling up natural resources at an ever-increasing speed. Furthermore, the new materials, nanorobots, and nanocomputers of the "coming age of nanotechnology" will turn other branches of our economy upside down, too, including agriculture, medicine, environmental protection, and transport.

The use of new materials in the construction of hothouses, and fertilizers produced from the air or from recycled products by nanomachines, together with cheap solar energy would increase the productivity of agriculture by an order of magnitude. Thus, healthy, pesticide-free food could be produced with a land use reduced by some 90%. Large areas could be returned to natural growth. Pollution would be practically eliminated, and the consequences of past pollution events could be reversed.

Present-day medicine, whose sharpest surgical tools compare to human cells like an ax to a microchip, would be replaced by "nanomedicine." Diseases ranging from cancer and AIDS to the common cold could be healed by nanomachines that would circulate in the bloodstream and hunt down harmful germs or cancer cells. Moreover, nanomachines could stimulate the formation of new, healthy tissue at injuries or operation scars, where today's surgeons can only sew and hope. Like a sheepdog rounding up the flock, the nanomachines would guard the body cells and make them grow together in the right places and in the right way. More daringly, Drexler predicts that even the very molecules of life can be repaired by nanomachines. If, for instance, a virus had smuggled its hereditary information into the DNA of the body cells, the nanomedical repair squads should be able to track down the offending DNA segments and remove them.

According to Drexler's visions, not only medicine will proceed from the stage of damage limitation, repair, and patching up to an active promotion of health, but similar progress will also be made in environmental protection. Not only would the new production methods avoid any further pollution, but the sins of the past could be made good. In one of the scenarios described in *Unbounding the Future*, a group of apprentice scouts tracks down the last traces of a chemical from the class of the PCBs (polychlorinated biphenyl compounds—well known for their nasty habit of forming dioxins during waste combustion). The youngsters are terribly excited about the rare finding, which earns them the privilege of taking part in the atomic recycling of this substance, which is by today's standards very difficult to degrade.

Removal of toxic and nondegradable man-made substances from the environment is a quite obvious target for environmental protection. Things are getting much more difficult if we consider a different aspect of the natural environment worthy of being maintained: the diversity of species. The trouble with biodiversity is that species come and go as a natural part of evolutionary history, hence there is no such thing as one set of species that is the "correct" biodiversity for our planet. Apart from the direct decimation of certain species by overenthusiastic hunting or pollution, humans have also messed up ecosystems through apparently harmless activities such as traveling. The best-known example is the story of the rabbits imported to Australia, where they became a plague because of the absence of natural enemies. Even the deliberate spreading of a viral disease among the rabbits didn't help, as virus and host quickly reached a textbooklike ecological equilibrium. As a means of protecting regional ecosystems from the invasion of foreign species, Drexler proposes the use of insect-sized nanorobots that he calls *ecosystem protector*. These could identify unwanted species by DNA analysis and eliminate them. Similarly, they could also keep weeds and parasites away from agricultural land, making pesticides obsolete.

As with much of Drexler's visions, with this idea, however, there is the major (political) problem concerning who will be allowed to program these guards, which could mean life or death for a given species. People less optimistic than Drexler may anticipate that the artificial insects will be more likely to further the profits of certain companies than to protect biodiversity.

Transport in the era of nanotechnology will, of course, be much faster and more efficient than today. Drexler speculates that the availability of novel machines and materials should enable us to build a fast and long-distance system of evacuated tubes, through which magnetically levitated vehicles could move with jet speed. Above ground, flights into space should become commonplace, and the resources "up there" should help us out when terrestrial supplies are running short. Not that they should, as perfect recycling would keep all of the resources in the cycle. And space will also provide new land for human settlements when our planet gets overcrowded.

Finally, *Engines of Creation* offered a way to immortality: People with diseases that would be lethal in our time could be kept frozen until a time when medical nanorobots will be clever enough both to ensure that the patient thaws without suffering frostbites, and to cure his or her hitherto "incurable" disease. This "biostasis," which Drexler praised as the "door to the future" in his first book, does not play a prominent role in *Unbounding the Future*.

Nanotechnology, it has to be feared, could invade the most banal aspects of everyday life. *Unbounding the Future*, for instance, promises the wall paint that would spread by itself onto exactly those parts of the wall where it is desired, repairs any damage by itself, and of course, will silently creep back into the tin once the wall owner gets tired of it. You will have guessed by now that the wallpapers of that era will change their pattern as soon as you tell them to, and can serve as TV screens or computer monitors if required.

Drexler and his followers have often been criticized for describing the potential benefits of the new technologies in great (and possibly arbitrary) detail, while glossing over the risks and problems for society. Potential problems range from 10 billion people getting terribly bored because the nanomachines are doing all of the work for them through to the possibility of nanomachines taking over the planet and eradicating all biological life including ourselves.

Responding to this kind of criticism, Drexler and his coauthors Chris Peterson and Gayle Pergamit have taken great care in *Unbounding the Future* to separate the speculative "scenarios" from the bulk text, to make clear that they are just illustrations of what might happen if everything went according to their plans (as it never does!).

In the politically ambitioned final part of the book, the authors explain why they emphasize the positive aspects of nanotechnology. They want to inform a wide audience about the potential benefits of the technology, in an effort to make sure that the development happens in the public domain and under democratic control rather than in secret military laboratories. In the latter case, one could easily imagine a new kind of weapon emerging that would be more dreadful than atomic, biological, and chemical weapons combined, and its spread would be even more difficult to control.

What's more, replicators could escape from the laboratory, and take over the planet. Both an unintentional loss of control or the deliberate psychopathic misuse of the technique could pose a substantial threat to the survival of humanity. While assemblers or machines that specialize in making assemblers should be easily controllable, there is a fundamental problem with the idea of self-replication. A nanomachine that could feed itself and make copies of itself would for all practical purposes count as a living organism. If left to its own devices, it could evolve through variation and natural selection and thus produce variants that may be able to evade any mechanisms that were designed to keep the replicators controllable.

Unlike Drexler, science fiction authors love indulging in the risks and potential side effects of nanotech—which come in very handy if you want to create some drama. In one episode of *Star Trek—The Next Generation*, for instance, nanorobots called *nannites* can repair damage within living cells. Sadly, some of these marvels make a dash for the starship's computer, where they take to explosive proliferation. (For more examples of nanotechnology-related science fiction, see the Further Reading chapter.)

Time will tell whether Drexler's optimistic scenarios will help to realize the better side of the potential, and whether the advances described will actually happen within the next 50 years, or rather take a few centuries. Even though Drexler from his prophet's perspective sometimes generously overlooks the difficulties we have today in our efforts to decipher the blueprints of the cellular nanomachines, and although his critics say that assemblers are in conflict with basic thermodynamics (see next section), there is little doubt that the direction in which he is pointing will probably be taken. Technology will keep advancing to smaller and smaller structures, and will one day—whenever it may be—arrive at the ability to manipulate molecules and atoms. Drexler is also right to anticipate that this breakthrough will cause major upheaval. And it is certainly better to consider the risks and opportunities of these coming developments before they just happen.

Maxwell's Demon—A Predecessor of Nanotechnology?

The Scottish physicist James Clerk Maxwell (1831–1879), one of the founding fathers of thermodynamics, came up with a mischievous riddle that remained unsolved for more than 50 years. In 1871, he designed a thought experiment that seemed to contradict the second law of thermodynamics, which Rudolf Clausius (1822–1888) had formulated just six years earlier.

The second law states that in the universe (or in any other "closed system"), the total disorder, a quantity that physical chemists call *entropy*, cannot decrease over time. This means, for instance, that two connected containers of gas will end up having the same temperature and pressure. You will never see the gas in one vessel heat up at the expense of the other, which cools down. Nor could most of the molecules accumulate in one vessel and leave the other at a lower pressure.

Similarly, although the process of braking a car converts the energy of its motion into heat, one could not get the car moving again by heating its tires. In all of these cases, the second law tells us in which direction a process is allowed to run. It is always the direction toward the greater overall disorder. In fact, the increase in entropy over time is the only physical law that allows us to define the direction of time's arrow.

Maxwell's thought experiment that puzzled physicists for half a century was based on two containers linked to each other and filled with gas (Fig. 2). At the nozzle between them sits a small being, later dubbed *Maxwell's demon*, which can block or open the way between the two containers for certain molecules, or for molecules with certain energy, and/or only in one direction. If, for instance, the demon only allowed fast-flying (high-energy) particles to go from the left to the right vessel, and only slow particles to go from right to left, what would happen? Starting from equal

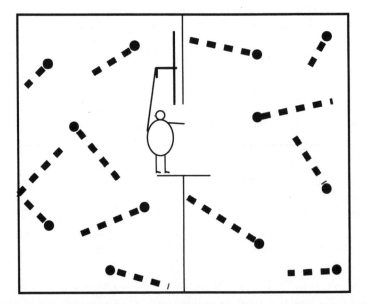

Figure 2:   Maxwell's demon is a strange little being that—in a thought experiment devised by James Clerk Maxwell—could detect the velocity of individual molecules and could use it to create a temperature difference between the two parts of a closed system. This would clash with the second law of thermodynamics.

conditions in both parts, the right-hand side would heat up by withdrawing energy from the left-hand side, which would cool down. Now this would create a more ordered state (with the available heat focused in a smaller volume) and thus violate the second law of thermodynamics. Similarly, if the demon could not be bothered to measure the energy of particles and restricted its activities to letting traffic through in one direction but not in the other, the gas pressure would increase in one compartment and decrease in the other, again violating the second law.

In the real world, the second law is still perfectly valid, and nobody has yet succeeded in constructing a real-life demon with the properties outlined by Maxwell. On the other hand, nobody could prove that such a demon was impossible, either. Thus, no one could be absolutely confident that the second law was really true—until the emerging computer science began understanding information as negative entropy. In 1929, the U.S. physicist Leo Szilard (1898–1964) pointed out that the demon would have to collect information about the molecules. Later still, other scientists identified the key step that brings the demon back to lawful behavior. If we want the demon to work continuously with a real-world (i.e., limited) memory, it would have to delete the information at some point. In doing so, it would increase the entropy of the system by the amount it has cheated out of it when it was sorting the molecules.

So what on Earth has Maxwell's demon got to do with nanotechnology? Quite a lot, according to David E. H. Jones, a chemist working at the University of Newcastle upon Tyne—better known to the scientific world under the pseudonym of "Daedalus." In a book review published in *Nature* (of Ed Regis's "Nano!"), he explains why he thinks Maxwell's demon was the first prototype of nanotechnology. Like the demon, Drexler's assemblers would have to collect information about the atoms and molecules to be manipulated, store it, and eventually delete it. If assemblers are to order atoms and molecules, they also have to create at least the matching amount of disorder, so as to obey the second law. The flaw in Drexler's concepts is, according to Jones, that he offers no way by which assemblers could dispose of the spare entropy. Jones points out that even the best computers available today produce a billionfold more entropy (mostly in the form of heat) than would be strictly required to match the information they are processing. Engineers designing the first assemblers will have to think of a way out of this dilemma to make sure the excess entropy does not go into heating of the newly assembled sample, which would probably mean disruption of the order they wanted to create.

Jones, whose credentials as a tongue-in-cheek technology prophet and chemical humorist include the prediction of fullerenes and carbon nanotubes, is furthermore very little amused by Drexler's generous use (or misuse) of chemical facts. He emphasizes that it is no coincidence that the IBM researchers chose the extremely inert atoms of the noble gas xenon for their nanometer-scale logo. Any other kind of atom would not have been so easy to push around, or to arrange at will. Atoms do come with chemical likes and dislikes, which one will have to take into account, even when one can move them one by one.

All of this of course does not mean that nanotechnology is bound to fail. We should just be aware that "remaking the world atom by atom" may be harder in reality than Drexler has dreamed of in his philosophy. I would expect the nanoscale technology of the future to be based not quite so much on positioning atoms as Drexler would have it, and more on molecules, self-organization, and weak interactions—those concepts with which nature has been practicing nanotechnology for 3 billion years.

The Future of Computation

One revolution is certainly happening right now, and will continue to happen for a few years more—the computer revolution. But will it continue at the same pace, will there always be a new computer in the shop offering you twice the power of last year's model at the same price? There are two important issues to be discussed in the future of computation. One is the rather down-to-earth technological issue of how far the current silicon technology can be pushed in terms of miniaturization. As I have explained in Chapter 6, there are reasons to believe that the miniaturization will get into trouble at a resolution of about 100 nm. The other issue—the requirement for parallelism—is more fundamental in that it arises from the depths of computer theory and therefore requires some additional explanations.

Conventional computers can perform simple calculations very rapidly. However, most calculations that are of practical importance are not simple. In computation theory, one distinguishes, in increasing order of "hardness," the following types of problems:

- Those for which the calculation time rises as a polynomial function of the number of variables (P), e.g., if an instance of the problem with n variables needed n^2 steps to solve

- Those for which a proposed solution can be verified "in poly-nomial time" (NP)
- Those in an especially tricky subset of NP, called *NP-complete*, that can be demonstrated by mathematical proof to be "at least as hard" as any other problem in NP
- Those for which the computational time rises as an exponential function of the number of variables
- The remaining problems which cannot even be solved in exponential time

Figure 3 shows how these sets fit together, like a Russian doll. That is, each can be regarded as a subset of the more general, and therefore harder to solve, group, except for that rather ugly and cumbersome set, NP-complete. Remember, these are problems for which you can check a solution that somebody whispered in your ear within a computation time that is a polynomial function of the problem size. And within the wider NP set, the NP-complete ones are the hardest problems. The trouble is that a lot of the computational problems involved in everyday tasks like, for instance, making a timetable for an airline, are NP-complete and have an awful lot of variables. A simple example of such a problem that is very popular with theoreticians is the Hamiltonian path problem explained in Fig. 4. In practical terms, this relates to the problem of a traveling salesman trying to find the shortest circular route connecting a defined set of cities.

Now the situation in Fig. 4 is so simple that you don't actually need a computer to find the solution. But what would you do if you had the corresponding problem with 500 cities and 20,000 links between them? As the problem is NP-complete, you know that your computer will not find the solution in a reasonable time. However, you also know that for each path that you guess, you could within reasonable time verify whether it is a solution to the problem. Thus, all you need is a few billion computers, and let each one check a few of the possibilities and they will let you know the solution within reasonable time. In other words, you need *massive* parallelism. As this degree of parallelism is not available as yet, people would in practice settle for a second best solution, e.g., a reasonably short route through 200 cities instead of the shortest possible route.

So the real challenge for the computer of the future will not be how to get it to calculate twice as fast as a present-day machine. The challenge is how to get it to act like a billion computers working in parallel. And this is a challenge that could one day spell the end of the amazing career of the silicon chip, as there are other methods of computation, which, although

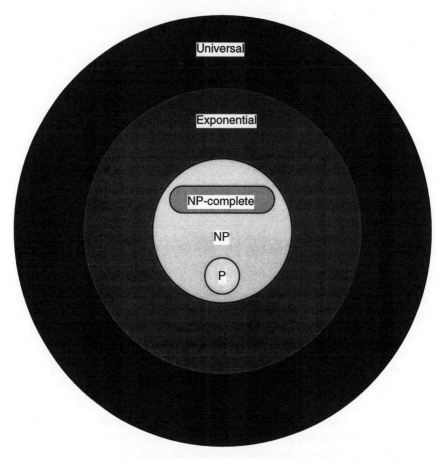

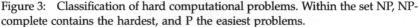

Figure 3:   Classification of hard computational problems. Within the set NP, NP-complete contains the hardest, and P the easiest problems.

weaker on speed and capacity, are stronger on parallelism than the conventional electronic approach. They may look like eccentric toys right now, but then, etching invisibly small specks out of a piece of silicon would certainly have appeared eccentric to the computer pioneer Charles Babbage (1792–1871), who built his calculating machine from metal cogs and wheels.

One way of achieving massive parallelism would be to use molecules. An ordinary test tube can easily hold 10^{19} different information-carrying molecules, which a chemist could "process" in parallel, and then proceed

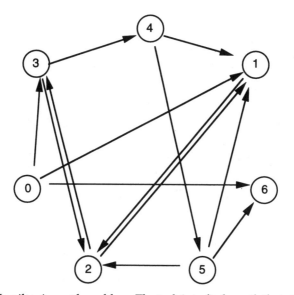

Figure 4: Hamiltonian path problem. The task is to find a path that starts at 0 and ends at 6, follows the arrows, and visits each number exactly once. (As one can easily work out even without a DNA computer, the path solving the problem links the circles in numerical order.)

to pick out those that represent the solution to the computational problem at hand. This is exactly what Leonard Adleman did with the Hamiltonian path problem, as I explained in Chapter 5. He used DNA molecules as the information carriers, and standard molecular biology procedures to read out the result.

While in this case, the "computation time" required to carry out the molecular biology required for the DNA computation compares rather unfavorably to the time an ordinary silicon chip would have needed to solve the problem, it was successful as a demonstration that molecules can be used for massively parallel computation. For technical applications, DNA may not be the ideal material as it is expensive to make and not that stable. Hence, there may be a need for novel, artificially designed computation molecules to fulfill the promise of molecular computation. One should bear in mind, too, that proteins in the living organism also carry out computational tasks, such as when they amplify an incoming signal by a certain factor during signal transduction. Thus, both the G proteins (Chapter 2) and the rhodopsin of the vision process (Chapter 4) could be regarded as computational molecules.

A second way of achieving parallelism has been worked out in some detail on paper, but has only recently been demonstrated experimentally: quantum computation. The basic idea is that quantum mechanics allows particles to reside in different states at the same time—until somebody does a measurement and finds them in one or the other. Back in the 1980s, the Oxford physicist David Deutsch could demonstrate by mathematical proof that a quantum computer—if anybody could ever build one— would be able to solve a certain kind of problem in a smaller number of steps than a classical computer.

Experimentally, however, quantum computers were a bit slow to come forward. Only in 1997, when two competing U.S. teams reported that an ordinary NMR spectrometer (see Ways & Means on pp. 80 and 81) can serve as a quantum computer if one feeds it with the right kind of molecules, did the field really enter a productive experimental phase. Less than a year later, Jonathan Jones and Michel Mosca from Oxford could for the first time carry out an actual calculation with a quantum computer, and they were followed hard on the heels by IBM's Isaac Chuang and his collaborators at MIT and Stanford. Jones and Mosca investigated the problem set by Deutsch and could indeed show that the quantum algorithm is more efficient in solving it than a classical algorithm.

While this achievement was a major step in that it brought the concept of quantum computation from the realm of theory into real life, one should be aware that these "computers" use the equivalent of two (yes, two) classical bits, or two qubits for the people in the know. Progress toward three, four, or five qubit realizations will certainly be made in a matter of a few years. It is, however, not yet clear whether the NMR approach will ever yield quantum computers in the range of hundreds or thousands of qubits, where real usefulness would only begin.

There may be other ways to achieve parallelism as well. In one particularly cost-efficient approach recently reported, a computer scientist went around his university and charitably picked up all 486 computers that departments were throwing out to replace them with Pentium II machines. Having collected a few hundred of these computers fallen out of fashion, he devised a clever way of getting them to share tasks and ended up owning not only the most efficient but also the cheapest supercomputer in the world.

10

Nanotechnology
Present versus Future

Now we know the sources from which nanotechnology derives its inspiration, and have discussed some ideas concerning the direction it may be taking. Having thus mapped out its course and the surrounding landscape, we're only left with the last task of sticking on a little arrow with the caption "You are here."

So, where are we standing right now? Nanotechnology is beginning to turn into an established research discipline. New institutes and research programs have names related to the issue, such as the "Cornell Nanofabrication Facility" (formerly the "National Nanofabrication Facility") in Ithaca, nanotech centers in Japan, a "Nano-Valley" in the Upper Rhine involving both German and French institutes and universities, and the "Nanotechnology Link Programme" in Britain. Moreover, the number of research papers produced in this field has been increasing significantly over the past few years (Fig. 1), with the most dramatic rise between 1994 and 1995.

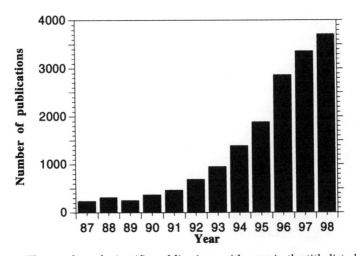

Figure 1: The number of scientific publications with *nano* in the title listed in the ISI Science Citation Index has risen dramatically between 1990 and 1998. The value shown for 1998 is the direct extrapolation (factor 1.5) of the number obtained for the months January to August.

While this sounds encouraging, it has to be said that the science of small things is far from becoming "big science," i.e., an internationally coordinated effort on the scale of the Human Genome Project, the space programs, or the particle accelerators. This situation is not very likely to change soon, even though the investment into smart, small things could prove more rewarding in the long term than any of the "big science" programs.

Even with regard to pure scientific investigation, nanotech is a research discipline "under construction." Some solid foundations have been laid. However, new methods will have to be developed, especially for directed synthesis on the nanometer scale, which thus far cannot keep pace with analytical investigations of the nanoworld. The Protein Database (at the Brookhaven National Laboratory in Upton, Long Island, N.Y.) contains the detailed three-dimensional structures of 7357 proteins (as of July 8, 1998), but the attempts at constructing similarly complex and efficient molecular systems synthetically are still far from perfect.

More information and communication work is needed to link researchers from neighboring disciplines to the new, interdisciplinary subject. Protein biochemists and material scientists, semiconductor physicists and biotechnologists, organic chemists and biophysicists would not normally communicate across the perceived boundaries between their disciplines. However, if nanotechnology is to be built up to something useful, all of these and a few more specialists from different disciplines will have to combine their efforts. The still remote goal of a new kind of production based on nanotechnology can be targeted in a "top-down" kind of approach—e.g., by further miniaturization of microfabrication—or by a "bottom-up" approach, which would mean building nanostructures by chemical synthesis and subsequent self-assembly. Either of these approaches or any combination of them can only be successful if they know of each other and work toward each other.

Moreover, scientists will have to develop novel methods of synthesis modeled on the best analytical methods available today. These methods will be the most important ingredients of the new technology, and they will thus play a crucial role in determining whether or not a revolution of the extent imagined by Drexler will take place.

The "Top-Down" Approach: From Micro to Nano

The top-down approach to nanotechnology essentially involves making the things that already exist on the micrometer scale even smaller by a factor of 1000 or so. While this line of development has been followed both in mechanical and chemical micromachinery (see Chapter 7) and in microelectronics with some success, its limitations are already becoming most obvious in the case of microchip fabrication, where there is an enormous commercial pressure to achieve further miniaturization.

The smallest structures on today's memory chips measure a few hundred nanometers (250 nm according to one source, but this number will certainly be outdated by the time this book reaches the shops). In the research and development labs there are gigabit chips boasting transistors only 100 to 200 nm wide. Mass production of such chips, however, may be extremely difficult. The conventional method of photolithography, which involves projecting the pattern of a larger mask onto the semiconductor surface using focused light, hits its limits in this area. Visible light with its wavelength range from 400 nm upward can no longer be used, and UV light is more difficult to use. X-rays are being discussed as an alternative (and are indeed being used for the LIGA method described in Chapter 6), but they cannot be focused as easily as visible or UV light.

If and when these production problems are overcome, conventional microchips can be further miniaturized down to a threshold of approximately 30 nm. Beyond this threshold, it is feared that tunneling effects would make the electronics error-prone. However, a chip built with a resolution of 30 nm would be small enough to fit into nanorobots the size of blood cells, so it would be suitable for fulfilling at least a few of Drexler's predictions.

We should remember, however, that the alternative approaches to fast and massively parallel computation discussed in the previous chapter may some day render the hunt for smaller semiconductor transistors obsolete. Until this happens, though, microchip manufacturing is among the most powerful incentives for the development of miniaturization.

The "Bottom-Up" Approach: Self-Organization Comes Together

As we have seen for a variety of examples in Parts II and III of this book, weak interactions and self-organization enable the construction of relatively large and complex molecular systems from small and simple building blocks. Although some chemists may still have problems with admitting that covalent bonds aren't everything in life, the playful approach of supramolecular chemists seems to be unstoppable. Be it Reza Ghadiri's peptides, which are doing the most amazing things, Jean-Marie Lehn's cleverly designed molecular jigsaws, or Fraser Stoddart's molecular train set complete with start and stop signals—it is always obvious that self-assembling structures carry the potential for complex function. Simple supramolecular compounds such as interlocking rings (Chapter 5) or rotaxanes (Fig. 2) could provide standard elements for tomorrow's technologies. Maybe we already have most of the right parts and only need to find an ingenious way of fitting them together.

Similarly, when Nadrian Seeman fits DNA molecules together to assemble complex porous lattices, it becomes clear that the material science of the future will also need self-assembly and perhaps some biologically inspired macromolecules.

From Old Materials to Advanced Materials

I sincerely hope that things have changed by now, but when I studied chemical engineering for half a year back in 1982, my obligatory course in

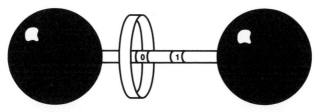

Figure 2: A rotaxane is a supramolecule consisting of a ring molecule and an axis threaded through it. To stop the assembly from disintegrating, the ends of the axis are plugged with bulky molecular groups. The axis can be designed such that there are alternative binding sites for the ring to dock onto under different conditions. This arrangement can serve as a molecular switch.

materials science was distinctly Victorian in its choice of subjects, and I wouldn't hesitate a second to name it the most boring university course I have ever attended. It was all about dozens of different kinds of steel, with their martensite, austenite, and perlite grains, a truckload of dead facts that one could certainly look up easily if one ever needed them.

After this traumatic experience, it took me almost a decade to realize that there is in fact intelligent life even in materials science. In 1988, the venerable German chemistry journal *Angewandte Chemie* developed a materials section that rapidly evolved into an independent journal, called *Advanced Materials*. Now, what is advanced about these materials? The "new" materials science associated with this name deals with exciting things (some of which we have encountered on our travels through nanoworld), like Langmuir–Blodgett films, polymer constructs mimicking biological membranes or proteins, or with coating procedures adapted from biomineralization, sol–gel transitions, aerogels, and many more. This new applied science is highly interdisciplinary in that it involves biological inspiration, chemical synthesis, and physical analysis. And it is closely related to nanotechnology, because many of the "advanced materials" will result from deliberate design on the nanometer scale rather than from big bucket chemistry or metallurgy.

Companies and application, oriented institutes are busy developing nanoscale coatings for everyday purposes, ranging from anticorrosion primers (see p. 165) to the self-cleaning window. Even though some of these applications may not fall into the range of what Drexler calls nanotechnology, for many consumers they may be the first products whose design was manipulated on the nanometer scale.

A Farewell to Factories?

One of the scenarios presented in *Unbounding the Future* introduces a married couple (how old-fashioned!) who are running the molecular manufacturing of furniture, computers, toys, and outdoor equipment with no human work force whatsoever. As disaster strikes, it only takes them a few hours to switch their "Desert Rose Industries" to making self-assembling prefab houses with all modern (twenty-first century) conveniences for the victims of an earthquake. I think that there can be little doubt that this scenario will remain science fiction for quite some time to come. Apart from the social problem—what on Earth are those people who are not running a fully automatic nanofactory going to do with their time?—there is little in today's technological development that would suggest such a radical change of production strategies to happen very soon.

One first step may happen when some new "laboratory on a chip" methods can make the step onward from analysis to synthesis. First it was separation techniques, which had hitherto required a benchful of equipment and could now be squeezed onto a microchip. Chromatography columns could be replaced by troughs only a few micrometers wide. Then, a synthetic method went small: the polymerase chain reaction (PCR) could be carried out in a chip-size channel winding its way back and forth between the two ends of a temperature gradient. In this way, the thermal cycler which is the core instrument of conventional PCR could be replaced by a constant-temperature device in which the necessary change of temperature is achieved by continuous flow of the sample. To make these microscale laboratories commercially viable, however, the supporting equipment such as pumps and computers will have to be miniaturized, too.

If these microlaboratories, possibly in combination with microfabricated sensors, will eventually lead to pocket-sized instruments for DNA sequencing or analysis of trace elements, this could certainly revolutionize certain areas of medical practice and environmental protection. And perhaps this trend would also include the synthesis of dangerous chemicals, which would be less threatening on many small chips than in one big reactor, and could be produced in a decentralized fashion exactly where they are going to be required. It may not be quite nano, but it could be very micro.

Nanotechnology: The Next Industrial Revolution?

During the late 1980s, when chaos theory was in vogue, we learned that even a perfect weather monitoring system, covering the globe with flawless instruments, would not allow us to make reliable and accurate predictions of the weather we will have 2 weeks hence. The deterministic world-view of Newton's physics (according to which bodies and forces interact in a fully predictable, clockworklike fashion) is not only wrong for small particles, where it is replaced by quantum mechanics. Strictly speaking it is only true for two bodies in an otherwise empty universe. The presence of a third object can already lead the system into chaos, meaning that small differences in the initial conditions can provoke huge and unpredictable differences in the consequences.

Similarly, what happens in a person's life, or in world history can depend critically on apparently small differences. As people and their vehicles tend to move rather rapidly in our time, a second's worth of hesitation can make all the difference between a fatal crash and a near miss. And 3 mm can separate a dead president from a wounded one, as Ronald Reagan realized in 1981. Although most small, chance events get drowned in the noise, some can literally change the world.

Therefore, it is no wonder that predictions concerning future developments in science and technology and their impact on society have a bad reputation among scientists. Experience tells us that life will always come up with surprises (that, for one, is a safe prediction!), and that there is an amazingly long backlist of predictions that have gone wrong in one way or the other. Steamboats, airplanes, submarines, motorcars, telephones, and robots were predicted alright, but so were levitation, time travel, and communication with the dead. And no one anticipated X-rays, atomic energy, radio, TV, photography, lasers, superconductors, superfluids, or atomic clocks. More embarrassingly, there are countless quotes from renowned physicists who at the beginning of this century thought physics was a scientific discipline nearing perfection. One would only have to correct the natural constants in the tenth decimal or so. No one predicted that quantum mechanics and relativity would turn the world-view of physics upside down within two decades.

Only 10 years ago, at an International Union of Pure and Applied Chemistry conference on physical organic chemistry, I attended a talk about those strange carbon molecules that some astronomically minded chemists had discovered in outer space. It all sounded quite fascinating, but then, these molecules were light-years away. Nobody stood up and predicted that within 3 years from that day, buckminsterfullerenes would be available in kilogram amounts here on Earth. Nobody could have anticipated anything like the fullerene fever, the fullerene superconductors, and all of the carbon nanotube spin-offs described in Chapter 6. I sometimes wonder what kind of reaction such a prediction would have caused in 1988.

Even if someone has the prophetic genius to determine the direction of a technical development, predicting its speed is even more tricky. H. G. Wells (1866–1946), who was quite successful with qualitative predictions, wrote in 1901 that men would fly before the year 2000, perhaps even before 1950. Clearly, he didn't see the Wright brothers coming, and even the more optimistic version of his prognosis, though qualitatively correct, was quantitatively wrong by a factor of 25.

So, bearing all of these problems in mind, what are we to make of the predicted nanotechnological revolution? Assuming the technical side of the predictions concerning nanotechnology are qualitatively correct, and we will in 20, 100, or 200 years be able to construct materials atom by atom, assuming further that the peaceful use of nanotechnology flourishes and the military misuse will be suppressed efficiently, and finally assuming that our planet and humanity will survive long enough to realize these opportunities—under all of these possibly optimistic assumptions, can we really anticipate the impact of a nanotechnological revolution on everyday life and society? Even though Drexler-style scenarios may be useful to get our imagination moving, they will not allow us to make an all-encompassing prognosis of life in the era of nanotechnology. If nothing else, the chaos ruling our non-Newtonian world will make sure things don't go according to plan.

A few partial predictions, however, are relatively safe. Energy doesn't have to be a scarce resource, if we had the technical requirements to make efficient use of solar energy. Developing an environmentally friendly and globally accessible energy supply on this basis would already be a technical revolution in its own right.

Things get more complicated when we come to the changes in production and economy that Drexler anticipates in his books. In the force field between science, economy, and politics, reliable prognoses cannot be made, and every technological revolution is at the same time a potential source of conflicts.

As soon as the new technology threatens traditional employment, there is bound to be social conflict and political dissension within each country affected. Globally, developing countries could become world powers overnight. The displacement of political equilibria both on a global and on a national or regional scale could lead either to catastrophes or to genuine improvements. There is absolutely no way of foreseeing which of the two will happen. Similarly, it is quite unpredictable whether products derived from nanotechnology will be successful in the marketplace, where they may be facing competition from biotechnology and perhaps from other new technologies that we cannot now even dream of.

These are the reasons why professional forecasters are generally very cautious. In the 1995, "technology foresight" report commissioned by the British government to predict developments in 15 areas from agriculture to computer science until 2010, no revolution whatsoever was predicted. The developments anticipated were basically cautious extrapolations of changes already under way or realizable with 1995 technology, such as banking from the home computer, shopping in virtual reality, personal substance sensors, or gene-manipulated trees to yield wood of a desired quality. (Note that even within the first 3 years of the 15-year time frame of the foresight exercise, major developments have occurred that were not predicted, such as the cloning of Dolly the sheep.)

Stuffy official reports don't normally anticipate revolutions. However, we should believe Drexler this one thing, if nothing else: Revolutions will happen. Of course they won't happen exactly in the way he has anticipated, perhaps they will happen faster, more slowly, or in an entirely different way, but technology and everyday life will continue to change in the future as spectacularly as they have changed through the impacts of motorcars, airplanes, and personal computers. This is something everybody should be aware of. Only those with a prepared mind will recognize the technological revolution when it comes and thus be able to respond appropriately and avoid being rolled over.

And even if the nanotechnological revolution does not materialize quite so soon in everyday life, and if a few more generations will have to work in traditional factories and paint their homes manually—it would be helpful if we could develop molecular motors as efficient as our muscles, data storage devices as compact as DNA, and a method for the reduction of molecular nitrogen at atmospheric pressure and room temperature. Because nature has taught us that these can be achieved.

Glossary*

Actin (2) A soluble protein found in muscle cells. It is the main component of the thin filaments.

AFM (atomic force microscopy) (6) A variant of the *STM* method. In AFM, the surface is probed mechanically rather than electronically.

Alpha helix (1) A screwlike arrangement of the linear protein chain. A typical element of *secondary structure*.

Amino acids (1) Small molecules containing both a carbonic acid and an amino group. A set of 20 different amino acids serve as building blocks for *proteins*.

Antibody (2) A large protein that specifically recognizes foreign structures such as bacteria or viruses and triggers an immune response against them.

Antigen (2) A molecule or part of a molecule that triggers an immune response following molecular recognition by an antibody.

---

*Numbers in parentheses indicate the chapter in which a term is first used. Italics highlight terms defined elsewhere in the glossary.

Archaebacteria (archaea) (4) One of the three domains of life, along with the eukaryotes (eukarya) and eubacteria (bacteria).

Assembler (9) A (nano)machine that can assemble atoms to molecules or materials.

ATP (adenosine triphosphate) (2) A building block for making *DNA* and *RNA*, ATP also is the most important carrier of chemical energy in all cells. To use the stored energy, the cell cleaves off the outermost of the three phosphate groups contained in the molecule, yielding ADP (adenosine diphosphate) and an inorganic phosphate ion.

Band gap (6) The energy difference between the states that electrons can populate in a solid material. The width of the band gap can be the decisive factor determining whether a material behaves like an insulator or like a semiconductor.

Beta sheet (1) An arrangement of the protein chain in which the backbone is spread out flat and two or more strands of the chain run in parallel.

Bioluminescence (7) Generation of light from metabolic energy. In addition to fireflies, bioluminescence is found in dozens of other species including fish, jellyfish, and mushrooms.

Catalysis (1) Acceleration of a chemical reaction by lowering the energy barrier achieved by a *catalyst*. The strict definition of catalysis requires that the catalyst not be affected by the overall reaction.

Catalyst (1) A substance able to perform *catalysis*.

Catenane (5) A set of interlocking molecular rings.

Chromophore (7) The part of a molecule that is responsible for its color or more generally for its response to light.

Cluster (2) A structure consisting of a small number of (metal) atoms.

Crown ether (5) Ring-shaped molecules held together by etherlike bonds (X–O–X), whose oxygen atoms can display very tight binding to metal ions located inside the ring.

Cyclodextrin (5) A product of starch degradation, containing 6, 7, or 8 glucose molecules linked to a ring with an inner diameter of 0.5–0.8 nm.

Cytoplasm (1) The liquid phase in the interior of a cell (excluding *organelles*).

Dendrimer (5) Branched *polymers*, often globular in shape.

DNA (deoxyribonucleic acid) (1) Biological chain molecule built from four kinds of building blocks, the nucleotides. DNA, normally found as a double helix spiral of two complementary strands, is the carrier of genetic information in all cellular life forms and many viruses.

Enzyme (1) A *protein* that can perform *catalysis*, i.e., speed up a chemical reaction without itself being affected.

Eubacteria (4) *Archaebacteria.*

Eukaryotes (1) *Archaebacteria.*

Expression (7) Realization of the genetic information encoded in *DNA* leading to the synthesis of a *protein* or a stable *RNA*. The term is used in particular when a foreign gene is introduced into a host cell, which then expresses the gene, i.e., produces a recombinant protein, or when the rate of synthesis is artificially enhanced (overexpression).

Genetic code (3) The (almost) universally valid rules by which three-letter "words" in *DNA* or *RNA* are assigned to amino acids to be incorporated into *proteins.*

Genome (3) All of the genes of a particular organism.

Glass state (7) If a substance is cooled below its freezing (crystallization) temperature but cannot rearrange its atoms or molecules in the way necessary to form an ordered structure, it remains a "vitrified" liquid. Common glass is transparent because it is a supercooled liquid.

Haber–Bosch process (2) Industrial process for the synthesis of ammonia from nitrogen and hydrogen, using high pressure and temperatures in the presence of heavy metal *catalysts.*

Heat shock proteins (3) A group of proteins that are synthesized in large amounts after a short overheating of a cell. Some of them have important functions in the context of protein folding (*molecular chaperones*).

Helix (1) Structure wound up like a screw. In biochemistry, helices are commonly found in proteins (alpha helix) and in nucleic acids (double helix).

Hydrophobic (1) Water-avoiding.

Hydrophobic interaction (1) Tendency of *hydrophobic* molecules or parts of molecules to cluster with other hydrophobic groups to minimize their exposure to water. Hydrophobic interactions are important factors for the stability of cellular structures such as the double layer membrane and the inner core of proteins.

Hyperthermophilic (4) Extremely heat-loving, normally used to describe microorganisms whose optimal growth temperature exceeds 80°C.

Immunoglobulin G (2) The most common class of *antibodies* present in human serum (i.e., liquid part of the blood).

Insulin (3) A hormone consisting of 51 amino acids in two polypeptide chains. Insulin reduces the glucose level in the blood. Failure to produce insulin is one of the causes of diabetes.

Ion channels (5) Pores in the cell membrane that allow and regulate the transport of ions across the membrane.

Kinesin (2) A motor protein used for transport processes within the cell and which migrates along the *microtubules*.

Langmuir–Blodgett film (6) A single layer of molecules that has been transferred from the surface of a liquid onto a solid substrate.

Levinthal paradox (3) If a fully unfolded protein chain had to test all possible conformations, the time required for the folding of a middle-sized protein would exceed the age of the universe.

Lysozyme (3) An enzyme that can be easily prepared from egg white and has therefore been used for many fundamental studies into the nature of enzymes. Lysozyme kills bacteria by perforating their cell walls.

Macromolecules (1) Relatively large molecules containing hundreds to ten thousands of atoms. Typically *polymers* of smaller building blocks.

Magnetotactic bacteria (4) Bacteria that can use the Earth's magnetic field for orientation. They contain minute crystals of magnetic iron minerals enclosed in a specialized cell compartment.

Messenger RNA (mRNA) (3) The information carrier used by the *ribosome* during *protein biosynthesis*. The mRNA arises from the process of *DNA* transcription. In contrast to *transfer* and *ribosomal RNA*, it is quite short-lived. The latter two, therefore, may be called stable RNAs.

Methanogenic bacteria (4) A group of organisms in the domain of *archaebacteria*, which convert carbon dioxide and hydrogen to methane and water.

Microtubules (1) Hollow tubes made of subunits of the protein tubulin. They serve both for structural stability of higher cells and as a "rail" for transport processes mediated by the motor protein *kinesin*.

Molecular chaperone (3) A protein that helps unfolded or freshly synthesized proteins to fold to the correct three-dimensional structure by suppressing unwanted side reactions.

Myosin (1) The motor protein that generates the force and movement in contraction of muscles.

Nanometer (1) Length unit corresponding to a millionth of a millimeter, or a billionth of a meter.

Nanotubes (5) Tubes with an inner diameter in the nanometer range.

Nitrogenase (1) An enzyme found in certain bacteria that can convert the chemically inert nitrogen gas present in air into compounds that the cell can use.

NMR (nuclear magnetic resonance) spectroscopy (2) A highly sophisticated method used for studying the structure and dynamics of molecules including small to middle-sized proteins. The method relies on the magnetic properties of certain atoms, which can be probed by the use of radiowaves and a strong magnetic field. It is closely related to the spin tomography methods used for noninvasive imaging in clinical medicine.

Organelles (1) Compartments of the *eukaryotic* cell, which are separated from the *cytoplasm* by a membrane and fulfill specialized function. Examples are mitochondria (energy metabolism) and chloroplasts (photosynthesis).

Oxidation (2) A reaction in which a particular molecular group gives electrons away (i.e., its oxidation number increases). The name relates to the fact that the first known examples of these reactions, such as the combustion of carbon compounds to carbon dioxide or the rusting of iron, involved oxygen. The reaction partner that accepts the electron is reduced, i.e., its oxidation number is decreased. The whole process can also be called a redox reaction.

Peptide (5) A chain molecule that consists of amino acids like a protein, but is usually too small to adopt a proteinlike structure.

Polymer (1) A molecule built from a large number of similar building blocks (monomers). Polymers that can be described as a regular repetition of one or a few monomers are called *homopolymers*. These include common plastics such as polystyrene and polyethylene. In contrast, biological polymers (*DNA, proteins*) tend to consist of an irregular (information containing) sequence of similar building blocks and are therefore termed heteropolymers.

Polymerase chain reaction (PCR) (1) A method for copying *DNA*, which can be applied to very small samples, provided the sequences flanking the gene of interest are known or can be guessed. By repetitive application of the PCR cycle, an exponentially growing number of copies of the original DNA can be made.

Polypeptide (1) Any polymer made of amino acid building blocks. Used in particular for those cases when the polymer is unstructured—as opposed to a *protein*, which is a polypeptide that normally adopts a well-defined three-dimensional structure.

Primary structure (1) First level of structure in proteins, comprising the order or sequence of *amino acids* in the *polypeptide* chain.

Proteasome (3) A multienzyme complex that catalyzes the degradation of proteins into amino acids.

Protein biosynthesis (1) The process of linking up *amino acid* building
   blocks to form a *protein* molecule. It is carried out by the *ribosome*
   together with a set of other cellular factors.

Protein folding (1) The process in which the linear chain of amino acids
   (i.e., *polypeptide*) arising from *protein biosynthesis* or from denaturation
   of a protein forms a three-dimensional structure stabilized by many
   weak interactions. Most proteins have to be folded to be biologically
   active.

Proteins (1) Chain molecules consisting of (dozens to thousands of) *amino
   acid* building blocks and carrying out a wide variety of tasks in the cell,
   including *catalysis* of metabolic reactions, transport of small molecules
   or ions, mechanical work, switch functions, and information transfer.

Q particles (6) Nanometer-sized particles of semiconductor materials,
   whose behavior is governed by quantum-mechanical effects.

Replicator (9) A (nano)machine that can make copies of itself, i.e., replicate.

Restriction enzyme (3) An *enzyme* cutting *DNA* at or near a certain sequence.

Ribosome (1) A complex of more than 50 *proteins* and several *RNA* molecules, which carries out the synthesis of proteins following the genetic
   instructions read from the *messenger RNA* with the help of *transfer
   RNAs* and various protein factors.

Ribozyme (1) An *RNA* molecule that can perform *catalysis*.

RNA (ribonucleic acid) (1) A biological chain molecule that acts as a
   mediator between the genetic information (*DNA*) and the function
   (*proteins*). The most important kinds of RNA are *messenger RNA*
   (mRNA), *transfer RNA* (tRNA), and the RNA of the *ribosome* (rRNA).

RNA world (3) A hypothetical stage in the early evolution of life, with
   RNA molecules as the only biological macromolecules playing the
   roles of both information carrier and function molecules.

Secondary structure (1) Certain structural features of proteins that can
   directly form from the linear protein chain. Secondary structure elements include alpha helices and beta-pleated sheets.

Side chains (1) The part of the *amino acid* building block that branches out
   from the linear string of the polypeptide backbone. The nature of the
   side chain determines the chemical properties of each amino acid, and
   in a complex way, the folding of the protein.

STM (scanning tunneling microscopy) (6) A technique that uses the
   quantum-mechanical effect called tunneling (i. e., that electrons can

jump through "forbidden" space across very short distances) to probe surfaces at nearly atomic resolution.

Synchrotron (2) A particle accelerator providing synchronized particles and high-energy X-rays.

Tertiary structure (1) Comprises the complete folded structure of a native protein, including through-space links (tertiary contacts) between separate elements of *secondary structure*.

Thermophilic (4) Heat-loving.

TMV (tobacco mosaic virus) (1) A rod-shaped plant virus that served as a model system for the study of self-assembly in biological systems.

Transcription (3) Copying of the genetic information from *DNA* onto *RNA* by the enzyme RNA polymerase. The regulation of transcription by specialized proteins, the transcription factors, is a central switchboard for all life processes in a cell.

Transfer RNA (tRNA) (3) Stable *RNA* molecules that act as specific carriers for the amino acid molecules to be incorporated in *protein biosynthesis*.

Translation (3) Another term for *protein biosynthesis*, used to emphasize the aspect that the ribosome "translates" the 4-letter *genetic code* used in DNA and RNA into the 20-letter *amino acid* code of the *proteins*.

Further Reading and Internet Links

Note: The author's personal homepage is at: http://www.ocms.ox.ac.uk/~mgross/

Chapter 2

About proteins in general, consult:

Creighton, T. E. *Proteins. Structures and molecular properties* (2nd ed.). Freeman, San Francisco, 1993.

Perutz, M. *Protein structure. New approaches to disease and therapy*. Freeman, San Francisco, 1992.

Stryer, L. *Biochemistry* (4th ed.). Freeman, San Francisco, 1995.

Molecular Motors

Allen, B. G., and Walsh, M. P. "The biochemical basis of smooth-muscle contraction," *Trends in Biochemical Sciences* 19, 362–363 (1994).

Finer, J. T., Simmons, R. M., and Spudich, J. A. "Single myosin molecule mechanics: piconewton forces and nanometer steps," *Nature* 368, 113–119 (1994).

Rayment, I., and Holden, H. M. "The three-dimensional structure of a molecular motor," *Trends in Biochemical Sciences* 19, 129–134 (1994).

Rayment, I., Holden, H. M., Whittaker, M., Yohn, C. B., Lorenz, M., Holmes, K. C., and Milligan, R. A. "Structure of the actin–myosin complex and its implications for muscle contraction," *Science* 261, 58–65 (1993).

Rayment, I., Rypniewski, W. R., Schmidt-Bäse, K., Smith, R., Tomchick, D. R., Benning, M. M., Winkelmann, D. A., Wesenberg, D., and Holden, H. M. "Three-dimensional structure of myosin subfragment-1: A molecular motor," *Science* 261, 50–58 (1993).

Schnapp, B. J. "Molecular motors: two heads are better than one," *Nature* 373, 655–656 (1995).

Schuster, S. C. "The bacterial flagellar motor," *Annual Reviews of Biophysics and Biomolecular Structure* 23, 509–539 (1994).

Spudich, J. A. "How molecular motors work," *Nature* 372, 515–518 (1994).

Svoboda, K., Schmidt, C. F., Schnapp, B. J., and Block, S. M. "Direct observation of kinesin stepping by optical trapping interferometry," *Nature* 365, 721–727 (1993).

Taylor, E. W. "Molecular muscle," *Science* 261, 35–36 (1993).

Xie, X., Harrison, D. H., Schlichting, I., Sweet, R. M., Kalabokis, V. N., Szent-Györgyi, A. G., and Cohen, C. "Structure of the regulatory domain of scallop myosin at 2.8 Å resolution," *Nature* 368, 306–312 (1994).

Nitrogenase

Georgiadis, M. M., Komiya, H., Chakrabarti, P., Woo, D., Kornuc, J. J., and Rees, D. C., "Crystallographic structure of the nitrogenase iron protein from *Azotobacter vinelandii*," *Science* 257, 1653–1659 (1992).

Kim, J., and Rees, D. C. "Crystallographic structure and functional implications of the nitrogenase molybdenum–iron protein from *Azotobacter vinelandii*," *Nature* 360, 553–560 (1992).

Kim, J., and Rees, D. C., "Structural models for the metal centers in the nitrogenase molybdenum–iron protein," *Science* 257, 1677–1682 (1992).

Orme-Johnson, W. H. "Nitrogenase structure: where to now?" *Science* 257, 1639–1640 (1992).

Rees, D. C. "Dinitrogen fixation by nitrogenase: if N_2 isn't broken, it can't be fixed," *Current Opinion in Structural Biology* 3, 921–928 (1993).

Smil, V. "Global population and the nitrogen cycle," *Scientific American* (July), 82–87 (1997).

Thorneley, R. N. F. "Nitrogen fixation: new light on nitrogenase," *Nature* 360, 532–533 (1992).

Protein Movies

Verschueren, K. H. G., Seljee, F., Rozeboom, H. J., Kalk, K. H., and Dijkstra, B. W. "Crystallographic analysis of the catalytic mechanism of haloalkane dehalogenase," *Nature* 363, 693–698 (1993).

G Proteins

Bourne, H. R., Sanders, D. A., and McCormick, F. "The GTPase superfamily: a conserved switch for diverse cell functions," *Nature* 348, 125–132 (1990).

Bourne, H. R., Sanders, D. A., and McCormick, F. "The GTPase superfamily: conserved structure and molecular mechanism," *Nature* 349, 117–127 (1991).

Bourne, H. R., and Stryer, L. "G-proteins: the target sets the tempo," *Nature* 358, 541–543 (1992).

Clapham, D. E. "The G-protein nanomachine," *Nature* 379, 297–299 (1996).

Kawashima, T., Berthet-Colominas, C., Wulff, M., Cusack, S., and Leberman, R. "The structure of the *Escherichia coli* EF-Tu EF-Ts complex at 2.5 Å resolution," *Nature* 379, 511–518 (1996).

Lambright, D. G., et al. "The 2.0 Å crystal structure of a heterotrimeric G protein," *Nature* 379, 311–319 (1996).

Linder, M. E., and Gilman, A. G. "G proteins," *Scientific American*, 52–59 (1992).

Nierhaus, K. H. "An elongation factor turn-on," *Nature* 379, 491–492 (1996).

Noel, J. P., Hamm, H. E., and Sigler, P. B. "The 2.2 Å crystal structure of transducin-a complexed with GTPγS," *Nature* 366, 654–663 (1993).

Wall, M. A., et al. "The structure of the G protein heterotrimer $G_{i\alpha\beta\gamma}$," *Cell* 83, 1047–1058 (1995).

Crystals Made to Measure

Addadi, L., and Weiner, S. "Control and design principles in biological mineralization," *Angewandte Chemie International Edition in English* 31, 153–169 (1992).

Groß, M. "Molecular recognition: crystallographic antibodies," *Nature* 373, 105–106 (1995).

Hanein, D., Geiger, B., and Addadi, L. "Differential adhesion of cells to enantiomorphous crystal surfaces," *Science* 263, 1413–1416 (1994).

Kam, M., Perl-Treves, D., Caspi, D., and Addadi, L. "Antibodies against crystals," *FASEB Journal* 6, 2608–2613 (1992).

Kam, M., Perl-Treves, D., Sfez, R., and Addadi, L. "Specificity in the recognition of crystals by antibodies," *Journal of Molecular Recognition* 7, 257–264 (1994).

Kessler, N., Perl-Treves, D., and Addadi, L. "Monoclonal antibodies that specifically recognize crystals of dinitrobenzene," *FASEB Journal* 10, 1435–1442 (1996).

Chapter 3

The Chaperonin Home Page: http://bioc02.uthscsa.edu/~seale/Chap/chap.html
TIGR database of microbial genomes: http://www.tigr.org/tdb/mdb/mdb.html

The Language of the Genes

Groß, M. "Linguistic analysis of protein folding," *FEBS Letters* 390, 249–252 (1996).

Pesole, G., Attimonelli, M., and Saccone, C. "Linguistic approaches to the analysis of sequence information," *Trends in Biotechnology* 12, 401–408 (1994).
Searls, D. B. "The linguistics of DNA," *American Scientist* 80, 579–591 (1992).

Death of a Dogma

Santos, M. A. S., and Tuite, M. F. "The CUG codon is decoded in vivo as serine and not leucine in *Candida albicans*," *Nucleic Acids Research* 23, 1481–1486 (1995).

Round and Round the Ribosome

Nierhaus, K. H. "The allosteric three-site model for the ribosomal elongation cycle: features and future," *Biochemistry* 29, 4997–5008 (1990).

Skiing the Energy Landscape

Dill, K. A., and Chan, H. S. "From Levinthal to pathways to funnels," *Nature Structural Biology* 4, 10–19 (1997).
Dobson, C. M., Evans, P. A., and Radford, S. E. "Understanding how proteins fold: the lysozyme story so far," *Trends in Biochemical Sciences* 19, 31–37 (1994).

Safeguarding Adolescent Proteins

Braig, K., Otwinowski, Z., Hegde, R., Boisvert, D., Joachimiak, A., Horwich, A., and Sigler, P. "The crystal structure of the bacterial chaperonin GroEL at 2.8 Å," *Nature* 371, 578–586 (1994).
Buchner, J., Schmidt, M., Fuchs, M., Jaenicke, R., Rudolph, R., Schmid, F. X., and Kiefhaber, T., "GroE facilitates refolding of citrate synthase by suppressing aggregation," *Biochemistry* 30, 1586–1591. (1991).
Buckle, A. M., Zahn, R., and Fersht, A. R. "A structural model for GroEL-polypeptide recognition," *Proceedings of the National Academy of Sciences* 94, 3571–3575 (1997).
Chen, S., Roseman, A., Hunter, A., Wood, S., Burston, S., Ranson, N., Clarke, A., and Saibil, H., "Location of a folding protein and shape changes in GroEL–GroES complexes imaged by cryo-electron microscopy," *Nature* 371, 261–264 (1994).
Martin, J., Langer, T., Boteva, R., Schramel, A., Horwich, A. L., and Hartl, F. U. "Chaperonin-mediated protein folding at the surface of GroEL through a 'molten globule'-like intermediate," *Nature* 352, 36–42 (1991).
Martin, J., Mayhew, M., Langer, T., and Hartl, F. U. "The reaction cycle of GroEL and GroES in chaperonin-assisted protein folding," *Nature* 366, 228–233 (1993).

Robinson, C. V., Groß, M., Eyles, S. J., Ewbank, J. J., Mayhew, M., Hartl, F. U., Dobson, C. M., and Radford, S. E. "Conformation of GroEL-bound alpha-lactalbumin probed by mass spectrometry," *Nature* 372, 646–651 (1994).

Recycling Scheme in the Cell

Ciechanover, A., and Schwartz, A. L. "The ubiquitin-mediated proteolytic pathway: mechanisms of recognition of the proteolytic substrate and involvement in the degradation of native cellular proteins," *FASEB Journal* 8, 182–191 (1994).
Goldberg, A. L., "Functions of the proteasome: the lysis at the end of the tunnel," *Science* 268, 522–523 (1995).
Löwe, J., Stock, D., Jap, B., Zwickl, P., Baumeister, W., and Huber, R. "Crystal structure of the 20S proteasome from the archaeon *T. acidophilum* at 3.4 Å resolution," *Science* 268, 533–539 (1995).
Peters, J.-M. "Proteasomes: protein degradation machines of the cell," *Trends in Biochemical Sciences* 19, 377–382 (1994).
Seemüller, E., Lupas, A., Stock, D., Löwe, J., Huber, R., and Baumeister, W. "Proteasome from *Thermoplasma acidophilum*: a threonine protease," *Science* 268, 579–582 (1995).
Weissman, J. S., Sigler, P. B., and Horwich, A. L. "From the cradle to the grave: ring complexes in the life of a protein," *Science* 268, 523–524 (1995).
Wenzel, T., and Baumeister, W. "Conformational constraints in protein degradation by the 20S proteasome," *Nature Structural Biology* 2, 199–204 (1995).
Zwickl, P., Kleinz, J., and Baumeister, W. "Critical elements in proteasome assembly," *Nature Structural Biology* 1, 765–769 (1994).

Chapter 4

Archaebacteria, *Methanococcus*

Bult, C. J., and Venter, J. C. "Complete genome sequence of the methanogenic archaeon, *Methanococcus jannaschii*," *Science* 273, 1066–1073 (1996).
Gray, M. W. "Genomics: the third form of life," *Nature* 383, 299–300 (1996).
Morell, V., "Life's last domain," *Science* 273, 1043–1045 (1996).
Woese, C. R. "Archaebacteria," *Scientific American* 244 (June), 94–106 (1981).

Magnetotactic Bacteria

Blakemore, R. P. "Magnetotactic bacteria," *Annual Reviews of Microbiology* 36, 217–238 (1982).

Sakaguchi, T., Burgess, J. G., and Matsunaga, T. "Magnetite formation by a sulphate-reducing bacterium," *Nature* 365, 47–49 (1993).
Williams, R. J. P. "Biomineralization: iron and the origin of life," *Nature* 343, 213–214 (1990).

Cell Wars (1): Taxol

Holton, R. A., et al. "First total synthesis of taxol. 1. Functionalization of the B ring," *Journal of the American Chemical Society* 116, 1597–1598 (1994).
Holton, R. A., et al. "First total synthesis of taxol. 2. Completion of the C and D rings," *Journal of the American Chemical Society* 116, 1599–1600 (1994).
Kingston, D. G. "Taxol: the chemistry and structure–activity relationship of a novel anticancer agent," *Trends in Biotechnology* 12, 222–227 (1994).
Nicolaou, K. C., Yang, Z., Liu, J. J., Ueno, H., Nantermet, P. G., Guy, R. K., Claiborne, C. F., Renaud, J., Couladouros, E. A., Paulvannan, K., and Sorensen, E. J. "Total synthesis of taxol," *Nature* 367, 630–634 (1994).
Nogales, E., Wolf, S. G., and Downing, K. H. "Structure of the $\alpha\beta$ tubulin dimer by electron crystallography," *Nature* 391, 199–203 (1998).

Cell Wars (2): Antibiotics

Bevins, C. L., and Zasloff, M. "Peptides from frog skin," *Annual Reviews of Biochemistry* 59, 395–414 (1990).
Coyette, J., et al. "Molecular adaptations in resistance to penicillins and other β-lactam antibiotics," *Advances in Comparative and Environmental Physiology* 20, 233–267 (1994).
Davies, J. "Inactivation of antibiotics and the dissemination of resistance genes," *Science* 264, 375–382 (1994).
Mor, A., and Nicolas, P. "Isolation and structure of novel defensive peptides from frog skin," *European Journal of Biochemistry* 219, 145–154 (1994).
Strynadka, N. C. J., et al. "Structural and kinetic characterization of a beta-lactamase-inhibitor protein," *Nature* 368, 657–660 (1994).
Webb, V., and Davies, J. "Accidental release of antibiotic-resistance genes," *Trends in Biotechnology* 12, 74–75 (1994).

Chapter 5

Nadrian Seeman: http://seemanlab4.chem.nyu.edu/
Jean-Marie Lehn: http://www.nobel.se/laureates/chemistry-1987-2-autobio.html
Reza Ghadiri: http://www.scripps.edu/pub/ghadiri/

Dendrimers

Hodge, P. "Organic chemistry: polymer science branches out," *Nature* 362, 18–19 (1993).

Issberner, J., Moors, R., and Vögtle, F. "Dendrimers—from generations and functional groups to functions," *Angewandte Chemie International Edition in English* 33, 2413–2420 (1994).

Jansen, J. F. G. A., de Brabander-van den Berg, E. M. M., and Meijer, E. W. "Encapsulation of guest molecules into a dendritic box," *Science* 266, 1226–1229 (1994).

Knapen, J. W. J., et al. "Homogeneous catalysts based on silane dendrimers functionalized with arylnickel(II) complexes," *Nature* 372, 659–663 (1994).

Mekelburger, H.-B., Jaborek, W., and Vögtle, F. "Dendrimers, arborols, and cascade molecules: breakthrough into generations of new materials," *Angewandte Chemie International Edition in English* 31, 1571–1576 (1992).

Tomalia, D. A., and Dvornic, P. R. "Catalysis: what promise for dendrimers?" *Nature* 372, 617–618 (1994).

Tomalia, D. A., Naylor, A. M., and Goddard, W. A. "Starburst-dendrimers— molecular-level control of size, shape, surface chemistry, topology and flexibility from atoms to macroscopic matter," *Angewandte Chemie International Edition in English* 29, 138–175 (1990).

Protein Design

Ghadiri, M. R., and Case, M. A. "De-novo design of a novel heterodinuclear three-helix-bundle metalloprotein," *Angewandte Chemie International Edition in English* 32, 1594–1597 (1993).

Groß, M., and Plaxco, K. W. "Protein engineering: reading, writing, and redesigning," *Nature* 388, 419–420 (1997).

Pessi, A., et al. "A designed metal-binding protein with a novel fold," *Nature* 362, 367–369 (1993).

Peptide Nanotubes

Echegoyen, L. "Synthetic chemistry: not through the usual channels," *Nature* 369, 276–277 (1994).

Ghadiri, M. R. "Self-assembled nanoscale tubular ensembles," *Advanced Materials* 7, 675–677 (1995).

Ghadiri, M. R., Granja, J. R., and Buehler, L. K. "Artificial transmembrane ion channels from self-assembling peptide nanotubes," *Nature* 369, 301–304 (1994).

Ghadiri, M. R., Granja, J. R., Milligan, R. A., McRee, D. E., and Khazanovich, N. "Self-assembling organic nanotubes based on a cyclic peptide architecture," *Nature* 366, 324–327 (1993).

Topological Molecules

Amabilino, D. B., Ashton, P. R., Reder, A. S., Spencer, N., and Stoddart, J. F. "Olympiadane," *Angewandte Chemie International Edition in English* 33, 1286–1290 (1994).

Bissell, R. A., Cordova, E., Kaifer, A. E., and Stoddart, J. F. "A chemically and electrochemically switchable molecular shuttle," *Nature* 369, 133–137 (1994).

Dietrich-Buchecker, C., Frommberger, B., Luer, I., Sauvage, J.-P., and Vögtle, F. "Multiring catenanes with a macrobicyclic core," *Angewandte Chemie International Edition in English* 32, 1434–1437 (1993).

Dietrich-Buchecker, C. O., Guilhem, J., Pascard, C., and Sauvage, J.-P. "Structure of a synthetic trefoil knot coordinated to two copper II centers," *Angewandte Chemie International Edition in English* 29, 1154–1156 (1990).

Useful Things to Do with DNA

Adleman, L. M. "Computing with DNA," *Scientific American* August, 54–61 (1998).

Chen, J., and Seeman, N. C. "Synthesis from DNA of a molecule with the connectivity of a cube," *Nature* 350, 631–633 (1991).

Clery, D. "DNA goes electric," *Science* 267, 1270 (1995).

Lipton, R. J. "DNA solution of hard computational problems," *Science* 268, 542–545 (1995).

Meade, T. J., and Kayyem, J. F. "Electron transfer through DNA—site specific modification of duplex DNA with ruthenium donors and acceptors," *Angewandte Chemie International Edition in English* 34, 352–354 (1995).

Zhang Y., and Seeman N. C. *Journal of the American Chemical Society* 116, 1661–1669 (1994).

Self-Replicating Peptides

Lee, D. H., Granja, J. R., Martinez, J. A., Severin, K., and Ghadiri, M. R. "A self-replicating peptide," *Nature* 382, 525–528 (1996).

Lee, D. H., Severin, K., Yokobayashi, Y., and Ghadiri, M. R. "Emergence of symbiosis in peptide self-replication through a hypercyclic network," *Nature* 390, 591–594 (1997).

Toward Artificial Enzymes

Anderson, H. L., Bashall, A., Henrick, K., McPartlin, M., and Sanders, J. K. M. "Crystal structure of a supramolecular dimer formed by pi–pi interactions between two interlocked cyclic zinc porphyrin trimers," *Angewandte Chemie International Edition in English* 33, 429–431 (1994).

Hirschmann, R., et al. "Peptide synthesis catalyzed by an antibody containing a binding site for variable amino acids," *Science* 265, 235–237 (1994).

Kirby, A. J. "Enzyme mimics," *Angewandte Chemie International Edition in English* 33, 551–553 (1994).

Koshland, D. E. "The key-lock theory and the induced-fit theory," *Angewandte Chemie International Edition in English* 33, 2375–2378 (1994).

Lichtenthaler, F. W. "100 years Schlüssel-Schloβ-Prinzip—what made Emil Fischer use this analogy?" *Angewandte Chemie International Edition in English* 33, 2364–2374 (1994).

Lindoy, L. F. "Molecular architecture: towards synthetic enzymes," *Nature* 368, 96 (1994).

Walter, C. J., and Sanders, J. K. "Free-energy profile for a host-accelerated Diels-Alder reaction—the sources of exo selectivity," *Angewandte Chemie International Edition in English* 34, 217–219 (1995).

Zhou, G. W., Guo, J., Huang, W., Fletterick, R., and Scanlan, T. S. "Crystal structure of a catalytic antibody with a serine protease active site," *Science* 265, 1059–1064 (1994).

Chapter 6

Ormecon (organic metals): http://www.ormecon.de/
George Whitesides: http://www.chem.harvard.edu/GeorgeWhitesides.html

AFM/STM

Bustamente, C., Erie, D. A., and Keller, D. "Biochemical and structural applications of scanning force microscopy." *Current Opinion in Structural Biology* 4, 750–760 (1994).

Gardner, E. "AFM fabricates a tiny transistor," *Science* 266, 543 (1994).

Hansma, H. G., and Hoh, J. H. "Biomolecular imaging with the atomic force microscope, " *Annual Reviews of Biophysics and Biomolecular Structure* 23, 115–139 (1994).

Radmacher, M., Fritz, M., Hansma, H. G., and Hansma, P. K. "Direct observation of enzyme activity with the atomic force microscope," *Science* 265, 1577–1579 (1994).

Thin Films

Bunker, B. C., et al. "Ceramic thin-film formation on functionalized interfaces through biomimetic processing," *Science* 264, 48–55 (1994).

Connolly, P. "Bioelectronic interfacing: micro- and nanofabrication techniques for generating pre-determined molecular arrays," *Trends in Biotechnology* 12, 123–127 (1994).

Edgington, S. M. "Biotech's new nanotools," *Bio/technology* 12, 468–471 (1994).

López, G. P., et al. "Imaging of features on surfaces by condensation figures," *Science* 260, 647–649 (1993).

Singhvi, R., et al. "Engineering cell shape and function," *Science* 264, 696–698 (1994).

Whitesell, J. K., and Chang, H. K. "Directionally aligned helical peptides on surfaces," *Science* 261, 73–76 (1993).

Whitesell, J. K., Chang, H. K., and Whitesell, C. S. "Enzymatic grooming of organic thin-films," *Angewandte Chemie International Edition in English* 33, 871–873 (1994).

Zasadzinski J. A., et al. "Langmuir–Blodgett films," *Science* 263, 1726–1733 (1994).

Q Particles

Kastner, M. A. "Artificial atoms," *Physics Today* 46, 24–31 (1993).

Weller, H. "Colloidal semiconductor Q-particles—chemistry in the transition region between solid state and molecules," *Angewandte Chemie International Edition in English* 34, 41–53 (1993).

Weller, H. "Quantized semiconductor particles: a novel state of matter for materials science," *Advanced Materials* 5, 88–95 (1993).

Chapter 7

Genetic Engineering

Rosenberger, R. F., and Holliday, R. "Recombinant therapeutic proteins and translational errors," *Trends in Biotechnology* 11, 498–499 (1993).

Santos, M. A. S., and Tuite, M. F. "New insights into mRNA decoding—implications for heterologous protein synthesis," *Trends in Biotechnology* 11, 500–505 (1993).

Spirin, A. S., Baranov, V. I., Ryabova, L. A., Ovodov, S. Y., and Alakhov, Y. B. "A continuous cell-free translation system capable of producing polypeptides in high yield," *Science* 242, 1162–1164 (1988).

Blue Genes

Eugster, C. H., and Märki-Fischer, E. "The chemistry of rose pigments," *Angewandte Chemie International Edition in English* 30, 654–672 (1991).

Holton, T. A., and Tanaka, Y. "Blue roses—a pigment of our imagination?" *Trends in Biotechnology* 12, 40–42 (1994).

Green Fluorescent Protein

Chalfie, M., et al. "Green fluorescent protein as a marker for gene expression," *Science* 263, 802–805 (1994).
Cody, C. W., et al. "Chemical structure of the hexapeptide chromophore of the Aequorea green fluorescent protein," *Biochemistry* 32, 1212–1218 (1993).

Squeezed Eggs

Groß, M., and Jaenicke, R. "Proteins under pressure: the influence of high hydrostatic pressure on structure, function and assembly of proteins and protein complexes," *European Journal of Biochemistry* 221, 617–630 (1994).
Mozhaev, V. V., Heremans, K., Frank, J., Masson, P., and Balny, C. "Exploiting the effects of high hydrostatic pressure in biotechnological applications," *Trends in Biotechnology* 12, 493–501 (1994).

Glass State

Franks, F. "Long-term stabilization of biologicals," *Bio/technology* 12, 253–256 (1994).

Chapter 9

Sean Morgan's Nanotechnology Pages: http://www.lucifer.com/~sean/Nano.html
Engines of Creation by K. E. Drexler: http://www.foresight.org/EOC/index.html
Nanotechnology in science fiction: http://www.erinet.com/prass/nanowars/ninsf/n_in_sf.html
The Foresight Institute: http://www.foresight.org./homepage.html
The Foresight Conferences: http://www.foresight.org/Conferences/
Cornell Nanofabrication Facility: http://www.nnf.cornell.edu
Drexler, K. E. *Engines of creation. The coming era of nanotechnology.* Fourth Estate Ltd., London, 1990.
Drexler, K. E. "Molecular nanomachines: physical principles and implementation strategies," *Annual Reviews of Biophysics and Biomolecular Structure* 23, 377–405 (1994).
Drexler, K. E., and Foster, J. S. "Synthetic tips." *Nature* 343, 600 (1990).
Drexler, K. E., Peterson, C., and Pergamit, G. *Unbounding the future.* Addison–Wesley, Reading, Mass., 1994.
Jones, D. E. H. "Technical boundless optimism (Review of 'Nano! Remaking the World Atom by Atom' by Ed Regis)," *Nature* 374, 835–837 (1995).
Müller, W. T., et al. "A strategy for the chemical synthesis of nanostructures," *Science* 268, 272–273 (1995).

Ozin, G. A. "Nanochemistry: synthesis in diminishing dimensions," *Advanced Materials* 4, 612–649 (1992).

Regis, E. *Nano. Remaking the world atom by atom.* Bantam Books, New York, 1995.

Service, R. F. "The incredible shrinking laboratory," *Science* 268, 26–27 (1995).

Stix, G. "Toward 'Point One,'" *Scientific American* February, 72–77 (1995).

Thomas, D. "Nanotechnology's many disciplines," *Bio/technology* 13, 439–443 (1995).

Index